DATE			

PAGES FROM THE PAST

History and Memory in American Magazines

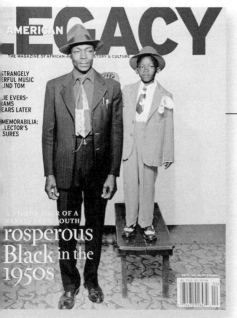

Pages from the Past

CAROLYN KITCH

The University of North Carolina Press   Chapel Hill

© 2005
The University of North Carolina Press
All rights reserved
Set in Scala types by Tseng
Information Systems, Inc.
Manufactured in the
United States of America

The paper in this book meets the
guidelines for permanence and
durability of the Committee on
Production Guidelines for Book
Longevity of the Council on Library
Resources.

Library of Congress
Cataloging-in-Publication Data
Kitch, Carolyn L.
Pages from the past : history and
memory in American magazines /
by Carolyn Kitch.
   p. cm.
Includes bibliographical references
and index.
ISBN 0-8078-2967-6
(cloth : alk. paper) —
ISBN 0-8078-5649-5
(pbk. : alk. paper)
1. American periodicals.
2. Journalism—Social aspects—United
States. 3. History in mass media.
4. Memory—Social aspects—United
States. I. Title.
PN4877.K58   2005
051—dc22   2005005926

Portions of this work appeared
earlier, in somewhat different form,
as "Twentieth-Century Tales:
Newsmagazines and American
Memory," *Journalism & Communication
Monographs* 1, no. 2 (Summer 1999):
120–55, published by the Association
for Education in Journalism & Mass
Communication (chapter 1); "'A News
of Feeling as well as Fact': Mourning
and Memorial in American Newsmagazines," *Journalism: Theory, Practice
and Criticism* 1, no. 2 (2000): 171–95,
published by Sage Publications (chapter
3); "Generational Identity and Memory
in American Newsmagazines,"
Journalism: Theory, Practice and Criticism
4, no. 2 (May 2003): 185–202, published
by Sage Publications (chapter 5); and
"Anniversary Journalism, Collective
Memory, and the Cultural Authority to
Tell the Story of the American Past,"
Journal of Popular Culture 36, no. 1
(Summer 2002): 44–67, published by
Blackwell Publishing (chapter 7), and
are reprinted here with permission.

cloth
09 08 07 06 05   5 4 3 2 1
paper
09 08 07 06 05   5 4 3 2 1

This book was published with the
assistance of the William R. Kenan Jr.
Fund of the University of North
Carolina Press.

It is either ironic or fitting that I was working on a book about memory while my mother, Aimee Lou Kitch, was courageously battling Alzheimer's disease. Her sister and my aunt, Melba Musser, was in the final years of her life as well during this period. By sharing their experiences and their recollections, both of them taught me to value and learn from the past and gave me wisdom for the future. They are truly the Greatest Generation, and this book is dedicated to their memory.

Contents

Illustrations

Acknowledgments

The proposal for this work was written with a Summer Research Fellowship from Temple University, and during the three years I spent writing the book itself I had support in the form of time and research assistance from the School of Communications and Theater and the Journalism Department, thanks to (respectively) Dean Concetta Stewart and Chair Patricia Bradley. Within the journalism department, I also have received professional support and invaluable personal encouragement from Edward Trayes, Andrew Mendelson, Fabienne Darling-Wolf, and Larry Stains.

A number of magazine editors were generous with their time and expertise, some of them sending me materials I could not find and sharing their own editorial research with me. They included Audrey Peterson, editor of *American Legacy*; Bettina Miller, editor of *Reminisce*; and Ken Tate, editor of *Good Old Days*. I am especially grateful to Richard Stolley, senior editorial advisor for Time Inc., for his wisdom, and for making the world's largest magazine company accessible to me. I further appreciate the help I received from numerous professionals in gaining permissions to reprint the illustrations that appear throughout this book.

Nearly all of the photography for the book was done by Georganne H. Hughes of Metrophoto in Hershey, Pennsylvania, and I am glad to have the benefit of her talent and professionalism. At the University of North Carolina Press, Editor Sian Hunter and Managing Editor Ron Maner have been extremely encouraging, providing an unusual combination of clear direction in shaping the book conceptually and sympathetic patience in helping me prepare it for publication. I am grateful as well for the careful eye of copyeditor Brian R. MacDonald and for the genuinely helpful suggestions offered by the anonymous reviewers of the manuscript.

The studies that form this book draw on text and images from more than sixty American magazines, and I am thankful for the existence of such rich source material from the industry in which I once worked. But I could not have analyzed much of that material without the enthusiastic help of several graduate research assistants, including Susan Robinson, Guillermo Avila-Saavedra, Rebecca Hains, Margaret Rakus, and Melissa Lenos. In particular, doctoral student Sue Robinson, who is a practicing journalist as well as gifted scholar, read the full manuscript and offered astute comments and significant structural advice, a level of feedback one would get from the best of professional editors. More generally, these and other graduate students in my "Media and Social Memory" classes have given me fresh insights that have sharpened my perspective on this field of scholarship.

I was inspired to pursue this topic and kind of research by Barbie Zelizer, who pointed me down memory lane nearly a decade ago, and my greatest intellectual debt is to her. Most of this work has been presented in some earlier form at scholarly conferences—the History and Magazine Divisions of the Association for Education in Journalism and Mass Communication, the American Journalism Historians Association, the International Communication Association, the Popular Culture Association, the Mid-Atlantic American Studies Association, and the Northeast Journalism Historians Conference—where I benefited from criticism and ideas from a broad assortment of scholars, whom I thank again now. A number of colleagues across the country who have heard or read earlier versions of this research have given me especially valuable feedback. They include Joseph Bernt, S. Elizabeth Bird, Frederick Blevens, Bonnie Brennen, Simon Bronner, Ray Browne, James Carey, Kathleen Endres, Scott Fosdick, Carol Holstead, Janice Hume, Sammye Johnson, Charles Kupfer, Jack Lule, Jane Marcellus, David T. Z. Mindich, Barbara Straus Reed, Leara Rhodes, John Soloski, Linda Steiner, Patrick Washburn, and Betty Winfield.

PAGES FROM THE PAST

Introduction

In academic circles and among social critics, it has long been a truism that journalism is ahistorical, especially so in America, the country presumably interested only in today and tomorrow. Yet in the opening years of the twenty-first century, the content of American journalism—and the broader national media culture—suggests the opposite: that we are a country obsessed with yesterday. Media treatments of yesterday may not be, strictly, history, yet the past permeates current journalism.

The backward glance of modern life is not merely a matter of media content. We are a nation of scrapbookers and family-reuniters who haunt antique stores looking for decorating touches of the "authentic" old days. We shop in boutiques selling vintage clothing that is as likely to be from the 1980s as the 1920s; we surf e-bay and cable-television channels in search of collectibles; we reenact military battles; we visit "living history villages" and heritage sites. A more somber side of this feeling for the past is our growing tendency to collectively memorialize the dead, with outpourings of grief over the loss of figures from Elvis Presley and John Lennon to Princess Diana and JFK Jr. The urge to memorialize was understandably intense and widespread just after September 11th. But now, because of the shape and rhetoric of those rituals, anyone who dies tragically in a public way is a candidate to be called a "hero" and to be "remembered" with flowers and candles and memorial plaques, by strangers as well as family.

These trends occur in the broader culture, but media play a part in their existence and enactment. It is, after all, from the media that we get many (perhaps most) of our notions about history as "heritage." And it is through news coverage that we learn how to behave publicly when tragedy occurs or famous people die. After former president Ronald Reagan died in early June 2004—one day before the sixtieth anniversary of D-Day—mournful-looking Americans lined up outside the national Capitol where he lay in state and lined the California highway route of his funeral motorcade. Yet despite the insistence of the news media, this behavior was not spontaneous: these ordinary mourners were covered by news media because they were there, but many of them were there because they were being covered by news media. Although Americans long have participated in memorial and civic rituals, the behavior of these modern-day mourners was specific to a mass-media setting. They had had plenty of rehearsal for how this event would be handled in journalism, plenty of experience with news coverage of other grief events. Those who could not remember television coverage of John F. Kennedy's funeral most likely had seen footage or photographs of his riderless horse and his cortege's procession to the Capitol in the dozens of media retrospectives about the assassinated president aired and published since 1963. They had read and watched journalists discuss the meaning of Ronald Reagan's presidency over a period of twenty years and had some sense of what his "story" might be in the end.

This book is about how that process unfolds in American journalism, how cultural narratives are constructed and reconstructed over time in ways that draw on the past to make sense of the present and future. These narratives—which we recognize even as we read them—are full of symbolic characters who represent what seem to be shared values. Their creation and retelling over time is a process not only of collective memory but also of collective amnesia, and the survival of certain stories has as much to do with today as with yesterday. To use the words of sociologist Maurice Halbwachs, who first described the concept of collective memory nearly a century ago, media memory is "a reconstruction of the past achieved with data borrowed from the present."[1]

Journalism has long played a role in the public articulation of American history. Betty Houchin Winfield and Janice Hume have traced the extensive use of historical references and reminiscent content in nineteenth-century newspapers and magazines, arguing that journalism was the first institution to create a public narrative about the nation's identity (preceding the writing of the first American history books).[2] Nor are memorial and nostalgia new in journalism. Harper's Weekly and other nineteenth-century periodicals grieved over President Abraham Lincoln's death as modern news media did over John F. Kennedy or Ronald Reagan. Beginning around World War I, cover artist Norman Rockwell and editor George Horace Lorimer of the Saturday Evening Post, then the nation's highest-circulation magazine, read by 2 million people each week, created a vision of a national past as a golden era of rural simplicity, an enduring ideal that was as wishful then as it is now and that remains intact in media today.[3]

Yet the nature and reach of reminiscent journalism have grown significantly since the middle of the twentieth century. In the 1950s two seemingly opposite yet actually complementary developments occurred that set the stage for this phenomenon: the magazine industry became more specialized, focusing on smaller but more homogeneous audiences defined in terms of shared identities and interests; and the new medium of television created a vast audience that reporters could imagine and speak to in national terms. The emergence of national broadcasting coincided with other social trends, including geographic mobility, family dislocation, and loss of regional identity—Americans' loss of "biographically distinctive moorings"—identified by sociologist Fred Davis in his discussion, more than a quarter century ago, of the turn toward modern nostalgia. Yet Davis ultimately concluded that the mass media were at the heart of this cultural transformation, declaring that "media products may now serve memory where once houses, streets, and persons did."[4]

Most of the media examples discussed in this book, therefore, were published during the past twenty-five years (though some are older). That evidence comes from sixty American magazines that have articulated several types of social memory. Unlike most scholarly studies on journalism and collective memory, which have tended to focus on newspapers and television news and on specific events (such as the Holocaust, the Kennedy assassination, Vietnam, or Watergate),[5] this study spotlights a critically neglected form of journalism while offering an unusually broad view of how memory is used across an entire medium. It further argues that, among all journalistic media, magazines have a special relationship with memory. Yet its overarching themes—the role of journalism in constructing shared ideas about the meaning of the past, and the role of memory in the creation of journalism—certainly apply to newspapers and television news as well.

In that larger sense, this study is meant to add to, and is based on, a growing body of scholarship addressing the social functions of journalism, particularly the narrative properties of news text[6] and journalistic uses of remembrance.[7] It also draws on the work of historians who have written on the role of narrative in understanding the past,[8] anthropologists and semioticians who have studied the structural nature of human communication,[9] and sociologists who have studied the cultural framework for journalistic production, as well as the appeal of nostalgia among audiences.[10]

Following the lead of the many textual studies in this interdisciplinary body of literature, this study uses rhetorical and narrative analysis to examine a broad range of primary sources. Sonja Foss defines rhetoric as "the process by which our reality or our world comes into being." She explains that a scholar using this method "does not study a rhetorical artifact for its qualities alone. Instead, the critic is interested in discovering what the artifact teaches us about the nature of rhetoric. The critic moves beyond the particularities of the artifact under study to discover what it suggests about symbolic processes in general."[11] Narrative analysis of news is a search for the common thematic choices journalists make consistently over time and across media, a study of the "culturally specific story-telling codes" that conform to "readers' existing narrative conventions," as S. Elizabeth Bird and Robert Dardenne explain.[12] This type of analysis is more deeply rooted in the work of scholars such as Roland Barthes and Vladimir Propp,[13] considering the connotative as well as denotative meanings of media images—what is suggested more broadly about culture, as well as what it literally depicted—and the structure, language, and emphases of media texts.

Such methods are necessarily tied to theory: they are based on the notion that journalism is a form of both cultural production and communal practice, what James Carey defines as a "ritual view of communication" in which news media work toward "the maintenance of society . . . the creation, representation, and celebration of shared even if illusory beliefs."[14] This model for understanding journalism blurs the line between producers and receivers, since "ritual is not something one is audience to but something one is participant in," notes Eric Rothenbuhler.[15]

Media narratives are indeed dialogic: that is, although the stories are "told" by journalists, the story types at least partly come from and return to the audience. Bird compares this process to oral storytelling, in which the role of the audience "is to respond to the storyteller, helping her or him shape future versions of the tale."[16] As her phrase suggests, media memory narratives also have a ritual component of repetition. "In order not to forget [its] past," writes Robert Bellah, a social group must "retell its story, its constitutive narrative."[17] In modern society, journalism is central to that retelling, and it is central to social identity formation and affirmation. The following chapters explore the role of journalistic memory in creating (and challenging) public notions about race, gender, and generation, while also weaving those particular concepts into a broader national ideal.

News has long been told through what Walter Fisher calls "the narrative paradigm,"[18] and many scholars have studied the ways in which journalistic media routinely use the techniques of narrative and personalization to find lessons in the news. Journalists are even more likely to do so when making sense of the events and personalities of the past.

"Narrativity provides us with a handle by means of which we can get hold of memory in action," writes Barbara DeConcini.[19] As Hannah Arendt explained: "Action reveals itself fully only to the storyteller, that is, to the backward glance of the historian, who indeed always knows better what it was all about than the participants. . . . Even though stories are the inevitable results of action, it is not the actor but the storyteller who perceives and 'makes' the story."[20] In journalism as well as historical writing, details of occurrences make sense only when placed within a narrative structure in which, to use the words of historian Hayden White, "events seem to tell themselves."[21] "Journalists have always been aware of this," writes Robert Karl Manoff. "Narratives bring order to events by making them something that can be told about; they have power because they make the world make sense."[22]

Audiences recognize news narratives because we have heard similar narratives before: even though the details of news vary, we understand what "the story" is. Novelty and familiarity blend together in a process Halbwachs compared to retouching a portrait to create a picture in which "new images overlay the old."[23] Thus memory is a factor not only in media summaries of the past but also in reporting of current events. Even journalism ostensibly about the present creates what M. M. Bakhtin called "the future memory of a past,"[24] serving a future public who will use that coverage as a memory cue, and perhaps as a historical document.

Journalists working in the present do increasingly take on the role of public historians, supplementing the communicative and educational role in American society of institutions such as museums, archives, historical tourism sites, and war memorials. The fields of public history and social history (an understanding of the past as it was lived by ordinary people) gained prominence during the 1960s and 1970s as, to use John Bodnar's terms, vernacular antidotes to the official American historical narratives of great men.[25] Ronald J. Grele wrote of its transformative potential at the time: "By its name, public history implies a major redefinition of the role of the historian. It promises us a society in which a broad public participates in the construction of its own history."[26] "Vernacular culture," writes Bodnar, "represents an array of specialized interests that are grounded in parts of the whole. . . . The term 'ordinary people' best describes the rest of society that participates in public commemoration and protects vernacular interests. They are a diverse lot, are not synonymous with the working class, and invariably include individuals from all social stations."[27]

Extending these concepts to mass media is problematic in that it is hard to argue that media do not support the status quo. Indeed, one common thread throughout the following chapters is the way in which media memories, no matter what their theme or time frame, culminate in a small and consistent set of unifying narratives about what it means to be American. On the other hand, media articulate ideas about the national present and past in diverse ways, given their sheer number and their respectively diverse audiences. Because of their focused themes, magazines in particular fit Bodnar's description of vernacular culture. And their audiences inarguably are ordinary people who, as this study reveals, are active in the construction of their own media memories.

In her President's Annual Address to the National Council on Public History in 1997, Diane F. Britton noted: "The images that we preserve to remember our collective past are reflected in the historical messages that confront us in our daily lives, thus reinforcing a sense of shared historical consciousness."[28] Yet—while surely such images include our daily encounters with various forms of media—historians have resisted including media in definitions of public history.

One exception is the growing number of historians who have become interested in film.[29] Their body of work[30] embraces Robert Brent Toplin's declaration that "the messages filmmakers communicate, directly and subtly, resonate with audiences in powerful ways, often shaping their ideas about the past's influence on the present."[31] Some writers in this vein call for new ways of thinking: "Instead of maintaining a disciplinary divide," writes Marcia Landy, "film scholars and historians need to pool their knowledge and work together in the interest of developing new methods for understanding history through images and fictional forms."[32] But the general tone of this scholarship is one of professional dismay. While acknowledging that film "can make history come alive more readily than commemorative addresses, lectures, exhibitions or museums," Anton Kaes writes that "history itself, so it seems, has been democratized by these eerily accessible images, but the power over what is shared as popular memory has passed into the hands of those who produce these images."[33] A presumed hierarchical relationship between historians and film makers is evident in an essay by two public historians who warn that historians "should not willingly continue to delegate the tasks of presenting historical narratives" to media producers.[34] Indeed, as historian Gerald Herman notes, "A kind of mutual disdain exists between historians and media professionals. Many historians regard history-based media producers as manufacturers of popular myths that overly simplify and distort 'true' history. And many media producers regard professional historians as nit-picking pedants who speak only to one another, shifting the discipline's center away from the human stories that make the past both interesting and important to audiences."[35]

This debate is the backdrop for two primary goals of this study: first, to add journalistic media, and specifically magazines, to this discussion, claiming a place for them on the terrain of public history;[36] and, second, to argue (without suggesting that film is not a legitimate conveyor of memory and history) that, perhaps more so than fictional media, journalistic media are a useful meeting ground for historians and media professionals, who do not work in such different realms and toward such different outcomes after all.

The public-history function of journalism was apparent in the many century-review issues and programs published or aired around the year 2000, which "revisited" people, events, and phenomena of the past by weaving them into a coherent narrative that made sense about the century as a whole. When publications or television programs celebrate their own anniversaries, or mark the anniversaries of milestone events, they also make historical generalizations, not just about what happened in the past, but also about what we now know it "meant" to "us."

Memory also resides in journalism that has been saved and preserved. Durable media are physical repositories for news and memory; as Barbie Zelizer puts it, "The media offer memory its own warehouse."[37] Yet carefully preserved newspapers reporting the Pearl Harbor attack or the moon landing, or old issues of the *Saturday Evening Post*, are something more than saved information; they become, for many people, treasured possessions that recall the owners' past, "the context of which they were once a part."[38] For Americans who did not save the initial reports of historic events, they have become available again, as newspapers reprint "Pages from the Past"[39] and as publications such as *Life* reprint historic issues (recently, for instance, it reissued its reports, complete with grainy photographs and original typefaces, on the Kennedy assassination and the Woodstock music festival).[40] The latter magazine also periodically issues "magabooks" (a hybrid paperback book and magazine for sale on newsstands) that are designed as history books summing up the American identity, such as a fall 2004 production titled *The American Immigrant: An Illustrated History*.[41]

These archival and touchstone functions are performed especially well by magazines, which have greater physical permanence than newspapers or television news reports and are manufactured in ways (with a glossy finish and perfect binding) that make them more likely to be collected and saved. To certain types of readers, collections of magazines are both an encyclopedia (for instance, think of how many homes contain shelves of *National Geographic*) and an identity statement. In its fortieth-anniversary issue, *Sports Illustrated* printed a letter from a charter subscriber who had "saved every copy of the magazine for the last 40 years. I have also made wooden boxes for all the volumes to keep them in mint condition."[42]

As "collectibles," magazines are commodities, arguably more so than newspapers (which don't cost as much, and their purchase is often thought of as a duty or habit rather than choice) or television news (which is technically free). Therefore, many critics consider them a commercial venture, pop culture for sale with content devised for profit, rather than a form of journalism. This is particularly the case with special issues, which sometimes are supplemental to, and may remain on sale for longer periods than, regular issues. Time Inc. offers not only themed compilations from historic issues of *Time, Life*, and *Sports Illustrated*, but also framed covers as a chance for readers to acquire "a piece of history" or, in the case of the first title, to "Own Your Moment in *Time*."[43] Magazines urge readers to collect the multiple covers they publish on special occasions: *TV Guide* ran four versions of Elvis Presley on the twentieth anniversary of his death, and *Vibe* published ten different covers, each featuring a different music star, on its own tenth anniversary.[44]

These special issues do indeed sell well. As of 1998, three of *Time's* four best-selling issues ever were cover stories about celebrity deaths, the theme of chapter 3.[45] And, as evidenced by "tributes" to dead celebrities (especially on anniversaries, years after the sadness of their actual deaths), certain types of media memory are arguably more commercial than others. Even the venerable *New York Times* has launched an online "store" in which it markets its extensive collection of historic photographs, as well as reprints of its own coverage of historic events, with phrases such as "Image Conscious" and "Photographic Memories"; it's also possible to buy a framed 1939 "homemaking cover," a scene of a family arriving at grandma's house for dinner, from *McCall's* magazine (which the *Times* briefly owned).[46]

Yet the very popularity of these kinds of journalistic media products, combined with their relative expense, suggests that they have personal and collective value, as material culture as well as information and imagery, to those who buy them. Even, or perhaps especially, as a commodity, a magazine can have profound social meaning to readers who identify with its contents, who treasure and save it as an object, and who believe and remember the story it tells.

Readers' loyalty to this medium is further strengthened by the editorial language magazines use. Their editors and writers address readers in a conversational way, anticipating their reactions and incorporating their impressions, especially in summary issues. A reflexive and inclusive style is apparent on the editor's page, where, often, the staff is pictured and readers are given an explanation of the content. Writers and editors tend to use the word "we" to link themselves with the audience, confirming James Carey's assertion that when a journalist looks back over time, "he abandons his pose as critic, adversary, and detective and becomes a member of the community."[47] In these ways, magazines can be seen as the most dialogic of all journalistic media.

Somewhat paradoxically, this identification with their readers increases magazines' authority to assess the meaning of American life and to define the "imagined community of the nation."[48] The editors of some of the twentieth century's foremost magazines have understood this. Describing its own influence after fifty years, *Life*'s editors wrote, "The magazine imparted a feeling that a vast nation could be brought together as a community."[49] In its seventy-fifth-anniversary issue, a columnist described *Time* as the "keeper of a certain American self-image and expectation" and as a "moral counselor."[50]

Newsmagazines' self-appointed status as national leaders is the subject of chapter 1, which examines summary issues published throughout the second half of the twentieth century at the ends of decades, and then, finally, at the end of the century itself, by *Time*, *Newsweek*, *U.S. News & World Report*, and *Life* (which at midcentury was a newsweekly). Read individually or as one body of work, these issues served as a form of public history, chronicling the facts of the past in a way that made sense of their order and placed them within "core plots" that recurred from era to era and created a larger story.

The twentieth-century story the newsmagazines told leading up to the year 2000 created a narrative template for the biggest story of the new century. Chapter 2 explores how American magazines explained the events of September 11th and their aftermath in terms of recognizable national mythology and a specific narrative about masculine heroism. Initially symbolized by the firemen who participated in the rescue effort, and in many cases died, at the World Trade Center, this hero

sprang from earlier media narratives about midcentury American heroism during World War II. The chapter traces the construction of this
symbolic figure in magazines ranging from *People Weekly* and *Parade* to
Sports Illustrated and the *Atlantic Monthly*. It then considers how other
tragic figures subsequently in the news were placed into the fireman
narrative, and how this heroic template set the stage for journalistic
coverage of American soldiers in Iraq.

The subjects of Chapter 3 were not ordinary heroes, but twenty celebrities whose deaths have been the most publicly mourned over a period
of more than forty years, from Marilyn Monroe in 1962 to Johnny
Cash in 2003, in magazines ranging from *TV Guide* and *Entertainment
Weekly* to *Rolling Stone* and the *New Yorker*. This study identifies common themes that emerge in magazine tributes to such figures (despite
how they differed from each other in life) and examines how media use
the act of memorial to define the celebrity as "one of us." It considers the
role of celebrity in American culture as well as the way in which memorialization changes the individual life stories of public figures. And it
challenges media critics' assertion that such extensive media mourning
and memorialization began with "the Diana phenomenon."

Chapter 4 explores the role of race in collective memory as told
through media. One of those magazines is the oldest surviving consumer magazine for African Americans, *Ebony*;[51] the other is *American Legacy*, which is just a decade old and focuses specifically on African American history. More so than others, this chapter explores the
importance of visual imagery in social-group identity—in fulfilling the
need for "testimony" and for documentation of ordinary life, as well as
notable accomplishments, within a minority community. These magazines reveal how African Americans have used journalism as one means
by which to become a part of the official American historical narrative
while also challenging and changing that narrative through "counter-
memory."

Chapter 5 offers a look at how magazines have defined the American population and their own audiences in terms of generational identity. Particularly since the 1980s, journalistic media have devoted significant attention to "the Baby Boom," "Generation X," "Generation Y"
(or the "Echo Boom"), and an older group once called merely "seniors"
but now hailed as "The Greatest Generation." While it considers this
theme in several types of magazines, it focuses on trend reporting in
cover stories published by the leading American newsmagazines over a

twenty-five-year period. It identifies commonalities in their characterizations of these groups—chief among them, a sort of instant nostalgia
as soon as the generation is named—as a study in how social trends
seem to emerge, depart, and then reemerge in journalism. And with
specific regard to Boomers, it examines the media meaning of the past
for a generation that refuses to grow old.

The truly old are the primary audience for the publications examined
in chapter 6, two magazines specializing in nostalgia, *Reminisce* and
Good Old Days. The stories in these magazines paint a sepia-toned picture of a lost past that was a simpler and better time and place than the
present, even if life was harder. They are the most conversational of all
the magazines discussed in this book and the ones in which readers are
most involved in the content, contributing the reminiscences and seeming to talk with one another on the pages. The overtly nostalgic stories
they tell illustrate the process of collective amnesia as well as memory.
Yet they also illuminate the constructive aspects of memory revision as
an identity-affirmation and survival strategy for older audiences, especially women.

Finally, chapter 7 traces how thirty national consumer magazines
have celebrated their own anniversaries in ways that have allowed them
to speak not just for their own institutional histories but also on behalf
of "society." They range in age from 5 to 150 years old and in nature
from *Good Housekeeping, Glamour,* and *Gourmet* to the *Utne Reader, Fast
Company,* and *Vibe.* These magazines each characterize history in ways
specific to a theme (such as food, sports, entertainment, homemaking,
fashion, or music), yet they do so in strikingly similarly ways, revealing
a number of common editorial approaches to summarizing very different aspects of American life.

As a whole, this book offers evidence that magazines have become
important social commentators on American life, as well as public historians of national culture—that, as historian Michael Kammen acknowledges of media in general, they take on "an ever larger responsibility for explaining America, as well as the meaning of America, to
Americans and others."[52] When magazine journalists write in terms of
national memory, they produce reports that are meant to serve as keepsakes; in a mediated conversation with their audiences, they characterize the past in ways that merge the past, the present, and the future into
a single, ongoing tale. In both of these ways, they shift their professional
work away from the transience of news and toward the weight of official

record. The magazines that are the focus of the following chapters exemplify a new and accelerating kind of journalism: they are documentary texts and material culture that provide—as one Time-Life direct-mail piece put it—"a time and place where history and memory mingle in the story of our own lives."[53]

1 How We Lived

Summing Up the Twentieth Century

Historians like to bundle years in ways that make sense, provide continuity and link past to present. Hundred-year packages—centuries—are the most popular form, and close behind is the decade, as if God had designed the world on the decimal system.—*Life*, 1989[1]

It's an amazing tale, and like the very best literature, it grabs readers not only with its twists of plot and its resonant themes but also with a collection of characters that dance in our minds, the great men and women who with their lives wrote the history of our times.—*Time*, 1998[2]

The first statement above, written by historian Daniel Boorstin, appeared not in a scholarly journal of his own profession, but in a special issue of *Life* magazine reviewing the 1980s. Since their foundings in the early twentieth century, *Life* and other magazines have made a regular practice of "bundling years" at decades' end, and within less than a decade of Boorstin's comment, they offered an entire "hundred-year package" of magazine memory. This chapter examines newsmagazine journalism at a moment when, as *Time*'s managing editor puts it, Americans stood in "the vestibule of [a] new millennium."[3] As his language suggests, news media considered themselves historians of American culture at the end of the twentieth century and the second millennium, self-consciously taking on the role of selecting the most important people and events of the past and explaining their historical significance.

Such journalism also has served to organize the past itself into meaningful slices. Eviatar Zerubavel notes that, because time and history are continuous, the selection of a beginning and ending point to an era is a purely social decision, one with "profound collective meaning."[4] While days and years are naturally occurring divisions of time, decades and centuries are not; they are, instead, cultural constructs that "chain events together" and offer "social buoys for our orientation . . . on the endless 'bridge of time.'"[5] In its own series of six century-summary issues, the *New York Times Magazine* referred to such divisions, and to retrospective journalism based on them, as "the illusion that we can stop the clock and somehow, even at this late date, master space and time."[6]

Media century summaries began in the mid-1990s, and by the end of 1998, several books had been published on the theme. One of the most prominent, the bestselling *The Century*, was coauthored by a journalist, television-news anchor Peter Jennings, and was the basis for two television documentary series, one on ABC and one on the History Channel (a corporate cable sibling).[7] Yet no medium so commanded this topic and treatment as did American newsmagazines.[8] They had been honing the story of the century—declaring its themes, weaving them together, and speculating on their meaning—for decades.

This chapter examines that process in four U.S. magazines, *Time*, *Newsweek*, *U.S. News & World Report*, and *Life*, publications that, for much of the twentieth century, were considered news media and yet also were common sites for national reminiscence. Each of these magazines devoted issues to summarizing the twentieth century, and *Life* even published a special issue that reviewed the past *thousand* years. *Time* began a six-part "People of the Century" series (culminating in a

"Man of the Century") in 1998, and for two years this was, as its managing editor noted, "a true multimedia project," including spinoff television specials airing on CBS and PBS, a web site where readers could register their opinions on the magazine's choices, and eventually a book containing all of the profiles in its "Top 100" people of the century.[9]

While these reports promised a new perspective on the American past, they drew on a reportorial format and voice established some fifty years earlier in the half-century-in-review issues published by *Time* and *Life* (figure 1.1) and reiterated in all four magazines' decade summaries. At the end of the twentieth century, the four magazines had a combined paid domestic circulation of just over 11 million readers, with *Time* and *Newsweek* reaching the majority (a total of 7.3 million) of them.[10] Because the issues discussed in this chapter were special issues and were designed to be keepsakes, it is likely that their readership exceeded average circulation figures.

Although its emphasis was by then more on features than news, *Life* was included in this survey because it was conceived as a form of photojournalism and because during the middle decades of the century it was indeed a weekly newsmagazine and was much more widely read than the other three magazines.[11] *Life* also was the most active memory maker, labeling its special issues as "keepsakes" and "collectors' editions."[12] *U.S. News & World Report*, which emphasizes business news and service journalism ("news you can use"), did not do decade summaries until the 1980s, but it was included because during the 1990s it moved toward this type of reminiscence and it did undertake a century-review series.

Of the four magazines, *Time* is the oldest, founded by Henry Luce and Britton Hadden in 1923. Its success as a weekly medium that delivered the world to Americans spawned a corporate sibling, *Life*, created in 1936 to fulfill a similar purpose through photography. *Time*'s popularity also inspired two competitors that debuted in 1933. One was *News-week* (as it was initially punctuated); the other was *U.S. News*,[13] which gained a sister publication, *World Report*, thirteen years later and merged with it in 1948. All four were related in genre, and they dominated weekly newsmagazine journalism through the middle decades of the twentieth century. Especially before the advent of television news, they were influential national news media, and their emphasis was then more on news than on entertainment.[14]

Nevertheless, from their inceptions, these magazines have forsaken the traditional, detached language of newspaper journalism in favor of a

FIGURE 1.1
Life *cover, January 2, 1950*
(Credit: Life, January 2, 1950).

voice that was meant to establish their authority as national leaders and to forge a personal bond with their readers. Their goals were to explain, to synthesize, and to interpret as well as to inform. During its debut year, promotional advertisements for *Newsweek* defined the new publication's goal of "sifting, selecting, and clarifying the significant news of the week," explaining to prospective readers that the magazine "does not take the place of a newspaper . . . it is an indispensable complement to newspaper reading, because it explains, expounds, clarifies."[15] The first issue of *Life* described its editors' "job of making pictures behave with some degree of order and sense."[16]

Time's prospectus revealed that it would serve as a summary medium that honored the limited "time which busy men are able to spend on simply keeping informed" with a promise to "organize the world's news and give it to readers in short, easily digestible doses."[17] At the heart of this vision (the magazine later remembered) was "this truth: history may be complicated, as life is complicated, but the business of storytelling is simple. . . . Sort the world into stories and carry them (facts, personalities, ideas, images, dramas, quirks, gossip, the details and energy of life) from Out There, where things happen, to In Here, inside the reader's consciousness, where stories turn into wonder, entertainment, cautionary experience, useful memory."[18] On the magazine's twenty-fifth anniversary in 1948, *Time*'s editors confirmed the continuation of this philosophy: "Journalists who have resolved to tell the news through the actions, characters, and motives of people have committed themselves to dealing in narrative." They went on to quote a former managing editor of the magazine as explaining that "a *Time* story must be completely organized from beginning to end; it must go from nowhere to somewhere."[19]

During their earliest years, newsmagazines were part of a medium that had dominated American public communication, and the construction of a sense of national identity, since the mid-nineteenth century. By the early twentieth century, media had joined the institutions of education, religion, and civic life as an important disseminator of political and cultural ideals. Magazines were leaders in this process because they were the only medium capable of reaching a national audience and using illustrations and then photographs in a large-scale and dramatic way.[20] Newspapers had never had the same national reach or visual impact. Radio provided some journalistic competition, although broadcast news would not assume its modern format and authority until the 1960s. During World War II it was the newsmagazine medium—

notably *Life*—that would finally be able to convey the reality of Holocaust atrocity through visual documentation of the concentration camps as they were liberated, a story that seemed untellable in words alone.[21] Magazines faced their first real competition in articulating the meaning of American life from the medium of film, which told its own compelling set of stories ranging from the Depression-era struggles of the common man in the 1930s to dark visions of disaffected American youth in the 1950s.

The stories the newsmagazines told, though, were based in fact, and their consistency over time—combined with their documentary nature—created and reinforced a particular view of the national character. If film offered varying versions of national identity, the newsmagazines collectively crafted a unified, patriotic vision.[22] *Time* described itself as "an American institution, mentor to the questing middle class . . . America's superego."[23] *Life* proclaimed that it "dedicates itself to being a lively instrument of the National Purpose," expanding on Henry Luce's vow that in any political debate, the magazine would take "the side that makes for the enlargement and for the deepening of human freedom."[24] *Newsweek* spoke for the nation in similar language after two major wars, confessing its "bias" of "confidence in the future of the United States" in 1945 and, after Vietnam during the 1970s, embracing "the enduring American faith that problems can be solved, that most people want to do the right thing and that somehow, the country will come through."[25] *Life*'s editors proposed to create a visual conversation in which editors and readers *together* certified what was good about America. A former editor claims that "one could, figuratively speaking, find himself or herself in the magazine's pages, or recognize one's hopes, or stoke one's indignation, or appease one's need for self-improvement or the need to identify with the great long line of humanity reaching back to the caves."[26]

The newsmagazine editors stressed the importance of the audience in shaping the stories that were told in decade- and century-review issues. Reviewing the first half of the century, *Life*'s editors admitted, "We expect to be chided by some readers for leaving out favorite memories"; at the end of the 1960s, *Time*'s editors wrote, "We hope that readers will be intrigued by—even if they may occasionally disagree with—the judgments of our editors and critics."[27] The text of the summary issues frequently contained the first-person plural "we," imagining both journalists and readers as being simultaneously inside and outside the story, as participants and spectators.

Newsweek took such a dual perspective in this sports metaphor for the 1960s: "At every moment when we might have paused to try to figure out what exactly was happening, to absorb it, to brace for the next onset . . . something else had happened and we were off again, running and stumbling, cheering and cursing, agape at some new astonishment or aghast at some new horror."[28] *Life* used "we" in both nostalgic generalizations, as in its description of the first decade of the century as a time when "we were at peace [and] the world loved us," and accounts of specific "hard" news topics, as in its reference to U.S. soldiers in Vietnam as "our men."[29] *Time*'s managing editor referred to the subject of the magazine's special series as the story of "our century."[30]

It was in this conversational and communal voice that newsmagazine journalists created public memory in year-end and decade-end reviews throughout the twentieth century. They peopled the plots of recent news with characters who had survived the test of time. In *Life*'s review of the 1970s, the magazine's managing editor defined a decade as "a sequence of time that is marked forever by the actions and voices of the men and women who lived it."[31] All four magazines have reported the passage of time primarily in terms of people rather than events and issues, and of individuals rather than groups. Since 1927, four years after its debut, *Time* has summarized each year in terms of one person, its "Man of the Year,"[32] and this practice has spilled over into its decade reviews. Describing the recent past in terms of individual actors is a way of resolving what founder Henry Luce identified in a 1940 memo as the "tension between the particular problems of little people (all of us and our families) and the surge of great 'historic forces.'"[33]

The very choice of explaining events in terms of people endows the news (or history) with meaning, explains James Carey: "We assume that individuals are authors of their own acts, that individuals do what they do intentionally, they say what they say because they have purposes in mind. The world is the way it is because individuals want it that way."[34] Ernest Borman argues that we understand the news not just through people, but through characters with motives. Personalization in journalism "stems from the human tendency to try to understand events in terms of people with certain personality traits and motivations, making decisions, taking actions, and causing things to happen. . . . The public can most easily understand disturbing issues when speakers portray them by placing symbolic personae in dramatic action in which they contend with other personae symbolizing other positions."[35]

Reporters place newsmakers "into the existing categories of hero, villain, good and bad, and thus . . . invest their stories with the authority of mythological truth," write S. Elizabeth Bird and Robert Dardenne; through such roles, individuals participate in the "dramatization [that] is part of the journalistic imperative to make the world comprehensible."[36] Anthropologist Victor Turner similarly has noted that news often contains "stage business" and such "dramatic personae" as "traitors, renegades, villains, martyrs, heroes, faithful, infidels, deceivers, scapegoats." In this symbolic system, "meaning is apprehended by *looking back* [emphasis in original] over a temporal process."[37]

In the offices of *Life*, "the picture story was described as an 'act,' a reference . . . [that] implied that the magazine was a stage."[38] When it debuted in 1933, *Newsweek* explained its mission in theatrical terms: "Across the stage of human affairs today moves the news that affects you, your happiness and security, your country—a stage so vast that no one man alone and unaided can see it all, nor understand all that he sees. As interpreter and guide to this ever-shifting drama we offer you *News-week* [sic]."[39] Henry Luce defined *Time*'s journalistic territory as "a world whose knaves and good men, fools and heroes play their parts on a stage whose backdrop is literally life-and-death."[40]

Indeed, the individuals written about and pictured in newsmagazine decade reviews filled recognizable dramatic roles, and heroes were rewarded with a new chance at life, while villains died literal or figurative deaths. Reviewing the 1920s, *Life* told the story of the Hall-Mills murder case as a melodrama[41] in which a New Jersey minister and a choir singer were doomed lovers brought down by a vengeful wife.[42] In a story meant to represent the 1930s, *Time* cast Louisiana politician Huey Long in the role of a cunning villain trying to take advantage of the common man in times of trouble—and his 1935 assassination as the logical outcome.[43] World War II provided a surplus of heroes, villains, and victims, both world leaders (Churchill, FDR, Stalin, Hitler) and anonymous people: *Time*'s half-century review depicted the Holocaust as a pile of skeletons at Buchenwald, and it named "The American Fighting-Man" as its "Man of the Year" for 1950, a reference to the entire 1940s, both World War II and the start of the Cold War.[44]

In the 1960s there were (to use the magazines' words) "Martyrs," John and Bobby Kennedy, Martin Luther King Jr., and Malcolm X; "Murderers," their respective assassins; and "Mourners," Jacqueline and Ethel Kennedy and Coretta King,[45] while the slain president was cast as a Hamlet-like "departed prince."[46] According to the section titles in *News-*

week's 1970s summary, "Trouble" was symbolized by passengers in a field after an airplane crash, "Scandal" by Spiro Agnew and various Watergate conspirators (who suffered political deaths), and "Terror" by a ski-masked gunman at the 1972 Munich Olympics.[47]

Less deadly but equally striking was *Time*'s theatrical metaphor for the close of the following decade: "The 1980s came to an end in what seemed like a magic act, performed on a world-historical stage. Trapdoors flew open, and whole regimes vanished." This stage terminology was particularly apt since what was being discussed was the falling (or raising) of the Iron Curtain. The piece went on to call Soviet premier Mikhail Gorbachev the "impresario" behind the show, though he was also cast as its "superstar." He was "a nimble performer who can dance a side step, a showman and manipulator of reality, a suave wolf tamer."[48]

Time's naming of Gorbachev as its "Man of the Decade" was an example of newsmagazines' use of world leaders to stand for world events. The magazine had made a similar gesture forty years earlier when it named Winston Churchill "Man of the Half-Century," telling the story of World War II through his trials and triumphs.[49] Such famous individuals filled the pages of newsmagazines' decade reviews, particularly in photos, representing the events or issues of which they were a part. America's new role as world peacekeeper was depicted by *Newsweek* in 1959 through President Dwight Eisenhower shown smiling with various world leaders, as well as American-flag-waving schoolchildren in Rome.[50] In all the 1970s reviews, the resigning president Richard Nixon symbolized America's loss of faith in political leaders, while the handshake of Egyptian president Anwar Sadat and Israeli premier Menachem Begin symbolized hope for peace in the Middle East. *Life*'s 1980s review cast the end of the Cold War as the story of two men, Mikhail Gorbachev and Ronald Reagan, identified in a title merely as "Misha and Ron"; *U.S. News & World Report* called them the decade's "spin doctors."[51]

For each decade, the newsmagazines turned their spotlight not just on political actors, but on a wide cast of celebrities who personified larger events and themes. Chief among the heroes were athletes, from Jack Dempsey to Jackie Robinson, from the 1969 Mets to the 1980 U.S. Olympic hockey team. Those particular competitors were celebrated not only because they won but also because they were underdogs. Of Jack Dempsey, one newsmagazine wrote: "In the 1920s, when Americans worked hard, drove their cars hard, drank hard and played hard, they liked to go out to sporting events and cheer the man who hit hard. . . .

Dempsey had three things that millions of Americans found irresist-ible: he could hit, he never quit and he was a poor boy making good. As the stone-broke, hobo son of a poor Western family, he fought for years. . . ."[52]

Stage and screen actors also were routinely portrayed as representa-tive of their times, even if it was only the characters they played who stood for broader characterizations of decades. Thus singer Rudy Vallee and movie-star flapper Clara Bow embodied the "carefree" 1920s; *Satur-day Night Fever*'s John Travolta and *Annie Hall*'s Woody Allen and Diane Keaton represented the narcissistic 1970s; and Sylvester Stallone as Rambo stood for the militaristic 1980s.[53] During the 1980s, business leaders took center stage as heroes and villains in a play about ambition and greed. The heroes included computer visionary Bill Gates, down-to-earth Wal-Mart founder Sam Walton, and flashy real-estate magnate Donald Trump; the villains included income-tax-evading hotel queen Leona Helmsley and inside-trader Ivan Boesky.[54]

Political leaders, celebrities, and business tycoons have played key roles in the decade stories told by American newsmagazines. Yet so too have ordinary people, who are perhaps the most symbolically impor-tant players of all on this journalistic stage. As the introduction to *U.S. News & World Report*'s 1980s summary noted, "Decades are never simply about the greats."[55] The inclusive voice of the community—the "we," journalists and readers looking back over time together—underscores the central role of the common man in summary journalism.

So important is the typical American that the magazines have used him in grand metaphors. The opening photograph in *Life*'s 1936 debut issue was that of a newborn baby (who, as a middle-aged man lean-ing over a blazing birthday cake, occupied the magazine's fiftieth-anni-versary-issue back page).[56] In their half-century review issues, *Life* de-scribed the "adolescent spirit" of America before the world wars, noting that "now we have come to responsible maturity," while *Time* portrayed the country as a man at middle age who "did a good deal of laughing at himself, knowing that he had come far in a hurry and was somewhat ludicrously unsure of what he was or where he was going."[57]

More often, though, the newsmagazines have featured actual people in their review issues as a way of personifying specific events. These ordinary characters act as stand-ins for the audience, notes Wendy Kozol in her study of *Life*'s depiction of middle-class families: "Even though they [are] 'strangers,' as representatives their easily recognizable social roles [make] them deeply familiar."[58] This device also enables journalists to turn the spotlight away from themselves, as the audience becomes the author of news, as well as history.

The magazines' use of theatrical metaphors elevates those audience members to types, recognizable characters who embody values and events. Looking back on the 1960s (which it called an era when "few had time to listen or pause for dialogue"), *Life* declared, "Americans living through the drama of these years performed—on camera—a running scenario that was nearly always fantastic, at times unbelievable. The photographs on these pages recall scenes from the American drama."[59] In summary journalism, stories become what Victor Turner calls "social drama" that turns on shared values, "a play a society acts about itself—not only a reading of its experience but an interpretive reenactment of its experience . . . a public way of assessing our social behavior."[60]

Visual images of anonymous people enacting news events have filled the pages of decade reviews. In the 1970s, a decade with few political or celebrity heroes, the magazines' photographic emphasis on Everyman and Everywoman was especially noticeable: a young woman cried out over the body of a shot Kent State student, a symbol of domestic conflict over Vietnam; a man filled a gasoline can during the oil crisis; a female firefighter and navy "midshipman" represented the women's movement; another woman demonstrated against pornography; and attractive young adults emblematic of the "Me Decade" jogged, relaxed in hot tubs, and danced to disco music.

The meaning of such figures was magnified when the magazines juxtaposed contrasting photos from the same era, making them symbols of tensions as well as trends. In *Life*, a smiling crowd extended handshakes toward a campaigning John F. Kennedy, while an angry crowd made obscene gestures outside the 1968 Chicago Democratic National Convention; in *Time*, a majorette twirled a baton in one scene, next to another showing a naked couple from the Broadway play *Oh! Calcutta!*; in *Newsweek*, a man dressed as Uncle Sam marched in a Bicentennial parade, while another used the American flag as a spear in a Boston race riot.[61]

A single feature in *Life*'s 1980s issue demonstrated the technique of combining photos of ordinary people to tell a complex story while, at the same time, painting a portrait of America as a pluralistic community. A writer-photographer team had driven across the country on 2,900-mile Interstate 80 "to examine the joys and concerns of those living along it and to document how they have weathered these past 10 years." Each individual or group who appeared in photos and text symbolized some aspect of American life in this decade: a Chinese immigrant woman sewing an American flag in a factory, an abortion protester, a bedridden man with AIDS, a homeless woman and her children, a group of people praying outside a crack house, the inhabitants of a dying small town, mourners near a car demolished by a drunk driver, and a couple with three children they'd had through $180,000 worth of in vitro fertilization.[62]

Not only photos but also words of ordinary people were invoked to describe important events. Several of *Life*'s decade-review issues featured recurring sections titled Voices, in which hundreds of Americans commented on the milestones of their eras. *Time*'s 1970s summary contained only two pages of text written by the magazine's staff; the rest of the issue consisted of photographs captioned by quotations from individuals who had found themselves involved in headline-making events, such as a survivor of the mass suicide in Jonestown, a women's rights activist, and the soldier who made the last military dispatch from Saigon in April 1975. "Typical" citizens were quoted in state-of-the-nation polls *Life* and *Newsweek* conducted at the end of the 1960s and 1970s.

The opinions of ordinary people were at the heart of *Time*'s feature on "The Middle Americans," a hypothetical married couple it selected as its "Man and Woman of the Year" for 1970. This choice, the editors explained, was a reflection on the preceding year as a response to all of the 1960s, as well as to the coming decade: "Mr. and Mrs. Middle America are the ones who sent President Nixon to the White House and the astronauts to the moon, who feel most threatened by the attacks on traditional values." They were the type of people who "sing the national anthem at football games—and mean it." One of them, a forty-three-year-old General Electric worker who had fought as a Marine in World War II "and can still do 400 sit-ups," claimed, "There is a movement in this country to discredit our nation." Other representative "Middle Americans" spoke out in this feature, including a forty-seven-year-old librarian who proclaimed, "Dissent is disgusting," and a thirty-four-year-old mother of four who wanted "my children to live and grow up in an America as I knew it, where we were proud to be citizens."[63]

The same issue contained an emotional portrait of other ordinary heroes: nine working-class young men who had grown up together in an Arizona small town and had gone into the Marines "in the patriotic camaraderie typical of Morenci's mining families." Six of them who had died in Vietnam were lauded in terms physical ("tall and husky, he was popular with Morenci's girls"), psychological ("a quiet but competitive youth [who] most enjoyed riding his two horses . . . through the secluded countryside"), and heroic ("an all-state linebacker whose jolting tackles would have brightened the Saturdays of any college coach").[64]

Common people stood for the issues of their day and for American values that endured over time. Sometimes, like the GE worker, they themselves referred to the past, though more often the magazine writers and editors made this connection, positioning modern-day citizens against the backdrop of a generalized American heritage. In its 1960s review, *Life* offered a very different version of the ordinary American than *Time* had, yet invoked the same values of a time gone by. The issue featured an unidentified family of six who had "dropped out" of mainstream life and were living in a commune. The text presented them as symbols of their time while also placing them within a larger historical narrative: "It was a scene from an earlier America—the nobly bearded patriarch and his family clustered together in the evening in a rude dwelling. . . . In search of some dream of honesty and simplicity, these young people, along with hundreds of others, had left city life to settle in primitive communities where they could live closer to the land." These were not counterculture hippies; they were a nuclear family "honor[ing] a tradition of American utopianism going back to Brook Farm and Walden."[65]

Life's half-century review contained perhaps the most striking example of this use of a representative American belonging to "public time."[66] That issue characterized the entire first half of the twentieth century as one man: "Mr. Midstream, the average man of the past 50 years." Mr. Midstream was an actual person, Junius Shaw, a St. Louis auto-parts salesman who had been born at twenty seconds after midnight on January 1, 1901. Outlining Shaw's life against the backdrop of "the Roaring 20s," Prohibition, and the Depression, the writer offered this portrait: "His life has been very typical of his era. He got married when everybody else did, got divorced, got drunk, went broke, made a comeback, bought a new car, all at the proper times. It is difficult to hear him tell his story without the eerie feeling that it is not one man who is talking but a million men. Shaw is a prototype. He is like the familiar face that constantly appears and disappears on a crowded street, the tune that is always half heard and half recognized but then fades out. He is the man everyone knows intimately but yet has never met—Mr. Midstream."[67]

Like the 1960s "utopian" family, Mr. Midstream was (and is) a symbolically powerful journalistic device because his story is one audiences like to recognize as their own. The saga of the American individual is one of the several standard story types that string decades together into a more comprehensive and lasting narrative.

Just as the same character types have appeared in newsmagazine summary issues, the types of stories they have told similarly have recurred from decade to decade. Sociologist Fred Davis called these "core plots," scenarios in which, "despite our knowledge that the details are new, we nevertheless feel certain we have heard 'the same story' many times before."[68] As Lance Bennett and Murray Edelman observe of such stories, "Each iteration of the symbolic process reinforces the cycle and prepares the . . . audience for the next time."[69] Throughout the twentieth century, the "core plots" of stories told in newsmagazine decade reviews included:

- *The virtue of individualism.* As evidenced by the magazines' relentless conflation of people and events, national issues are literally embodied in the individual. This archetypical American pulls himself up by his bootstraps and takes responsibility for his actions (and thus, also, for the events he represents—the news itself). He is the ultimate symbol of the country's independence.[70]
- *The rise of the underdog,* as previously noted in the stories of sports heroes such as Jack Dempsey. President Jimmy Carter was portrayed in all the 1970s reviews as the underdog-outsider who restored Americans' faith in political leadership, while Pope John Paul II was described as "the Polish dark horse who had conquered Rome."[71]
- *The fall from grace of the greedy or immoral,* and the resulting "righting" of the moral order. Perhaps the biggest story fitting this plot was that of Richard Nixon, whose resignation (as remembered in all the magazines) symbolized the country's expurgation of corrupt leadership, not merely the fall of one man. In the 1980s this plot was applied as well to Leona Helmsley, whose conviction for tax evasion was a vindication for tax-paying citizens, and baseball great Pete Rose, whose gambling problem tarnished the image of the all-American game.[72]
- *The triumph of democracy.* In all four magazines, this plot was acted out by world leaders in the stories of the Allied victory in World War II, the end of the Cold War, and the fall of communism in Eastern Europe. It also was inscribed in homey celebrations of patriotism.[73] Reviewing the 1976 Bicentennial, *Life* published photos of

revelers dressed in red, white, and blue and wrote: "The people of George, Wash., baked a 60-square-foot cherry pie. In Miami 7,000 became U.S. citizens at once. All day long, from sea to shining sea, we marched down Main Street [and] set off firecrackers."[74]

· *The survival of the small town.* This plot is an extension of the virtue of individualism, since the small town is the symbolic home of the Common Man. Across decades, the small town has stood for the survival of the American way, portrayed in terms of both community ties and self-sufficiency. *Life* turned its spotlight on the inhabitants of particular towns to show how they were thriving (Boonville, Missouri, in 1950) or endangered (Chugwater, Wyoming, in 1989). *Time* depicted the churchgoing residents of Port Jefferson, New York, as symbolic of the values rejected by the 1960s counterculture. *U.S. News & World Report* discussed America's change from a manufacturing economy to a service economy in terms of the rebirth of Park City, Utah (transformed from a mining town to a tourist site).[75]

· *The role of technology in making the world a better place.* This core plot could be seen in *Life*'s 1950 salute to the automobile as a defining invention of the century's first half, and in *Newsweek*'s 1970 treatment of the space program and moon landing. More lighthearted but equally clear was *Time*'s 1990 photograph (explaining the 1980s) in which computers and other consumer electronics were arranged in the form of a smiling face.[76]

These common themes in newsweekly decade reviews parallel the "values in the news" that sociologist Herbert Gans enumerated in his study of *Time* and *Newsweek* (along with network-television news) in the late 1960s and early 1970s. Among the values he identified were "individualism" and "small-town pastoralism" in journalistic depictions of a "good life" characterized by "cohesiveness, friendliness, and slow pace." He explained: "The news seems to imply that the democratic ideal against which it measures reality is that of the rural town meeting—or rather, of a romanticized version of it."[77] Journalists' acknowledgment of these ideals places the specifics of news within the context of the ongoing American experience. What has gone before will come again. The details of these stories vary, yet they vary in consistent ways over time. As Fred Davis noted, "the historic plots and stories that symbolically fix a decade in our minds encompass not just a single decade but several at once. Moreover, these are linked thematically in certain patterns of inversion, complementarity or negation which make it difficult to change the thematic representation of one without markedly altering the definitions of others as well."[78]

The complementarity of these journalistic linkages can be seen in *Time*'s midcentury explanation of how the 1910s, 1920s, and 1930s had led to a Second World War: "The decade which ended in 1920 had seen a war that was to prove inconclusive. It had seen a revolution that was to lie quiescent after establishing itself in the largest country of the world. The decade which ended in 1930 was one of confusion and wasted energy — the wasted energy of gambling and gin-drinking in the U.S., of civil war in the Far East, of misdirected revolutionary effort from the U.S.S.R., of the attempt in Europe to hold resurgent peoples in check. The decade which ended this week [1940] saw the failure of that attempt and the unleashing of ruthless war."[79] Similarly, in *Life*'s 1970s issue, social critic Tom Wolfe explained that decade's narcissism as the culmination of a larger trend begun in the 1940s, "a development so stupendous, so long in the making, and so obvious": the great expectations that resulted from wartime spending, postwar prosperity, and the Baby Boom and "business boom" of midcentury decades.[80]

Inversion and negation are illustrated by the magazines' efforts to create a logical trajectory between the 1960s and the 1980s. *Newsweek*'s 1970s summary began with a nod to the previous decade: "After the tumult of the angry '60s, it was supposed to be a quiet time — a pause to reflect, regroup and recover."[81] *Time* wrote that the 1970s were "erected upon the smoldering wreckage of the '60s": "Now and then, someone's shovel blade would strike an unexploded bomb; mostly the air in the '70s was thick with a sense of aftermath, of public passions spent and consciences bewildered. The American gaze turned inward." Yet the magazine found cause for optimism and renewal in the coming 1980s, declaring that Americans had "fac[ed] up to crises (a lost war and a broken presidency) that might have turned other societies rabid or anarchic. . . . There is an impression now of national unity, a feeling that the U.S. is emerging from the privatism and divisions of the Me Decade. . . . the '80s may even prove to be the Us Decade."[82]

While inversion suggests causality between contrasting events and values of consecutive decades, negation is something more — not just a balancing of the previous decade, but a denial of what seemed to be its consequences. For this reason, narrative linkages, in a story told over time, are particularly important in the historical work done by newsmagazines. It is worth considering not just what stories *were* told about decades, and what people emerged as symbolic of eras, but also what stories were not told, and what people were not included in those tales.

Because the overall narrative was a positive one, certain historic episodes, while covered, were explained away as aberrations, as problems that were solved by progress. In the conservative *Time* (though less so in *Newsweek*), periods of political dissent, such as the antiwar, civil rights, and women's movements of the 1960s and early 1970s, were described as national illnesses, rifts in the social fabric that were ultimately healed. Beyond such finessing were outright erasures: some events and eras that did not fit well into a narrative of progress were simply left out of the story. In reviewing the first half of the century, *Time*, *Life*, and *Newsweek* devoted more attention to the 1920s than the 1930s, virtually ignoring the Great Depression. Only *Newsweek* reviewed the 1950s—a decade that in 1960s summaries was remembered as a time of postwar, suburban domesticity and prosperity, rather than McCarthyism and Cold War. Also missing were actors whose stories contradicted the core plots delineated here: losers (that is, ordinary people who have *not* succeeded, even despite hard work); Americans who have opposed democracy and capitalism, such as the Socialists whose party gained national prominence in the 1910s, or radical American political parties since then; and groups (particularly those with political and economic concerns), as opposed to triumphant individuals.

The absence of these alternative actors and plots illustrates how news media shape America's collective amnesia as well as its collective memory. Their omission, decade by decade, also helps to explain the erasure of radicalism, of feminism, of class and poverty issues, and of ethnic, racial, religious, and regional tensions (as opposed to "melting pot" blending) from the American story that was told at century's end. While these omissions have political implications, they most likely have narrative causes: it is not the unpopular but rather the incongruous that gets left out of these summary stories.[83] The content of decade-summary issues over time suggests that aberrant events and characters are useful to summary journalism only when they offer a lesson that propels the larger narrative forward—that links events and eras together in a logical way.

Narrative linkages enable journalists not just to explain the logical unfolding of the past but also to claim authority as predictors of the future. In 1950 *Time*'s editors called their half-century review "a story of how the present grew out of the past and how the future is growing out of the present."[84] In *Newsweek*, columnist George Will (borrowing from Shakespeare) wrote, "We scrutinize the past for its elements of prologue."[85]

Newsmagazines have, in fact, frequently engaged in decade *previewing* in conjunction with their practice of reviewing.[86] From one decade to another, such short-term predictions have been unsurprising. *Newsweek*'s preview of the 1960s was a veiled review of the 1950s.[87] For the 1970s, *Life* "forecast" trends that were clearly in evidence at the end of the 1960s: overpopulation, a growing interest in spirituality, continuing space exploration, and advances in technology.[88] Similarly, aspects of American life apparent in the late 1980s—grass-roots environmentalism, the aging population, the global spread of capitalism—were parts of *U.S. News & World Report*'s predictions for the 1990s.[89]

At the start of that decade (well in advance of their century reviews), both *Time* and *Newsweek* devoted special issues to predicting the coming century, and the latter magazine did so again in early 1997. These editions were characterized by the same voice and techniques of decade summaries, using the first-person plural in speculating about American life in the next century and focusing on what will happen to the average person. Because all of these issues used polls as evidence for their forecasts, ordinary citizens played a role in shaping this vision.

Time predicted that, as the population continues to age, the nuclear family will give way to the extended family, and that this change will reshape American society. The same conflation of American life and family life was the theme around which *Newsweek* built its 1990 issue titled *The 21st Century Family*. Like *Time*, it expected a "geezer boom" and varied family structures. But its editors added a caveat that assumed a shared past among readers: "Americans will not turn their backs completely on the idealized family we remember fondly. Thus, we must create accommodations that are new, but reflect our heritage."[90]

The magazines' prediction issues also delivered the unifying moral leadership that had been a part of their founders' vision and had marked the ends of decades, an inclusive optimism in which editors spoke for the nation's future. In its 1997 special issue titled *Beyond 2000: America in the 21st Century*, *Newsweek*'s editors wrote: "We Americans are an introspective lot, arguably more given than most other nationalities to seeing warts on the body politic as nothing less than cancer. So it is probably inevitable that the national mood as the millennium approaches is a bit uneasy—as if, with the flip of a calendar page, we begin some long decline in all the blessings that make America exceptional and the future worth living for. . . . The genius of America is its ability to face its difficulties and make creative social adjustments. All it takes is faith in the future—a form of confidence that is the most American trait of all."[91]

The authority to make such a pronouncement came from *Newsweek*'s understanding of the previous century, its editors implied. This prediction issue launched the magazine's "Millennium Project," a weekly department called Millennium Notebook plus a series of special issues that would "provide our readers with a rich and colorful account of the turbulent 20th century, as well as a taste of the world of the future."[92] *Time*'s summary series claimed to "present the story of the century."[93] The latter title solicited the opinions of readers (via its web site) as well as scholarly experts in making its content selections; both magazines contracted with television networks (*Time* with CBS and *Newsweek* with CNN) to air shows that expanded on their century reports.

Interestingly (given Time-Life's predilection for repackaging the past), *U.S. News & World Report* was the first of the magazines to offer a special section that recapped the twentieth century, though it was not part of the magazine's official century-review process. Published in 1995 and titled "Our Century," it reviewed eras and events through oral-history interviews with the nation's 52,000 centenarians. Employing the familiar first-person plural, the section's subheads were "How We Lived," "How We Played," "How We Traveled," and "The History We Lived." Its forward-looking conclusion, "A Century of Renewal," linked this century with the next by assessing the state of the country when the interviewees were born and by noting that "America came through—and is likely to do so again."[94]

In its later series called "Makers of the 20th Century," *U.S. News & World Report* recapped the twentieth century by focusing on "great" individuals organized by category of accomplishment, including "Strategists of War," "Prophets of Pop Culture," and "Masters of Discovery" (inventors).[95] Normally the most reportorial in style of the four publications, *U.S. News* told the stories of its "Strategists of War" in a narrative, even theatrical style. Its article on John J. Pershing began: "Long legs carried the tall man swiftly across the parade ground and held him fast in the saddle. His uniform was immaculate, his bearing erect. A neatly trimmed mustache completed an air of by-the-book efficiency, the look of an officer who was a good bet to perform impressively, get noticed by the right people, and be kissed by luck at every turn. A comer."[96] The next profile followed through, in content and style, almost seamlessly: "A new legend was rising among the warriors, an Army brat with an outré modus operandi that owed nothing to Black Jack Pershing's sober, by-the-books methods. Rules were for other people, not for Douglas MacArthur."[97] Its pop-culture issue profiled famous people yet emphasized their ordinary qualities: of "Bing and the King," it wrote, "Neither of them could read a note of music, but Crosby and Presley defined song for their generations."[98] And when it published its "Man of the Century" issue during the last week of 1999, *U.S. News* conferred that titled on Uncle Sam, a character (visualized as illustrator James Montgomery Flagg's famous war-recruitment poster) meant to stand for all Americans.[99]

Time similarly praised well-known individuals in its six century-review issues—titled "Leaders & Revolutionaries," "Artists & Entertainers," "Builders & Titans," "Scientists & Thinkers," "Heroes & Icons" (figure 1.2), and the final "Person of the Century" issue—while also admitting the potential of the ordinary American to be extraordinary. The first five issues were nearly identical in format, type of content, and explanation: each profiled twenty people (with runners-up in sidebars), summing up trends in essays and on timelines. Several of the lists included an additional entry for an "unknown" or "unsung" hero, and all four concluded by looking toward the future, predicting the issue's theme in the twenty-first century. *Time*'s final installment had a different format but the same focus on individuals, as suggested by the title of its cover story: "Who Mattered and Why." The issue profiled the "Person of the Century" (Albert Einstein) and runners-up; it also listed the top people of the millennium, with one choice for each of the previous nine centuries.[100]

Beginning at the end of 1997, *Newsweek* published undated special issues titled *2000: A New Millennium* that considered how the "greats"—both individuals and events—affected the lives of ordinary Americans. One issue recapped major inventions and discoveries (and the geniuses behind them) in terms of how they changed various aspects of American life, with sections titled "How We Work," "How We Live," "How We Fight," and "How We Heal"; each section concluded with a subsection titled "The Future."[101] Another told the story of the century as one of movies and movie stars, analyzed in terms of their impact on the lives of fans. The magazine's film critic (speaking not to, but on behalf of, filmgoers) wrote: "If there is a passion that enters the voice when people begin to talk about movies . . . it's because we're talking about who we are, and what the movies have made us. . . . From Hollywood movies we have learned how to live, how to love. . . . The movies let us time-travel in search of role models."[102]

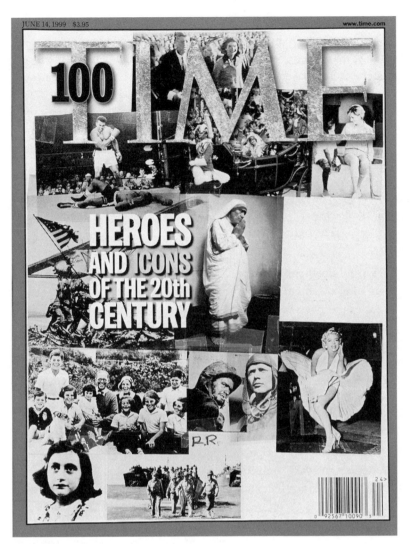

FIGURE 1.2
Time *cover, June 14, 1999*
(Credit: Time, *June 14, 1999).*

Newsweek also published a three-part series, with the umbrella title *Voices of the Century*, reversing this tactic, telling the story of great events through memories of ordinary individuals. Its opening installment covered the theme of war and instructed readers: "Listen now as the people who lived through these dramatic years, from the doughboys of World War I to the Great Men of World War II to the grunts of Vietnam, tell their stories."[103] These "oral histories" of "the eyewitnesses of the century" provided "accounts [that] are necessarily snapshots, just glimpses of history," the magazine admitted—yet when "gathered together, they bring the past alive in a way not often achieved in history books," enabling readers to "experience history as it really happened, with the men and women who shaped the way we live now."[104] *Time* instead commissioned articles (mixed among the work of its own staff writers) by today's "greats" who summed up their predecessors: Bill Gates writing about the Wright Brothers, Andrew Lloyd Webber on Rodgers and Hammerstein, Gloria Steinem on Margaret Sanger, Lee Iacocca on Henry Ford.[105]

All of the newsweeklies reiterated five of the six decade-summary "core plots" in their century-summary issues. Most striking was their emphasis on individuals. The Common Man was less well represented in these profiles, which focused on leaders, though frequently among the leaders were underdogs. By championing heroes who rose from humble beginnings through hard work and character (Elvis Presley, Colin Powell, Lech Walesa, Sam Walton), the magazines, by inversion, criticized the schemers of history and reinforced the moral difference between the two types of public figures. All of *U.S. News & World Report*'s "Strategists of War" were American—the heroes who ensured the triumph of democracy—and the "We" in *Newsweek*'s "How We Work/Live/Fight/Heal" sections offered a distinctly American definition of the advances of the twentieth century and the promises of the twenty-first. Similarly, the magazines' attention to business was a tale of the triumph of capitalism. *Time*'s "Builders & Titans" issue cover story began, fittingly, with a quote from the magazine's founder, Henry Luce: "Make money, be proud of it; make more money, be prouder of it."[106] In the following pages, capitalism was defined by profiles beginning with Henry Ford and ending with Bill Gates, thus perfectly conflating the triumph of American capitalism with progress through technology.

Confirming this ultimate aspect of the story of the American past was *Life*'s 1997 special issue (republished as a "collector's edition" book)[107] listing the most important people and events of the *entire millennium*—the past thousand, rather than hundred, years—and framing that era in terms of technology. Its number-one person was Thomas Edison; its most influential event was the invention of movable type (the Gutenberg Bible). Interestingly, the editorial voice of this issue differed significantly from the inclusive, conversational, and lighthearted voice of *Life*'s earlier decade and half-century reviews: perhaps because of its encyclopedic content, or perhaps because most of that content occurred before the lifetimes of the editors or the audience, the text had a formal, almost dutiful tone. Its editors' failure to describe this past as "ours" may have had to do with the facts that four-fifths of the events they covered occurred outside the United States, that only 14 Americans appeared on their list of the 100 most important people of the millennium (despite Edison being first), and that, having set up the issue as a historical summary, they were forced to march through the Middle Ages, the Mongolian and Ottoman Empires, the Renaissance, and the Reformation before arriving in America.[108]

Even such ambitious time summaries revealed a modern bias, however, confirming historian David Lowenthal's comment that "everything we see is filtered through present-day mental lenses."[109] In its issue on the arts, for instance, *Time* chose Bart Simpson rather than Mickey Mouse as its "cartoon character of the century," while *Life* proclaimed Louis Armstrong but not Mozart among the most important people in the world over the past thousand years.[110] What's more, the language with which the magazines characterized the century and the millennium conformed remarkably to their preference for personalization and narrative. In the first of its issues summarizing the twentieth century, *Time*'s editor in chief wrote: "In the end, this issue is . . . a collage of names, dates and emotions that produce not only a sense of the times but also a visceral reminder of all that is most terrifying in people and all that is most wonderful in humankind. In that important sense, the story *Time* tells this week isn't so different from the one the magazine has been telling for 75 years."[111]

The core plots emerged quite clearly in that issue, which labeled the century in terms of its "great themes": The Century of Freedom ("If you had to pick a two-word summation, it would be: freedom won."); The Century of Capitalism ("Democracy can exist without capitalism, and capitalism without democracy, but probably not for very long. Political and economic freedom tend to go together."); The Electronic Century ("a transition from an industrial age to an information age"); The Mass-Market Century (which it dated to "1913, when Henry Ford opened his assembly line. Ordinary people could now afford . . ."); The Genocidal

Century ("Why doesn't progress make civilizations more civilized?");
and The American Century (in which "America's clout in the world" was
explained as a matter not of military or economic power, but rather of
"idealism" and "values").[112]

All but "The Genocidal Century" were American stories that had
been told before in newsmagazines' decade reviews. *Time*'s 1992 issue
predicting the twenty-first century had characterized the twentieth century as a global fight for liberty, endangered first by Hitler and then
by Russia, with the ultimate triumph of democracy.[113] Six years later
the same magazine used the theme of technological progress to link
both centuries, anticipating "a transition from a mass-market world
to a personalized one" in an increasingly computerized society. (Similarly, more than a fourth of the 100 events *Life* considered most important in the past millennium were technological developments, while
Newsweek's 1997 century-prediction issue described nearly all aspects of
future American life in terms of technology—imagining, for instance,
politics as web-based "digital democracy" and medicine in terms of "re-
placement parts.")[114] And all of the magazines championed individualism as the ultimate act of patriotism. This, in fact, was the moral of the
twentieth-century tale, *Time* concluded: "The ultimate goal of democracy and freedom, after all, is not to pursue material abundance but to
nurture the dignity and values of each individual. That is the fundamental story of this century, and if we're lucky and wise, it will be the story
of the next one."[115]

Indeed, these special issues created some important precedents for
twenty-first-century journalism. Their long-term presence on newsstands (from 1998 to 2000) made this sort of production seem familiar,
setting a marketing precedent for more of the same, even when there
is no milestone event to justify it. When *Time* published an issue in the
spring of 2004 with the sole coverline "The Time 100," it appeared to
be a reprint of its century series. (Given its sheer length as well as its
six-part format, its century series could not have been published in a
single issue of the magazine; instead, it eventually took unified shape in
the form of a hardcover book.) The issue *Time* published in 2004 used
the same cover concept and the same category titles ("Leaders & Revolutionaries" and the other four) in order to profile current figures, including many who would not have appeared in the century review, such as
presidential candidate Senator John Kerry, singer Norah Jones, and "The
Google Guys."[116] Another example of the staying power of this summary
format was *U.S. News & World Report*'s 2003 special issue titled "Build-

ers of Dreams: The Visionaries and the Creations that Changed Our World." With its bold title over a dramatic, upward shot of the Chrysler Building, and no other coverlines (despite the fact that it was actually a regular, dated issue of the magazine), it had the look of a glossy American-history coffeetable book.[117]

The regularity of these kinds of cover stories in current editions of the newsmagazines suggests that they have acquired historical authority not previously associated with weekly journalism. In reviewing the twentieth century, *Time, Newsweek, Life,* and *U.S. News & World Report* increased their role as public historians, and they have continued to do this kind of cultural work in the twenty-first century. At the same time, the recurring editorial themes of those summary issues—the ideals of individualism, small-town values, and the triumph of democracy—provided the framework for coverage of American journalism's greatest reporting challenge in the early twenty-first century.

2 A Working-Class Hero Is Something to Be

The Lasting Story of September 11th

It's a fine, uplifting story, full of terror and suspense, grit and determination—a story that shows, as did the story of September 11th and its aftermath, that a working-class hero is something to be. . . . They prayed together; they shared the single sandwich that was their only food; they lashed themselves together so that in death their bodies would not be separated.
— *New Yorker*, August 2002[1]

Another disaster, playing out on the screen, and so soon. . . . But there is another side to all of this, one that is comforting, even uplifting. . . . they all become heroes, the latest addition to a long and glorious national roster. How long ago was it that we decried the lack of heroes? . . . There has been a leavening of attitude toward greatness: no one is disqualified.— *U.S. News & World Report*, February 2003[2]

If the story of the century was the product of decades of journalism, the story of September 11th—which at first seemed untellable—took shape quickly, seeming to emerge simultaneously in news media and in the broader American culture. A week later, at a concert dedicated to the nonviolence advocated by John Lennon, actor Kevin Spacey quoted Lennon's lyrics as he saluted "our city's everyday protectors who so valiantly attempted to protect the lives of others and in so doing sacrificed their own."[3] The Lennon song Spacey referred to was invoked again less than a year later (in the passage above) by the *New Yorker*—in a report on the men trapped and then rescued in a Pennsylvania coal mine during the summer of 2002. By the time the Space Shuttle Columbia exploded in early 2003, there was no lack of heroes in American media.

The use of the same rhetoric in seemingly different circumstances (and by a diverse group of cultural sources) suggests how quickly the heroic ideal of September 11th traveled through the public imagination, and how useful it became in explaining upsetting events in a changed world.[4] What's more, its reminiscent tone revealed that the "new" American heroism was not new at all; instead, it was described in media as a recapturing of values "lost" in the past. *Time* claimed: "We are seeing it in our nation and sensing it in ourselves, a new faith in our oldest values."[5] Yet the heroic past that was recalled in the new story was one that was in fact two generations old. Its resurrection required forgetting the recent past in order to "remember" an era that increasingly few Americans actually do remember.

Through memory, the story of September 11th—with, initially, a prototypical fireman as its central figure[6]—became a narrative template for media coverage of subsequent crisis events, which were reported in terms of the American character, the common man, and the notion of a "good war." The story reached back more than half a century not only to explain a particular event of the present, but also to tie together the events of ongoing crises within a story that made them seem logically connected. This nostalgic political and cultural reconstruction intertwined nationalism with ideas about gender and class in a heroic civilian story that foreshadowed a military one.

For more than a year following September 11th, images of firemen were ubiquitous in American popular culture. Fictional firemen peopled the plots of nighttime television dramas set in New York,[7] while real firemen were profiled on the NBC documentary series *Firehouse* and stood onstage with Paul Simon as he sang "The Boxer" to open the first post–September 11th *Saturday Night Live* show.[8] Images of firemen appeared on material culture from paintings to postage stamps to Christmas-tree ornaments. Perhaps the peak of the fireman-hero's media profile came with the "documentary" film 9/11, which aired as a production of CBS News on the six-month and one-year anniversaries. That film told the story of one rookie fireman and his company who responded to the disaster; it also was, in the words of the film makers, the story of "how a boy becomes a man."

Because magazines serve a wide range of audiences, the appearance of such images and stories across the medium confirmed their symbolic resonance to Americans despite their age, sex, race, education, income, political inclination, or geographic residence. From September 2001 to late 2002, the prototypical fireman appeared on the covers and in the articles of magazines ranging from *People* and *Parade* to the *Atlantic* and the *New Yorker*, from *Reader's Digest* to *Men's Health* to *Newsweek*. He quickly became not just a symbol of one event, but a mythic figure, culturally useful in other ways. Jack Lule defines myth as "a sacred, societal story that draws from archetypal figures and forms to offer exemplary models for human life," adding that "myth—and perhaps news —[is] an important way a society expresses its prevailing ideals, ideologies, values, and beliefs."[9] Michael Schudson further notes that "myths necessarily have multiple meanings; in fancier terms, they are 'polysemous.' They do not tell a culture's simple truths so much as they explore its central dilemmas."[10]

Betty Houchin Winfield dates the emergence of a specifically American hero in news media to coverage of explorers in the early nineteenth century. Whereas "heroes of the old world were of noble birth," she explains, "the new nation's hero was an independent citizen who served the country with ingenuity, perseverance, enterprise, bravery, and valor. . . . An American hero had to be selfless . . . a republican hero, marked not by the exceptional intellectual ability or elite birth of the founding fathers, but rather as a publicly spirited, sacrificing citizen, regardless of origin."[11] Janice Hume, who has studied media constructions of heroism in the nineteenth and twentieth centuries, writes that in the latter era the American hero has been presented "not so much as a 'great man' but as a symbol of his culture. . . . Heroes stand on a pedestal, true, but in our egalitarian society, that pedestal must be reachable for everyone; in America, a 'hero' is not royalty or deity, but an average person who, through adversity, strives to reach society's highest potential."[12]

According to Susan J. Drucker and Robert S. Cathcart, the "hero myth" of any particular culture "is transformed in the telling and re-telling, according to the time and place, and, most importantly, by the means of conveying *the story* [emphasis in original]."[13] That story must be told in a public forum: "Public places are required by hero worship-pers as sites for retelling tales of great deeds, for enacting ceremonies of hero worship, and as a locale for public statues erected to honor the hero."[14] Today that town square, the site of our heroic storytelling and statue building, is the arena of mass media, particularly journalism.

The most honored average American hero of the twentieth-century appeared at midcentury during World War II, and in recent decades he has been the subject of celebration during fiftieth- and sixtieth-anniver-sary media "remembrances" of that war, as well as the dedication of the American World War II Memorial. In her 1999 bestseller, *Stiffed: The Betrayal of the American Man*, Susan Faludi recalls this ideal through a famous work of photojournalism: "A band of marines struggling to erect a flagpole in the flinty ground of Iwo Jima would become the supreme expression of the nation's virtue. A team of anonymous, duty-bound young men successfully completing the mission their fathers and their fathers' fathers had laid out for them, defeating a vile enemy and laying claim to a contested frontier—this would be the template for postwar manhood."[15]

Historian Edward Linenthal notes, "Like the Minutemen, the G.I.'s were . . . seen as 'pioneer stock,' and underdog heroes. The soldiers, heirs of the experience of the thirties, were seen like their predecessors, as hard workers."[16] The admirable World War II soldier was heroic in his typicality. He was "prepared to do the job of fighting [and] believed that action spoke louder than words," writes historian Joe Dubbert.[17] His anonymity also was central to his symbolic meaning in a "good war," as Paul Fussell contends: "For the myth-making memory, the principle of anonymity is one way of sanctifying the war. The myth requires that 'ser-vicemen' be depicted, at least in photographs, as virtually anonymous. Because the war was a common cause, no one in it has a right to appear as anything but anonymous."[18]

Faludi explains, "There was nothing fancy about that type . . . [of man who was] made visual in Bill Mauldin's wartime cartoons of Willie and Joe, his 'dogface' soldiers," and starred in the newspaper columns of Ernie Pyle, who wrote, "War makes strange giant creatures out of us little routine men who inhabit the earth." She notes that in Pyle's col-umns "the foot soldier was elevated into a masculine emblem—a man who proved his virility not by individual feats of showy heroism but by . . . supporting the welfare of his unit. . . . 'It was beyond their power to quit. . . . They were good boys.'"[19]

A generation later, the sons of World War II veterans had their own war, though with a very different public climate and media portrayal. Although the common soldier was still depicted with sympathy, he received less media attention than antiwar protesters at home, and journalistic media—including leading photojournalism magazines such as *Life* and *Look* as well as television news programs—contained graphic images of injury, showing American soldiers as victims rather than heroes of a foreign conflict. Writing on films about Vietnam, Marita Sturken contends that "the grunt in these films is posed as a figure of the 'real' American, the spirit of American men that was destroyed in the war."[20] Susan Jeffords sees this same victim status in the soldier-characters of 1970s films, arguing: "Consequently, the Vietnam War and its veterans became the springboard for a general remasculinization of American culture that is evidenced in the popularity of figures like Ronald Reagan, Oliver North, and J. R. Ewing . . . images of strength and firmness with an independence that smacks of Rambo and confirms their faith in a separate culture based on a mythos of masculinity."[21]

As Jeffords notes, however, these new masculine media figures were lone rangers, rather than a band of brothers, and media (as well as academic) warnings about a "crisis of masculinity" grew in number and volume. In 1988 anthropologist Ray Raphael worried, "The image of man-the-protector, like that of man-the-provider, has . . . been seriously eroded. . . . If we are no longer hunters or warriors, then in which sense are we really 'men'?"[22] *Esquire* published a special issue in October 1991 titled "The State of Masculinity" with articles that surveyed the new "men's movement"; in one essay, titled "Battle Hymn: My Last War," a Pulitzer Prize–winning journalist "look[ed] back on a life spent dodging bullets and keeping the dirt from his soul."[23] Bookstores carried psychologist-authored titles such as *Knights without Armor* and *In a Time of Fallen Heroes.*[24]

At the time, historians Michael Kimmel and Michael Kaufman warned: "The retreat to find a revitalized and recharged manhood . . . is a retreat to a highly selective anthropological world of rituals that reproduce men's cultural power over women and that are now used to facilitate a deeper nostalgic retreat to the lost world of innocent boyhood."[25] Indeed, out of this late-twentieth-century "crisis" came the boys-will-be-boys voice of *Maxim* and nostalgic military tributes such as *Saving*

Private Ryan and journalist Tom Brokaw's *The Greatest Generation*. Writing about the latter texts, Barbara Beisecker claims that "recent cultural representations of the 'Good War,' from blockbuster movies to cable television series, best selling books and museum displays, together constitute one of the primary means through which a renewed sense of national belonging is being persuasively packaged and delivered to U.S. audiences for whom the question what does it mean to be an American has, at least since the Civil War, never been more difficult to answer."[26] They also appeared at a time when the question of what it means to be a man was equally a matter for public discussion. What Beisecker calls the "present recuperations of WWII" set the stage for the emergence of the fireman-hero, and for the reemergence of a common-man military ideal, in popular media.

Like G.I. Joe, of course, the public symbol of the fireman was based on real men who died in real and horrific circumstances. Yet this figure also stood for the "recovery" of certain ideals. And like G.I. Joe, the fireman became not merely a central and recurring character in news coverage of a national crisis, but a mythic figure in the broader culture of which journalism is a part.

In media portrayals today and half a century ago, this figure is paradoxical in the sense that his "privileged" and "exemplary" status comes from his ordinariness, his inarticulateness, and his reluctance to be labeled a hero. Moreover, he is a very particular ideal: a physically strong, stoic, working-class man who finds his calling and his identity among other men, his "brothers." Michael Kimmel notes that "American men define their masculinity not as much in relation to women, but in relation to each other. . . . As one Army general put it, every soldier fears 'losing the one thing he is likely to value more highly than life—his reputation *as a man among other men*.'"[27] In his coverage of World War II, Ernie Pyle wrote: "The ties that grow between men who live savagely together, relentlessly communing with Death, are ties of great strength."[28]

The same assertion, expressed in similar military rhetoric, emerged as a central theme in the coverage of the heroes of September 11th. Firemen became the primary type of working-class hero in news media as early as September 12, 2001, when many newspaper front pages carried the photograph of three firemen raising an American flag at the World Trade Center site (figure 2.1). Now an iconic image itself, this photo was, at the time of its publication, what sociologist Barry Schwartz calls a "frame image," a picture that has meaning because it recalls another

FIGURE 2.1
Newsweek *cover, September 24, 2001*
(© 2001 Newsweek, Inc. All rights reserved. Reprinted by
permission/© 2001 The Record *[Bergen Co., N.J.]).*

well-understood cultural image—in this case, the Iwo Jima flag-raising photograph.[29]

Less than a week after the attacks, the same photo appeared as *Newsweek*'s cover. That magazine contained a feature with a photo of a car painted red, white, and blue parked in front of a suburban house in Franklin Square, New Jersey, and with this title and blurb: "Hitting Home: Mike Kiefer was a suburban kid who dreamed of fighting fires in the big city. He is among the thousands missing in the towns where ground zero's victims lived."[30] The article was illustrated with childhood photographs and cast Kiefer as Everyman—or rather as Every Boy whose unasked-for, courageous sacrifice had made him a man, much like Ernie Pyle's "good boys" who became soldiers. In this story, the construct of Everyman included nonfiremen as well, "ordinary" people who were described, in this case, through a military metaphor and the lenses of both upward mobility and small-town nostalgia:

> In the rosters of the missing are surprisingly few titans of finance or industry; instead, the disaster struck at the foot soldiers of Wall Street, men and women who sat at computer terminals and answered their own telephones. But those people are also the backbones of communities. . . . By and large, it isn't the managing partners of big investment banks who run the Boy Scout troops or manage the church bake sales—or staff the volunteer fire departments. . . . so many of [the town's] sons and husbands go off to work . . . every day as cops and firefighters, saving lives in a city their grandparents left a half century ago.[31]

Other early coverage also focused on "civilian" (i.e., nonuniformed) heroes and regained social values. Many of these initial statements had nothing to do with gender or class status. "New York, my city, remains like a small town, where people are tender with those they love and understanding of the fragility of strangers," wrote the editor in chief of the *Ladies' Home Journal*.[32] A Columbia University professor was quoted in *Talk*: "The city suddenly felt very small. . . . There was this sense of instinctive heroism and community and people volunteering."[33] The *New Yorker* reported: "On the afternoon of that day . . . New Yorkers walked the streets . . . with the kind of tender necessary patriotism that lies in just persisting."[34]

The American Association of Retired Persons' *My Generation* was one of many magazines to use a red, white, and blue cover, with the coverline "Our Search for Meaning" (figure 2.2), and its editor's letter

December 2001

MY GENERATION

REACHING 3.6 MILLION HOMES

NEW FROM *AARP*

OUR SEARCH FOR MEANING

Just as this issue went to press, our nation was shaken by

the unspeakable acts of September 11. Now, the country,

using all its resources and drawing on the past, struggles

to make sense of the tragedy and its aftermath. And

with true American spirit we go forward.

$2.95

WWW.MYGENERATION.ORG

FIGURE 2.2

My Generation *cover, December 2001*
(American Association of Retired Persons).

referred to New Yorkers and Americans in general: "In the days after the tragedy, strangers found time to talk with one another. . . . The point was to reach out and connect."[35] *Business 2.0* magazine celebrated the spirit of the ordinary office worker in extraordinary circumstances: "Words and glances passed between colleagues took on life-or-death consequence. Co-workers clasped hands and decided to flee, or, in some case, perish together. . . . The stories of people helping one another inside the doomed towers . . . were affecting enough. But it wasn't until the following Monday when the area around ground zero returned to economic life, that work took on a hue we rarely see. Asked what impelled them to return to the job, people struck a common refrain: A sense of duty. . . . for a brief moment, the simple act of going to work seemed, somehow, heroic."[36]

Some magazines painted broader pictures of patriotism. *People Weekly* declared: "As the Twin Towers and the Pentagon smoldered in ruins, Americans wept for our dead, feared for our lives and raged at an insidious foe. But when the initial shock subsided, the nation emerged with renewed energy, passion, and resolve. New Yorkers and Washingtonians displayed a can-do gallantry. . . . Across the country flags draped the windows of tenements and mansions alike."[37] *Newsweek* praised the recovery spirit of Americans in general: "There are many strands in the national fiber. Bold ones like heroism and solidarity and sense of purpose, which were on such impressive display after the attack. And also more modest ones, like individuality, humor, frivolity and fun."[38] These eulogies echoed the nature and tone of the *New York Times'* "Portraits of Grief" obituary series, in which, according to Janice Hume, "the larger qualities were the simplest ones—love of family, a work ethic, generosity, humor, good health. These victims became icons of familiarity, of the egalitarian virtues of the 'everyAmerican.'"[39]

Yet as the first few weeks of cleanup in New York and Washington passed—and as the United States began to mobilize soldiers—the media "story of September 11th" shifted from a civilian one to an essentially military one, focusing on the firemen who had "fought" in the attacks and containing military language. In its tribute to the lost members of its neighborhood fire company, *Entertainment Weekly* quoted their commander as saying, "They were so young, so eager, so proud to be members of the department. We firefighters have an expression, 'See you at the big one.' These guys figured it was the big one and they had to be there."[40] *New York* magazine chronicled one fireman's experience in cinematic present tense: "He is running. He is running up West Street

in clunky knee-high rubber boots that cut into the backs of his knees
. . . with a 30-pound air cylinder strapped to his back. . . . A shrapnel
storm of steel and glass and stone is smashing all into the ground. . . . He
travels at least 50 feet in the air."[41] Other firemen's first-person accounts
were published in *Gear, Rolling Stone*, and *Men's Journal*; the latter publication ran the sole coverline "The Firefighters: Their Own Stories" over
a photograph of one gazing upward toward the wreckage (figure 2.3).[42]
Maxim's editor called firefighting "the noblest profession there is."[43]

As these examples suggest, such stories appeared especially in magazines with male or primarily male audiences, including sports magazines. ESPN *The Magazine* ran a black cover with this text: "These were
the days when heroism and villainy were redefined. This was the week
when sports went dark, when its spotlight swung around to the firefighters who ran up the stairs. . . . Clichéd descriptions we so freely bestow on our athletes—words like courageous, tireless, inspirational—
have taken on deeper meanings" (figure 2.4).[44] *Savoy*, which targeted
African American men, made the connection more subtly, putting a
sweating Muhammad Ali on its November 2002 cover over the coverline "Spirit of the Fighting Man."[45]

Sports Illustrated's first issue after the attacks contained a feature on
the three New York City firemen-brothers of New England Patriots football player Joe Andruzzi, who called himself "the black sheep" of the
family.[46] These magazines echoed gestures being made in the sports
world itself in which athletes (like actors and rock stars) donned NYFD
hats and praised firefighting as a higher calling than their own. (One
player invited to the NFL draft was quoted as saying: "For some, the draft
is all about creating new heroes. But those guys were real heroes, not
the kind of hero that wears capes and jumps off buildings, but guys with
real courage.")[47]

The cover subjects of *Sports Illustrated*'s year-end special issue, under
the coverline "Everybody's All-Americans," were four New York City
firemen representing the various sports teams of the NYFD, in football,
baseball, basketball, and hockey. Its closing feature profiled the fallen
men on those teams, with a subplot of how the Mets' Mike Piazza be-
friended the son of one dead fireman who had become a fan at age five
when the Mets improbably won the World Series in 1969. The piece
nostalgically compared firemen with athletes: "Playing ball and fighting
fires, there's a link there, has been forever. *What do you want to be when
you grow up? A ballplayer. A fireman*. Those two jobs, changed world and
all, still fill a million childhood dreams."[48]

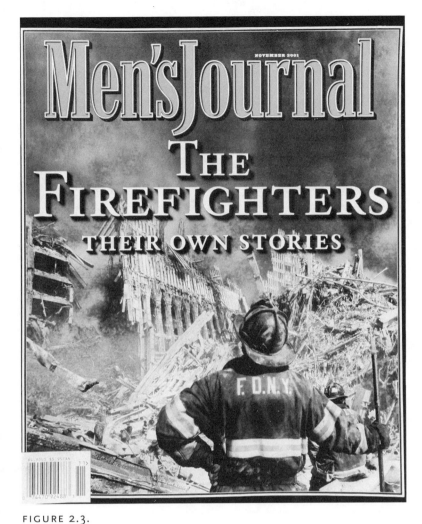

NOVEMBER 2001

Men's Journal

THE
FIREFIGHTERS
THEIR OWN STORIES

F.D.N.Y.

FIGURE 2.3.
Men's Journal cover, November 2001
(Cover photo by Matthew McDermott from Men's Journal,
November 2001 From Men's Journal LLC 2001.
All rights reserved. Reprinted by permission).

THESE WERE THE DAYS
when heroism and villainy were redefined.
This was the week when sports went dark,
when its spotlight swung around to the firefighters
who ran up the stairs, the police and EMS
crews who braved the showers of destruction, the
laborers who sifted through the debris of a cataclysm
to find evidence of someone's life. The clichéd descriptions
we so freely bestow on our athletes—words like courageous,
tireless, inspirational—have taken on deeper meanings ...

The Magazine
espnmag.com 4.20
October
01 2001
$3.50 US/$4.50 CAN/FOR

FIGURE 2.4
ESPN The Magazine *cover, October 1, 2001*
(© ESPN, Inc. Reprinted courtesy of ESPN *The Magazine).*

A family of firemen was the focus of the main feature of *Newsweek*'s year-end double issue, titled "The Day That Changed Us All." It told the story of Bill Feehan, a veteran New York City fireman and former chief who was killed, opening with an illustration of him reaching forward to help someone (out of the frame of the illustration) in front of the burning Trade Center towers. The long essay closed with a spread showing photos of Feehan's son and son-in-law wearing fire gear and his two grandsons, little boys shown wearing firemen's helmets. Its text ended with a quote from Alfred, Lord Tennyson's "Charge of the Light Brigade" ("Theirs not to reason why / Theirs but to do and die") and an anecdote about one of Feehan's grandsons, who now has a chunk of the Trade Center rubble as a memento.[49]

Given the prevalence of World War II nostalgia in popular culture at the time of the September 11th disaster, Bill Feehan's status as a grandfather is especially powerful in this story: we are meant to understand that he stands for a long-ago work ethic that was nearly lost, but was saved through heroism during crisis, a model that may be taken up again by a new generation. "'Your grandfather was a hero, and he was killed by this,' Brian told his son. 'You must never forget him.' It's doubtful Connor could. . . . Connor tells almost anyone he sees that when he grows up, he is going to be a fireman, too."[50]

Although coverage of the disaster and its aftermath became less frequent in magazine journalism after the new year, firemen continued to make appearances in this medium. *Men's Health* set aside its practice of featuring super-fit and shirtless male models on its cover when it put Eddie Cibrian, an actor who plays a New York City fireman on NBC's fictional program *Third Watch*, "wearing his own authentic FDNY 'Ladder 3' T-shirt," on its April 2002 issue.[51] For the one-year anniversary, *Newsweek* rephotographed the three firemen who were shown raising the flag on the magazine's cover just after the disaster. Under the title ". . . And Our Flag Was Still There," the editors explained: "We think the new image—of brave men standing strong—is, like the first picture, a metaphor for a country that's also unbowed" (figure 2.5).[52] The special issue also contained an article titled "The Brotherhood Now," written by a fireman and concluding with a quote from another, who named "one thing that 9-11 can't change, and that is that this is the best job in the world."[53] The sentiment was echoed in *People*'s profile of a New York City man who had joined the fire department to replace his brother, who had been killed in the disaster. "Although I lost my blood brother, I feel I gained 12,000 brothers," he told the magazine.[54]

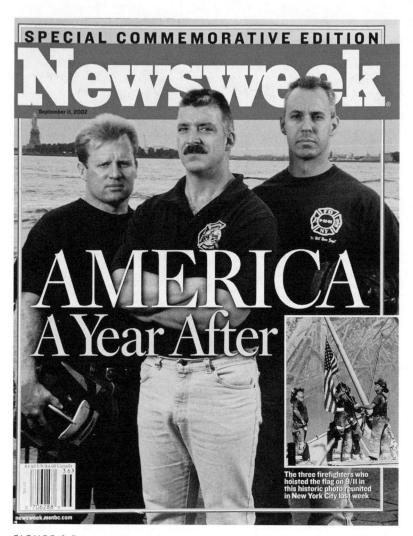

FIGURE 2.5
Newsweek *cover, September 11, 2002*
*(© 2002 Newsweek, Inc. All rights reserved. Reprinted by
permission/© 2002 The Record [Bergen Co., N.J.]/
© 2001 The Record [Bergen Co., N.J.]).*

Journalists were not simply choosing fireman themes; in many instances, they were covering events in which newsmakers or public officials themselves drew attention to such themes. It was not journalism that determined that the memorial march to the World Trade Center site on the one-year anniversary would be led by bagpipers, or that the rescue effort there would end, in late May 2002, with a symbolic fireman's funeral. Yet those rituals were conducted within a cultural climate in which firemen had come to stand for national values, and journalistic media had played a large part in the creation of that climate. Each retelling of a fireman story added to the depth and the naturalness of all fireman stories as "the American story."

One result was that, within the first year after the attacks, the public identity of those lost in the disaster had changed from a mixed group of random victims whose role had been a passive one (the attack happened to them) to a band of brothers whose role had been an active one (they had died in a battle against evil attackers). This narrative shift made class and gender major factors in the definition of American heroism: even though most victims were white-collar, corporate workers (of both sexes), the figure symbolizing "the fallen" was a working-class man "fighting" for his country. Moreover (even if somewhat illogically), "the fallen" were cast as heroes rather than victims, a transformation that allowed a corresponding shift in the status of the nation itself—no longer a victim of attack but an avenger.

Especially because living firemen were folded into the heroic tale (whether or not they were involved in the event), the focus on firemen enabled journalistic media to quickly rewrite "the story of September 11th" from one of vulnerability, fear, and death to one of strength, courage, and survival. This adjustment involved a new image of American working-class masculinity based in collective memory of the World War II era and created against a backdrop of popular culture that for a decade had bemoaned a "crisis" of American masculinity. In both senses, this was a recovery narrative. Yet this new story also was forward-looking, setting the stage for journalistic coverage of future events, especially those seen as emblematic of the nation's identity after September 11th.

The first national story that fit into the fireman-hero template was news coverage of the August 2002 rescue of nine miners who had become trapped in a western Pennsylvania coal mine. Coal-mine accidents have occurred regularly for a century, and without the cultural and political context of September 11th, this story would likely have yielded simply a report of the collapse and an upbeat feature on the rescue. Instead, it became a multiweek story, and the saved men were interviewed by newspapers from across the country and appeared on television shows.

Referring to the miners as "lunch bucket heroes,"[55] journalists described their rescue as both a continuation of the heroism of the passengers aboard Flight 93, which had crashed just ten miles away on September 11th, and a redemptive correction to that story as well as to the futility of the rescue effort at the World Trade Center site. There was extensive press coverage of President George W. Bush's visit, during which he referred to their rescuers as "first responders" and proclaimed of the miners: "It was their determination to stick together and to comfort each other that really defines kind of a new spirit that's prevalent in our country . . . that in order to succeed, we've got to be united; that by working together, we can achieve big objectives."[56] *People* magazine wrote: "In the midst of plenty of bad news—greedy business moguls, a shaky economy and the ongoing war on terrorism—here was a story of shared effort, good luck and saved lives."[57] *Newsweek* quoted friends and relatives in Somerset, Pennsylvania, who called them "the salt of the earth" and said, "You just can't ever count a miner out."[58]

For Christmas 2002 issues, the story was retold as a lesson in small-town and family values. *Good Housekeeping* interviewed the miners' wives and mothers in a feature that focused on the religious faith that had sustained the trapped men.[59] The *Ladies' Home Journal* interviewed Leslie Mayhugh, whose father and husband both had been trapped in the mine and at whose rescue "the nation rejoiced."[60] As the youngest and best-looking of the miners, Leslie's husband, Blaine Mayhugh, received the most photographic coverage, and he was at the symbolic center of the story—a family story that also celebrated small-town industrialism and a certain type of masculinity. "Theirs is a kind of reverse elite, a bluer-than-blue-collar, hypermasculine subculture," the *New Yorker* explained. "The miners dip snuff, chew tobacco, drink beer, and hunt. . . . A woman in their workplace is considered bad luck. . . . The miners routinely joke about their low station (Merle Travis's line in the song 'Sixteen Tons' about 'a mind that's weak and a back that's strong' is often quoted), but the self-deprecation is of a piece with a fierce pride in their work."[61]

It was not much of a stretch for news media to place the miners into working-class hero mythology. Yet less than a year later, the same characterization was made of astronauts. When the space shuttle Columbia exploded in February 2003, journalists linked the incident to September 11th by profiling the astronauts as devoted family men and women and mourning them as a group "united by a single bond—to dedicate their lives to making the rest of ours better."[62] *People* noted that shuttle commander Rick Husband was "a baritone in his church choir back in Clear Lake City, Texas" and that astronaut Laurel Clark "seemed to have no trouble sorting out her priorities. . . . 'I tell my son all the time that my most important job is being his mother.'" The same magazine concluded: "They went out as a crew and came back as a family."[63] A column in *U.S. News & World Report* contained this remarkably patriotic passage:

> It seems as if we cannot catch a break. It feels as if our luck has run out. It appears that to live in the land of the free, you really do have to dwell in the home of the brave. . . . we are at risk because we will not change. After September 11, we did not trim our sails; instead, we spread our wings. . . . Why do we do it? Because we can. To be an American is to dare. . . . We fear, we grieve, we sometimes feel as if we are at the breaking point. But we do not break, and we do not doubt. We are a nation with its face perpetually turned toward the light, not the darkness. And if these days our sunny optimism has been replaced with grim resolve, the resolve will see us through until the sun shines brightly once again.[64]

The miners' and astronauts' casting as American heroes provided a rhetorical bridge from September 2001 to February 2003, when the United States began its war against Iraq—a conflict that (whether or not it was an outcome of them) was narratively connected to the events of September 11th in many ways. Most striking were the unvarying proclamations, in general public rhetoric as well as news media, that, no matter what one thought of the war itself, all Americans stood united in their support of the troops. Finding similar rhetoric, particularly in journalism, requires a trip back through time to at least War World II (or to "our" collective memory of the War World II era, a knowledge that is itself now largely based on media storytelling).

American soldiers in Iraq were portrayed in news as common people who had set aside their individual lives to respond to shared duty. (The reporters embedded with them acquired a similar status.) For three consecutive weeks in April 2003, American newsmagazines used cover photos of ordinary soldiers in battle fatigues.[65] One characterized the conflict as "the grunt's war," borrowing a theme from Ernie Pyle and Bill Mauldin: "As the generals debated strategy, the pogues and dogfaces were grinding it out in the desert." This cover story explained: "Their triumph is at heart human, not strategic. The men are not especially brilliant or bold, and they gripe like all solders, but they are inventive and straight with each other."[66]

References to "the men" on the battlefield were common in journalistic coverage, even though some 15 percent of American troops in Iraq were female.[67] Soldiers were portrayed, in photographs as well as text, as male and virilely physical. *Newsweek* ran a coverline that read, "Wanted: More Men and Muscle," and this pull quote appeared within the cover story: "The buff soldier stripped off his filthy battle garb and bathed in the water at one of Saddam's palaces."[68] At the same time, soldiers were portrayed as typical family men. *People* profiled a thirty-four-year-old master gunner named Jeff Bush: "Bush says he is excited to be fighting in Iraq. Though he joined the Army when he was 18, this is his first deployment in a combat zone. All the same, he asks that a message of love be relayed to his wife and daughter. . . . His favorite photo of his family is one he received recently showing Ruby holding Maya, both with big smiles. That is the image he holds in his mind as he nods off to sleep."[69]

Interestingly, however, it was the story of a woman that most closely linked coverage of this war with earlier crises. *Newsweek* used a photograph of rescued POW Jessica Lynch, wearing army fatigues and posed in front of an American flag, with the sole coverline "Saving Private Lynch," a phrase used by other news media as well.[70] Like the story of the Pennsylvania miners, this initially was a recovery narrative, in which Lynch herself was not a heroine but a symbol of what could be recovered by heroes. "Lynch, a onetime Miss Congeniality winner in the beauty pageant at her county fair, enlisted in the army out of necessity, to help pay for the college education she needed to become a kindergarten teacher," *Time* explained.[71] *People* reported: "Back at his base, Marine Gunnery Sgt. Joe Morehead wrote an e-mail to his mother in Pennsylvania: 'Awesome Victory!!! I just wanted to let you know that we are finally war heroes. We pulled out the POW last night. Makes me feel as if it was all worth it.'"[72]

When Private Lynch returned to her West Virginia hometown in July 2003, wearing the Bronze Star and the Purple Heart, she too was placed into the ordinary-hero template: the *New York Times* quoted one observer as saying, "She embodies the small-town image of the person who does the right thing."[73] Eventually, however, news coverage would reframe her as the all-American girl(-victim), especially when she made appearances at camps set up "to help children cope while their parents are away in the armed forces."[74] In her analysis of this story, Deepa Kumar argues that "the construction of Lynch as a hero/victim has all the markings of the military's long held ambivalent attitude towards women" and writes, "The military strategically constructed a particular narrative in which Lynch was an object about which stories were told."[75] The same case can be made of journalistic coverage of that narrative, and of news media's reluctance to engage with the more complicated truths of her capture and "rescue," even when Lynch herself denied the accuracy of the original story.

Also during July 2003, a *New York Times Magazine* writer revisited the site of the Quecreek coal-mine accident on its one-year anniversary. What had been "the biggest news of the summer, a nostalgic tale of brawn and ingenuity and survival set in a small town . . . a story Americans needed to hear at that moment," had instead become a local story of resentments over fame and lawsuits over blame.[76] This treatment paralleled Will Langewiesche's three-part series in the *Atlantic Monthly*, published a year after the September 11th attacks and later issued as a book, in which some firemen and their families were portrayed as opportunistic and squabbling.[77] Yet on the anniversary, the ABC television network replayed its fictionalized, made-for-TV movie version of the Quecreek Mine rescue, and footage from CBS News's *9-11* was reused two months later on the two-year anniversary of September 11th.

The narrative thread of ordinary-soldiers-at-war also threatened to tear. Jessica Lynch's homecoming was not representative of the experience of most American soldiers, who remained in Iraq and, despite the president's declaration of "mission accomplished," continued to die by bombing, gunfire, and suicide. Still, news media continued to feature typical soldiers as representative of the war and to describe them as family men and women. This narrative consistency had an ironic effect: it recast the central character from volunteer hero to reluctant victim, yet it retained characters and a plot with which millions of Americans could identify. In an issue that featured soldiers on its cover, *Newsweek* reported that "the mothers of American soldiers watch the hellish images of TV and listen to the gloomy commentators and want to know when their children are coming home."[78]

Nevertheless, at the close of 2003, anonymous soldiers in battle fatigues appeared on the covers of the year-end issues of *Parade* and, more notably, *Time*.[79] While *Time*'s coverage of the war had been bylined by reporters stationed in Iraq, this cover story was written by Nancy Gibbs, the same staff writer who had summarized the events of September 11th for the magazine's cover story at the end of 2001 (and who had written all of its cover stories on September 11th for the first four weeks after the attack).[80] Her article opened with a reference to disaster ("It is the bad news that comes with a blast or a crash, to stop us in mid-sentence to stare at the TV, and shudder") and concluded, "For the challenge of defending not only our freedoms but those barely stirring half a world away, the American soldier is *Time's* Person of the Year."[81]

It was the first time the magazine had made such a gesture since it had named "The American Fighting-Man" its "Man of the Year" fifty-three years earlier, published at the start of America's involvement in Korea. Despite their appearance more than half a century apart, the two covers were visually quite similar, if symbolically specific to their times: the older one bore an illustration of a white man, looking something like Gregory Peck, in battle fatigues and with a gun, while the most recent one was a photograph of three unidentified men in fatigues and with guns, one white, one African American, and one presumably Latino.[82] If one were to substitute "terrorism" for "communism," the text of the 1951 cover story could be placed into an issue today:

> Most of the men in U.S. uniform around the world had enlisted voluntarily . . . few had thought they would fight, and fewer still had foreseen the incredibly dirty and desperate war that waited for them. . . . No matter how the issue was defined, whether he was said to be fighting for progress or freedom or faith or survival, the American's heritage and character were deeply bound up in the struggle. More specifically, it was the U.S. which had unleashed [*sic*] gigantic forces of technology and organizational ideas. Communism was a reaction, an effort to turn the worldwide forces set free by U.S. progress back into the old channels of slavery.[83]

The article quoted from a letter one such midcentury soldier had sent home to his mother: "I'm no hero, but . . . if these people aren't stopped here on their own ground, we will have to share the thing which so many have died to prevent their loves ones from sharing."[84]

This broader notion about the purpose of the American military was invoked again during the late spring of 2004 in coverage of the dedication of the World War II Memorial in Washington, D.C., and of the sixtieth anniversary of D-Day. During the preceding weeks, news media had been full of photographs of American soldiers abusing Iraqi prisoners. Yet those images of young soldiers in the Middle East with leashes and attack dogs were quickly displaced by photos of old soldiers wearing medals—as well as by Robert Capa's blurry photos of soldiers landing on Normandy beaches, which appeared on the cover of the *Time* issue celebrating "that one day, when luck and fate and genius and nerve worked to give Freedom her victory."[85]

Following immediately after the D-Day anniversary, the week-long funeral of former President Ronald Reagan displaced nearly *all* other news in American media, and—in a striking contrast with the Pentagon's ban on news coverage of the return of dead soldiers' bodies—the country saw one flag-draped coffin repeatedly. Though he himself had not seen combat, the dead president's life was conflated with the courage and accomplishments of "the Greatest Generation," and journalistic nostalgia for his "optimism" and unwavering opposition to an "evil empire" helped to repair the image of the country's current heroes at war. Moreover, his life was recalled as the American Dream, a Horatio Alger tale of a boy who rose from humble beginnings, in an era when evil could be identified and overcome, and when men still could be self-made.

Such rhetoric echoed (ironically) feminist Susan Faludi's characterization of the American masculine ideal that seemed, to many men, "lost" after midcentury. Writing in 1999, she claimed that "[Ernie] Pyle's bugle call is still a summons for a generational transformation, waiting to be heard."[86] That call was sounded, in journalism as well as other American institutions, on September 11, 2001. The answer was the construction and elevation of a symbolic working-class hero who remained useful in coverage of subsequent events because his story was both old and new.

In this broader narrative, the ideal American is an ordinary person (or, even if he is privileged or well educated, he has the same values and work ethic as ordinary people) who nevertheless is the nation's backbone. He has experienced, or has the potential for, upward mobility gained through hard work and commitment to ideals. He is a devoted family man who does good, even great, deeds with quiet humility. He is a team player, and he puts the needs of his "brothers" (his neighbors, co-workers, and fellow countrymen) ahead of his own. He chooses work that puts him in danger or makes him vulnerable because the work is for the public good. At a crucial moment in his life, he suffers a trial—the kind through which "a boy becomes a man"—and it is these qualities that save him. It turns out that these qualities are not merely his strength; they are the strength of his country.

For the two years following September 11th, not just firemen, but also coal miners and astronauts, a president[87] and a mayor, rock stars and athletes were to varying degrees placed into this news template. This process has occurred in media but is central to national identity. It allows, even ensures, that in times of crisis, individual people and events and issues are woven into an American story that naturalizes individual phenomena and restores sense to the life of the nation. The fact that this story has a clear shape gives it an illusion of permanence and historicizes its details through commemoration. "Commemoration silences the contrary interpretations of the past," note David Middleton and Derek Edwards. "The silent remembrance of those who died in battle also silences outrage at the courses of action entailing such loss."[88]

The overall commemorative tale does indeed emphasize certain characters and events, certain motivations and outcomes, and certain cultural and political ideals. In the journalistic coverage discussed in this chapter, a particular disaster was represented and explained in a way that justified a controversial war. The media story of September 11th also naturalized definitions of typical American values based on specific notions about gender and class, seen through the lens of nostalgia at a current conservative political moment in American life. It became a public narrative with staying power and yet also with flexibility that made it adaptable to many types of crisis news events, and it seems likely to be used to tell future stories as well. As Claude Levi-Strauss noted, "Mythic thought does not effect complete courses; it always has something more to achieve."[89] It is for this broader reason that this moment in journalism is worth careful critical attention, well beyond September 11th.

3 A News of Feeling as well as Fact

Public Mourning for the Dead Celebrity

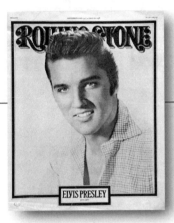

Elvis contained more of America—had swallowed whole more of its contradictions and paradoxes—than any other figure. . . . [He was] a sort of force, as a kind of necessity: that is, the necessity existing in every culture (or anyways ours) that leads it to produce a perfect, all-inclusive metaphor for itself. —*Rolling Stone*, 1977[1]

The communal expression of grief is not a form of mass hysteria, but a recognition that we too are sick and we too must die; for once we have been made to understand that the bell that tolled for Diana, Princess of Wales . . . tolled also for us. That is what is meant when people—ordinary, working-class people—say, "She was one of us": She shared the human condition.—*TV Guide*, 1997[2]

Public mourning occurs spontaneously upon the news of terrorism such as September 11th and the Oklahoma City bombing, or terrible accidents such as the Challenger and Columbia explosions, and news media widely cover those outpourings of grief. This is not surprising. What is striking is how similar these outpourings and their coverage are, and how well Americans—reporters and citizens alike—know what to do. We know to erect sidewalk shrines with pictures, candles, teddy bears, flowers, and beads; we know to converge in public parks with lit candles.[3] For decades, we have had rehearsals through events that are less nationally consequential and yet, sometimes, are perceived as public tragedies: the deaths of famous people. On these occasions, too, journalistic media shed the illusion of objective reporting and engage in emotion and tribute. Such a shift is expected when national leaders die and there is a political script for national mourning, yet it is equally true of the media coverage of movie stars and musicians and athletes, whose death coverage may exceed that of official dignitaries.

Moreover, the deaths of celebrities are described, in media tributes, as meaningful in a deeply personal way to ordinary people. When country-music legend Johnny Cash died in October 2003, *Rolling Stone* summarized the appeal of this kind of journalism—and paid him the highest compliment—by calling him "a legend who never stopped being a common man."[4] Much like the fireman-heroes of September 11th, celebrities who are most and best remembered are those whose lives can be told in a way that stands for all of "us," and whose deaths can be understood as a moment to stop, in journalism, to assess who "we" are.

Celebrity-death coverage has been the subject of critical attention, and it has been critical indeed. The increasing quantity of this type of content in news media is seen by journalists as well as academic critics as something inevitable (after all, we live in a celebrity culture, and fans will be upset) yet embarrassingly unfortunate. When John F. Kennedy Jr.'s airplane crashed into the waters off Martha's Vineyard in July 1999, news coverage included such self-conscious criticism, even as it recalled Kennedy's childhood and showed piles of flowers at his apartment building. A columnist in *Newsweek* accused Americans of wallowing in "virtual grief," an inauthentic form of "media-orchestrated empathy, abetted by celebrity-charged curiosity, bordering on voyeurism"; another in *Time* regretted "tear-drenched mass-media renderings of . . . tragedies."[5]

The latter magazine also contained the opposite point of view. "No doubt there will be many who will say the media have gone overboard.

... Maybe so, but people feel the way they feel because ... they do," one reader wrote. "The media help many people grieve over a loss such as this."[6] *Time* columnist Roger Rosenblatt agreed, claiming, "Those who feel that journalism's coverage of his death has been overdone do not understand that there is a news of feeling as well as fact."[7] Writing on the death of Princess Diana,[8] communication scholar Janice Hocker Rushing makes a similar case, criticizing "academic paparazzi" who "freeze-frame our textual prey" and calling for "a more empathetic criticism" and an admission that we sometimes are "one with what we study, if only for a little while."[9]

This chapter offers a look at celebrity-memorial journalism over time, and across a range of types of personalities, by examining magazine coverage of the deaths of twenty celebrities over the past four decades.[10] Such a broad survey confirms critics' contention that celebrity memorialization is an accelerating trend and an increasingly profitable enterprise. Yet it also provides evidence that such journalism has a useful social function, and that it rises out of cultural (not just commercial) instincts shared by journalists and audiences.

In a society in which fame has become a kind of "secular religion,"[11] it is rhetorically significant that we call the famous "celebrities" and that the word celebration is common in coverage that provides not just a report of their deaths but also an affirmative reenactment of their lives. The material examined in this chapter sheds light on how media construct celebrities in a way that endows them with sacrificial symbolic status, that allows them to live and die for all of us. It also reveals that "the Diana phenomenon"[12] in news is hardly new—its media roots go at least as deep as Graceland in 1977[13]—and that it embraces a range of types of celebrities. When race-car driver Dale Earnhardt was killed in a crash in 2001, NBC News anchor Brian Williams wrote in *Time*: "The flowers and personal notes that piled up last week outside his headquarters briefly threatened to make him America's Diana with a push-broom mustache."[14]

The death of Earnhardt and Diana and JFK Jr. was the same journalistic story as the passings of other figures as diverse as Judy Garland, John Wayne, John Lennon, and Kurt Cobain. It is an instructive tale in which the life of the celebrity, ritually reviewed, is an occasion to discuss the values of "everyone." Through media, audiences come to feel as if they know celebrities; it makes sense, then, that they can fully mourn them only through media.

James Carey writes that the function of journalism is "not the act of imparting information but the representation of shared beliefs" in a "sacred ceremony that draws persons together in fellowship and commonality."[15] In an age of family and cultural dislocation, news media increasingly offer a public forum in which to express and experience what once were deeply private feelings. This shift has occurred at the same time that memorial has become central to modern attitudes toward death: according to Philippe Ariès, as people have become less willing to accept the naturalness and inevitability of death, the rituals of burial, and particularly the celebration of the deceased, have taken on greater importance.[16]

Journalists perform this ritual: to borrow the terminology of anthropology, they conduct the rite of passage from life to death, a three-stage process that involves the community as well as the deceased, beginning with separation (the death itself, a rift in society) and ending with reincorporation (the community's acceptance of the death and reaffirmation of group values, a healing). Much of the funeral ritual occurs during the middle stage, a "liminal" period in which social hierarchy is replaced by what Victor Turner calls "communitas." He explains that "if liminality is regarded as a time and place of withdrawal from normal modes of social action, it can be seen as potentially a period of scrutinization of the central values and axioms of the culture in which it occurs."[17] According to Arnold van Gennep, this examination "reunite[s] all the surviving members of the group . . . in the same way that a chain which has been broken by the disappearance of one of its links must be rejoined."[18]

In his study of public responses to John Lennon's death, Fred Fogo uses these ideas to explain the generational identity of the Baby Boomers who came of age in the 1960s. To him, this generation itself was liminal, a "moment" of *communitas* in which American values were resisted and reevaluated, and journalistic discussions of the meaning of Lennon's life and death were actually articulations of the Boomers' acceptance of an adult identity (reincorporation).[19] Similarly, Sharon Mazzarella and Timothy Matyjewicz found generational themes in news coverage of the deaths of Lennon and Jerry Garcia (for the Baby Boom) and Kurt Cobain (Generation X).[20] This chapter extends these arguments and the underlying theoretical concept—the notion of the death as an unstable public moment in which people feel compelled to assess their identities and beliefs—to the meaning any major celebrity holds for any social group.

When famous people die, magazine editors promote their coverage with labels such as "commemorative edition," "special report," and "collectors' issue." Inside the magazines are documentary photos of milestones in the person's life, fans' shrines made with flowers and candles, crowds of mourners assembled in public places. The covers function as a kind of tombstone, listing birth and death years over a photo that is not just a picture but a portrait to be preserved: Princesses Diana and Grace wearing their tiaras (figure 3.1); Jacqueline Kennedy as a young First Lady, in pillbox hat and pearls; John F. Kennedy Jr. as a three-year-old saluting his father's casket; a casual Frank Sinatra, coat slung over one shoulder, tipping his hat; a tired but sober, black-clad Johnny Cash squarely facing the camera in gritty black-and-white (figure 3.2).

These images recognize the celebrities as people everyone knows, seemingly erasing the reality that the audience did not, in fact, personally know them. Joshua Meyrowitz uses the term "media friend" to describe "the sense of intimate knowledge and empathic connection" people feel with celebrities, "a direct, one-to-one tie to a media friend that exists apart from, and almost in spite of, how widely known the person is."[21] Richard Dyer further explains: "Stars are obviously a case of appearance—all we know of them is what we see and hear before us. Yet the whole media construction of stars encourages us to think in terms of 'really'—what is [the star] really like? . . . Stars articulate what it is to be a human being in contemporary society; that is, they express the particular notion we hold of the person, of the 'individual.' . . . Much of the construction of the star encourages us to think . . . [that] we have a privileged reality to hang on to, the reality of the star's private self."[22] Joshua Gamson makes the same argument with specific regard to coverage of celebrities in twentieth-century American magazines. "The public discovers and makes famous certain people because it (with the help of the magazines) *sees through* the publicity-generated, artificial self to the real, deserving, special self."[23]

This is a media illusion; in a literal sense, audiences' connection with stars is a fantasy (as is the spectacular nature of ongoing media coverage of celebrities). Writing about the iconic status of "The Dead Rock Star" in *Rolling Stone*, celebrity-author Marilyn Manson noted the exoticism of such figures, in life and death: "The people who live their lives close to death, or who die tragically, are the ones we're going to fantasize about the most. It is escapism, it's voyeurism, it's living vicariously. Or dying vicariously."[24]

Yet the audience's connection with stars is real, too, in the sense that it allows people to form their own individual and collective identities and values, a transformation that occurs on the reception rather

FIGURE 3.1
People Weekly *cover, September 15, 1997*
(Credit: People Weekly, *September 15, 1997).*

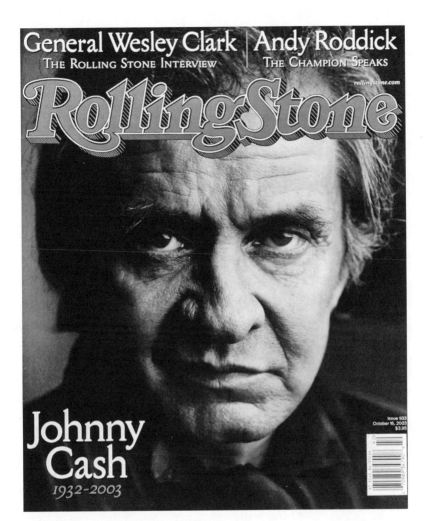

General Wesley Clark | Andy Roddick
THE ROLLING STONE INTERVIEW | THE CHAMPION SPEAKS

rollingstone.com

Rolling Stone

Issue 933
October 16, 2003
$3.95

Johnny
Cash
1932-2003

FIGURE 3.2
Rolling Stone *cover, October 16, 2003*
(Cover photo by Mark Seliger from Rolling Stone,
October 16, 2003. © *Rolling Stone* LLC *2003.*
All rights reserved. Reprinted by permission).

than production end of media imagery. Anthropologist John Caughey explains: "People characterize unmet media figures as if they were intimately involved with them, and in a sense they are—they engage in pseudo-social interactions with them," relationships that continue "when the TV is turned off, the book closed, or the newspaper thrown away." In most cases, the celebrity "becomes the object of intense admiration" but also an object of identification: "The admired figure is typically felt to have qualities that the person senses in himself but desires to develop further. The admired figure represents an ideal self-image."[25] Writing about John Wayne, historian Garry Wills contends that he "fill[ed] some need in his audience. He was the conduit they used to communicate with their own desired selves or their own imagined past."[26] Richard Stolley, the founding editor of *People* magazine, provides much the same explanation of why the magazine's top four best-selling issues have been cover stories about dead celebrities: "We buy them to mourn [and] . . . we're mourning ourselves, our own past, as much as we're mourning the celebrity. We want to relive the part of our life that we remember through that celebrity."[27]

The stories that media tell and audiences "know" about celebrities are moral tales about how Americans might live their lives, individually and collectively. "A 'star' reputation is thus also a 'moon,'" writes literary scholar John Rodden, "refracting—if through a glass darkly—the enlarged self imagined by an individual or group. . . . We have met the images and they are ourselves."[28] *Time* columnist Rosenblatt made this point when he wrote of JFK Jr., "For the observing public, he was useful as a figure to dream into."[29] When Frank Sinatra died, *TV Guide* discussed the phenomenon of iconic celebrities in the same way: "We project on them our own hopes and fears, experience through them our dreams, even our losses and pains, for we understand somewhere within ourselves that the lives of the great bear human scars like our own."[30]

When such a person dies, Joshua Meyrowitz explains, "The pain is paradoxical: It feels personal, yet it is strengthened by the extent to which it is shared."[31] A writer for *Rolling Stone* explained of John Lennon: "We *knew* him. . . . We knew what he meant. . . . Through the Beatles—and, I think, primarily through John—I was able to share with millions my thoughts and their thoughts—*our thoughts*—about growing old, falling in love, seizing happiness, transcendence. . . . Part of the grief we feel about his murder is our longing to once more belong to something larger than ourselves, to feel our heart beat in absolute synchrony with hearts everywhere."[32]

If celebrity is a cultural space in which Americans negotiate their values and identities, through which they become something larger than their individual selves, then a celebrity's death is a moment for public discussion of shared ideals and identities. Magazine coverage of late-twentieth-century celebrity deaths illustrates how this period of *communitas* plays out in American media, and to what extent their role has grown in recent years.

Certainly such coverage has accelerated across the magazine industry. Although magazines commented widely on the popularity of James Dean—what *Life* called "delirium over [a] dead star" and the *Saturday Review* called "mass hysteria"—following his 1955 fatal car crash, this phenomenon was reported with surprise in articles published a year later; at the time, his death itself merited only a seven-line item in *Time*'s "Milestones" column and an eight-line item in *Newsweek*'s "Transition" department.[33] Seven years later, the two leading newsweeklies together devoted five pages of coverage to the death of Marilyn Monroe (chronologically the first person included in this study), though that level of coverage seems scant today.

Apart from slain political leaders, the twenty celebrities discussed in this chapter are the ones whose deaths received the most magazine-cover-story attention over the past half century—but more than half of them died in the ten years before this book was completed (2004). After his death in 2001, George Harrison appeared on three times as many magazine covers as John Lennon had in 1980. Some magazines now publish tributes to dead celebrities on an ongoing basis, such as the Salute sections of *Life*'s annual "Year in Pictures" issue and *TV Guide*'s year-end "Tribute" issue, as well as *People* magazine's new series of "magabooks" (each about a particular person) under the *People Tributes* logo. While we expect celebrity tributes in those magazines, what is perhaps more striking is the acceleration of coverage in newsmagazines. During the 1960s, *Time* and *Newsweek* barely noticed the passing of Monroe and Judy Garland, and while they paid more attention to the deaths of Elvis Presley and John Wayne in the 1970s, neither merited a cover. Even *People* magazine largely ignored Presley's death, with the only cover tribute coming from *Rolling Stone* (figure 3.3). The week Presley died, *Newsweek* gave its cover to the political scandal of federal budget director Bert Lance; eighteen years later, it chose Jerry Garcia over a presidential scandal (Whitewater). Two of the three current newsweeklies devoted even more space to coverage of JFK Jr.'s 1999 death than they had to Princess Diana in 1997.

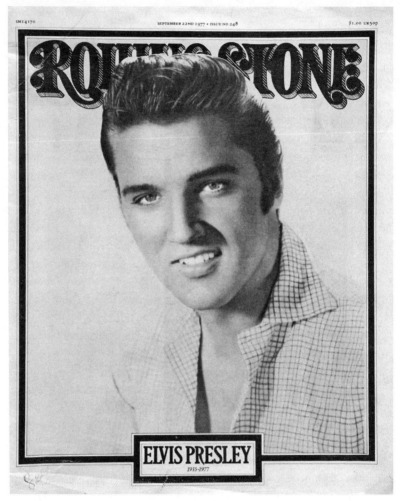

FIGURE 3.3
Rolling Stone *cover, September 22, 1977*
(Cover photo by unknown photographer from Rolling Stone,
September 22, 1977. © Rolling Stone LLC *1977.*
All rights reserved. Reprinted by permission).

This trend parallels journalistic media's growing attention to celebrities in general, a shift that has occurred across news media over the past several decades. Some critics see newsmagazines' move toward celebrity coverage as a move away from political coverage,[34] but as David Marshall notes, political figures themselves increasingly can be understood only in terms of celebrity.[35] Bruce Gronbeck points to reporters' interest in the "character" of political leaders, a quest that parallels the public's desire to know the "real" person behind the star.[36] Celebrities embody this tension: just as their images symbolize the intersection of the individual and society, they "live on a fault line between the public and the private," writes Catharine Lumby, who claims that "it's precisely this undecidability of where the public stops and the private begins that defines the fascination of contemporary celebrity."[37]

When they cover celebrity deaths, journalists seem to stand on this fault line: they speak to, and on behalf of, the public, while openly sharing their own reactions. They act as healing spiritual leaders—this was religion scholar Roland Boer's suggestion in describing coverage of Princess Diana's death as a "global manifestation of civil religion"[38]—yet they also are mourners. *Life* wrote after Judy Garland's death, "We laughed with her and cried with her and begged for more in a marriage of requited love never before experienced in the theater."[39] Thirty-two years later, *Rolling Stone* wrote of George Harrison, "We are richer for the time that he lived with us. May he go in peace."[40]

This rhetoric is frequently testimonial. *Life* printed the impressions of a writer who had previously profiled Monroe: "If Marilyn Monroe was glad to see you, her 'hello' will sound in your mind all of your life," he wrote, quoting the star as insisting that "'most people really don't know me.'"[41] Though few journalists ever got to know Monroe's husband, Joe DiMaggio, *Time*'s writer shared a childhood memory—"I not only saw the Yankee Clipper play in person; I got his autograph twice"—that established his authority while making him one of the "us" who had lost something at the baseball great's passing.[42] *New Yorker* editor Tina Brown recounted her lunch with Diana, revealing that the princess had "found a place to channel all that unrequited love, and [was] learning to be sustained by it."[43]

The coverage also is emotional and sentimental. After Frank Sinatra's death, *Newsweek* turned to the language of pop-psychology, confessing that "we're having trouble saying he *died*. Because losing him means losing too many worlds that we're not willing to give up yet."[44] Peggy Noonan memorialized Jacqueline Onassis as a heroine in *Time* by invoking memories of the slain president's funeral three decades earlier. "I wish I could see someone's little boy, in a knee-length coat, lift his arm and salute," she wrote.[45] That image referenced the toddling JFK Jr.'s 1963 salute, which itself reappeared as a *Time* cover when the younger Kennedy's plane crashed in 1999. As Roger Rosenblatt suggested, emotion *was* the "news" in JFK Jr.'s death, with twenty-four references to that salute in two weeks of the newsweeklies' coverage and frequent use of the first-person plural. "We mourned with him, we grew up with him," *U.S. News & World Report* wrote.[46]

While such language unites journalists and readers in terms of perspective, the use of a narrative format places the death within a story we already recognize from previous news coverage of the person's life (as well as from entertainment-industry mythology). Here are two leads from *Time* published twenty-one years apart:

> As the legend goes, Elvis Presley had only a year's passing familiarity with a recording studio when he cut that record in the winter of 1955. He had wandered into Sun Records with his guitar, two summers before, plunked down $4 to sing a couple of tunes to his mother, Gladys.

> "Get that!" the story goes. "His name is Sinatra, and he considers himself the greatest vocalist in the business." This is the bandleader Harry James talking in 1939, when Frank Sinatra, of Hoboken, N.J., had not yet moved the world. "No one's ever heard of him! He's never had a hit record, and he looks like a wet rag, but he says he's the greatest." Said it. Meant it. Proved it. Harry James must have sensed it too, because he had hired Sinatra.[47]

In the case of Princess Diana, the magazines had a story type available. *Newsweek* called her life "a grim fairy tale that had come true" and likened it to a farce, the princess and the pea: "For this princess, no mattresses could mask the kernel of resentment at being plunged into a role for which she had never been prepared and from which there appeared to be no escape."[48]

Even so, Diana's story was really the same as the story of the other female icons. She was cast in the same role as Princess Grace, with the subthemes of not just royalty, but also tragedy and irony, as suggested by nearly identical leads that appeared fifteen years apart in different magazines. In *Time*, "[Diana's] final ceremonial progression through the streets of London raised haunting memories of her first a brilliant morning 16 summers ago . . . borne in a carriage toward an enchanted future"; in *Newsweek*, "The last journey of Princess Grace was one she had taken often in life, the 600 yards from her pink-walled palace to the great white Cathedral of St. Nicholas."[49] Both women's life stories were told in a visual narrative as well, with photo features tracing their life stages: privileged child, young beauty, princess, devoted mother, caring philanthropist. The same technique was used to chronicle the life of Jacqueline Onassis, who was also described in royal terms, and whose pictures set in place a visual trajectory for Diana: shy but stunning bride, at first hesitant in public but then beloved, a pillar of strength facing adversity, and eventually the jet-setting companion of a wealthy playboy.

The uniformity of the stories of Diana, Grace, and Jackie is hardly surprising, considering that they held essentially the same public roles. Yet these stories echoed the memorialization of Marilyn Monroe and Judy Garland. Monroe's and Garland's lives were told through parallel plots: an unhappy childhood; talent and youthful innocence exploited by Hollywood; marriages that did not fill the emotional void; a cultlike following; and death by an overdose of sleeping pills. *Life* noted that "Judy, like Marilyn, was a victim of a system she couldn't beat."[50] Both this characterization and *Newsweek*'s description of Judy Garland as a woman "who had struggled to the other side of the rainbow and found nothing there"[51] also defined Princess Diana. The magazines saw the eating disorders of Garland and Diana as a cry for help and equated the blonde beauty of Monroe and Diana with innocence and gentleness. In some coverage, Diana's story was an inversion of those of Garland and Monroe: she had beaten her problems and survived. In *Newsweek*, Princess Grace was directly contrasted with Monroe, described as a 1950s actress–sex symbol who had escaped the Hollywood machine. But in the magazines' final interpretation, all four women had the same destiny—to be killed by their own fame.

So did JFK Jr., and, of the men, his story most closely corresponded to the core plots of the women's lives. He was frequently compared with both his mother and Princess Diana; he too survived great sorrow and enormous pressure in his youth; he too was remembered in terms of his family ties and his physical attractiveness. While the stories of the other men were told chronologically, the stages of their lives were defined professionally rather than personally. There were examples of inversion—both John Lennon and Jerry Garcia were praised as having avoided the fate of Elvis Presley—but, in general, their lives merged into one tale.

Despite very different backgrounds and philosophies, John Wayne,

John Lennon, Jerry Garcia, Frank Sinatra, Sammy Davis Jr., Joe DiMaggio, and Johnny Cash were remembered as the same type of hero, a man whose genius survived despite a life of arrogance or misbehavior, who had multiple relationships with women, yet whose identity was formed among men. Lennon, Sinatra, Wayne, DiMaggio, and Dale Earnhardt also were praised for their determination to negotiate the world on their own. *Time* wrote that Earnhardt "would never take his foot off the gas. That is why they loved him. Ironhead, the Intimidator, Earnhardt: he had massive, irresistible appeal. . . . What roiled inside him usually came out, sometimes in fits of temper or unruly behavior behind the wheel." The magazine quoted one male fan as saying: "'He was the John Wayne of NASCAR. He was a kick-ass, take-names kinda guy. A guy's guy.'"[52] In a similar vein, *TV Guide* observed: "Throughout his life, Sinatra broke all the rules and did as he pleased, sometimes paying the price . . . he was willing to take the risk for 'All or Nothing at All,' as most of us wish we had the courage and opportunity to do."[53]

These men's stories conveyed what Caryl Rivers identifies as a standard news theme, "that the best of us are those that stand alone." Referring to Sinatra, she claims that in American journalism, "our heroes tend to be 'My Way' kind of guys, loners."[54] At the same time, these loners were celebrated as role models: their standoffishness, ironically, inspired strangers to identify with them.[55]

Indeed, one element of the memorial story is the extent to which, in life, the celebrity was as common as (or even more common than) the reader. *Rolling Stone* began its account of Johnny Cash's life story this way: "Apart from his mother's unshakable belief in his musical talent—'God has his hand on you, son,' she told him when he was a boy, 'don't ever forget the gift'—little in Cash's impoverished background suggested that the extraordinary life he would lead was possible. He was one of seven children, born to a sharecropping family in Kingsland, Arkansas. . . ."[56]

As in Cash's story, magazine memorials list the hardships celebrities overcame, laying the foundation for the Horatio Alger theme that runs through so many of these memorials. *Newsweek* noted that John Wayne began life as "Marion Morrison, a big shy fella from Winterset, Iowa," that Frank Sinatra was born the son of a fireman and a barmaid "in the rough, working-class town of Hoboken, N.J.," and that Elvis Presley, whose "father worked at odd jobs," "was born dirt poor in the small rural town of Tupelo, Miss.," adding, "The instigator of raunch-revolt was a good boy who loved his mother."[57] *People Weekly* revealed that John Belushi "was the child of poor Albanian immigrants" and that Jerry Garcia "was 5 when he witnessed the drowning death of his father, José . . . [and was] raised by his mother, Ruth, who ran a saloon next to the merchant marine union hall near the San Francisco waterfront."[58] Us Weekly reported that George Harrison's "father, Harold, was a bus driver," while People noted that John Lennon's father had abandoned the family and that "these early years were . . . a deep psychic wellspring from which he could draw reserves of hard truth."[59] Rolling Stone documented Kurt Cobain's early years in "a hard-hit lumber town," as a child of divorce "passed" among relatives, a "misfit" who was "scorned and beat upon both by those who should have loved him and by those who hardly knew him."[60]

Sports Illustrated eulogized Dale Earnhardt in a rags-to-riches tale that explained his appeal in terms of common frustrations. Its cover story called him

> a superstar the average blue-jean-wearing fan could identity with. . . .
> Underdogs appreciated how he had worked his way up from humble
> beginnings, tinkering with cars in a makeshift garage that his dad,
> Ralph, a short-track whiz, built in the barn behind the family's house
> on Sedan Avenue in Kannapolis, N.C. . . . Then there were the tough
> guys, the ones who couldn't get enough of the way he refused to let
> anyone slow him down on the way to his destination. "I think every-
> body in the country is angry about having to drive in urban areas,"
> said [speedway owner H. A.] Wheeler in 1995. "They hate the traffic
> with a passion. Earnhardt drives through traffic too. And he won't put
> up with anything. He's going to get through. That's what they want
> to do—but they can't. So Earnhardt is playing out their fantasies."[61]

Remembering Sammy Davis Jr., People wrote: "Born in 1925 in Harlem, the son of a tap dancer and a Puerto Rican chorus girl who ran off while he was still a tot, Davis was only 3 when he began doing vaudeville turns with his father. . . . Sometimes, on nights when there was barely enough money for a meal, the roar of the crowd was the only comfort the boy would get."[62] All the magazines stressed Joe DiMaggio's beginnings as the son of an Italian-immigrant fisherman. U.S. News & World Report noted that he had chosen a game "played by working-class men mostly for blue-collar joes in bleacher seats" and quoted his explanation for his own success: "'A ballplayer's got to be hungry. . . . That's why no boy from a rich family ever made the big leagues.'"[63]

Though he *was* a boy from a rich family, JFK Jr. was loved for his ordinariness. *Time* called him "a black-tie aristocrat who took the subway" and noted that "the most famous son in the world wanted nothing more than to be a normal guy."[64] *People Weekly* recalled John Lennon at the time of his murder as a new father who had just "embarked on the most revolutionary undertaking of any rock star's career: an attempt to lead a normal life."[65] Two decades later, *Rolling Stone* observed that "George Harrison spent most of the last two decades . . . tending his gardens and raising his son."[66] *Entertainment Weekly* noted that Kurt Cobain "was regarded as a quiet but often kind introvert off stage" and that he was, according to a friend, a "great father."[67] *People* wrote, "Bearded and gray, a middle-aged man whose weight sometimes ballooned to 300 pounds, Jerry Garcia seemed the antithesis of what a rock star is supposed to be."[68] *Rolling Stone* wrote of Sinatra: "He sang about a profound loneliness that he knew well and that he spent his whole life trying to beat, in both wondrous and awful ways. Just as important, Sinatra sang to the loneliness inside others, and those who heard that voice sometimes found something of their own experience within its resonance."[69]

Female celebrities were remembered in the same terms, even if they had grown up wealthy, with an emphasis on their childhood unhappiness. *Newsweek*'s cover story on Onassis reiterated the poor-little-rich-girl theme in describing Jackie's parents, who divorced when she was eleven, as "a philandering lush" and "an icy social climber."[70] *Time* wrote, "Unlike Dorothy of *Oz*, Judy Garland never really had a backyard to call her own. . . . Judy was a vaudeville trouper at the age of five. Her father died when she was twelve, and her mother, as Judy remarked bitterly years later, 'was . . . the real-life Wicked Witch of the West.'"[71] *People Weekly* reported that the stepgrandparents who raised Lucille Ball "locked the poor kid into a dog collar and leashed her to an overhead wire in the backyard."[72] *TV Guide* described Diana as a "once-coltish girl from a dysfunctional family who had been unnurtured, undereducated, undercherished."[73]

It was Diana, whose life was the farthest removed from those of ordinary people, who was most pitied for her hard life and praised for her realness and accessibility. *Time* called her "the princess with the common touch" whose "nobility embraced everyone and whose life reflected the commonality of loneliness and of heartbreak. . . . Her death . . . robbed the world of the hope that her story—which was somehow everyone's story—would end happily ever after."[74] One *New Yorker* essay titled "Requiem" explained: "The more you know she was never perfect, the less you, who are not perfect either, are able to detach the loss of her from the loss of yourself"; another piece in the same magazine claimed that "Diana expressed, more poignantly than almost any other woman of our time, the melancholy solitude specific to many women's experience of marriage."[75] In *People*, Lucille Ball also was remembered as a symbol of what women must endure, recalling her husband's infidelities as well as her comic persona, "a Don Quixote in pin curls who tilted hopelessly but hilariously at the male establishments, a beguiling caricature of all those wistful hausfraus of the '50s who dreamed of conquering the great big world out there but time and again wound up bitchin' in the kitchen."[76]

Entertainment Weekly quoted actress Meryl Streep of saying about Katharine Hepburn, "She was the template upon which many smart 20th-century women modeled themselves." Yet she was the exception to the "ordinary" portrayal of female celebrities, precisely because of the qualification "smart," as *Newsweek* observed: "The patrician style—indeed, the very notion that America has a patrician class—evokes a complex reaction in our supposedly classless society, and Hepburn was both idolized and resented for that breezy Bryn Mawr accent, that effortless assurance that didn't stoop to curry our favor."[77]

Much as Diana and Lucy were seen as publicly living out the lives of all women, Frank Sinatra was cast as a fantasy Everyman. *Newsweek* wrote that "Sinatra's art spanned and shaped much of the century; his music defined how Americans loved—and lost. In movies and in song, raising hell or hanging with presidents, Sinatra, a drink in one hand and a cigarette in the other, knew how to connect with all of us."[78] *Entertainment Weekly* called him "the entertainer of the century," and *Time* wrote, "His way became the quintessential 20th century American way."[79]

Older icons symbolized not just the generation that came of age during World War II, but also a midcentury American spirit. When Katharine Hepburn died at ninety-six, *Entertainment Weekly* claimed: "The old gods are now gone. . . . Modern Hollywood, whose films are to the studio-era classics as videogames are to illuminated manuscripts, knows what it has lost. . . . It hardly needs to be said that with Hepburn goes not only old Hollywood but an older America as well."[80] In Joe DiMaggio, "the nation found a mirror for its best self," wrote *Newsweek*. "In the hard-knuckled '30s, he was the Sicilian immigrant's son who came from nothing, made it big. . . . In the war, he sacrificed his best years but came back as a winner."[81] *U.S. News & World Report* carried the same theme: "Like the very best stories and images, DiMaggio's are intensely evocative, talismans of an American past, of the way we were—

or at least wanted to be. Like Gary Cooper, Jimmy Stewart, and a handful of midcentury icons, DiMaggio was the face America wanted to see when it looked in the mirror."[82]

Another hero's name easily could have been added to that last sentence. "Celebrating the dead John Wayne, America was celebrating one of its gallant dead dreams—a dream of unflagging national virility, courage, moral righteousness and stone-fisted sincerity," Newsweek explained.[83] Jacqueline Onassis had provided a more refined version of the same values, "a connection to a time, to an old America that was more dignified, more private, an America in which standards were higher and clearer and elegance meant something," noted Time.[84] U.S. News & World Report saw Sinatra as another kind of role model who "reflect[ed] a particularly American image that was at once coarse and tender, swaggering and vulnerable. To a post–World War II nation suffused with success, the young crooner was . . . a vicarious ego boost to millions of fans, a distillation of what they hoped to see when they looked in the mirror: the swinger."[85]

Sinatra, Time explained, was a symbolic figure the next generation rebelled against: "In the Oedipal drama of the counterculture, Frank was the daddy-o who must die."[86] But Newsweek credited Elvis Presley with having "created the generation gap. Rarely does an entertainer so galvanize the unstated yearnings of an age and serve as a harbinger for the decade to come as Elvis did in the mid-1950s." The magazine noted that "when Elvis exploded, kids were no longer just individual appendages on millions of American families. . . . A tribe was born . . . and a kind of civil war was triggered."[87]

The "tribe" that rejected Sinatra and was mobilized by Elvis, and that dominated popular culture through the 1960s and 1970s, lost its first musical icons within three years of one another, Presley in 1977 and then John Lennon in 1980. Although Lennon was shot by a mentally ill fan, the magazines (staffed then by writers of Lennon's own age) found profound cultural meaning for his death. Time declared: "For much of an entire generation that is passing, as Lennon was, at age 40, into middle age, and coming suddenly up against its own mortality—the murder was an assassination, a ritual slaying of something that could hardly be named. Hope, perhaps; or idealism. Or time."[88] Rolling Stone wrote of his murder: "It was, of course, like the Sixties again, waking up, hearing of his death. . . . . It's like a hurricane suddenly returning after it was supposedly spent at sea."[89]

Readers as well as journalists found generational lessons in Lennon's story. "John Lennon told us we had survived the Vietnam War, Watergate and all the other tragedies of the past decade," wrote one *Newsweek* reader; another fan saw his death as "the last nail in the coffin of the '60s."[90] Fifteen years later, in 1995, *Newsweek* wrote of Jerry Garcia's death, "that this, at last, *finally* [emphasis in the original], was the end of the '60s."[91] Not quite. The generational significance of JFK Jr. was described not in terms of other people his own age, but rather in terms of older Baby Boomers' memories of his father. In their extensive use of the photograph of him saluting his father's casket, as well as photos of the young boy with the president, the newsmagazines mourned him less as a thirty-eight-year-old than as a three-year-old. *Time's* sole coverline beside the salute photo—"Ask Not . . ."—evoked not the son but the father; its text was more explicit, calling him "a hero sprung up from tragedy . . . whose life was meant in our minds to redeem that evil day in Dallas."[92] *Newsweek* printed a reader letter that summarized the perspective from which the editors saw the tragedy of his death: "We loved John Jr. because we loved his father. . . . his death has reopened some of the wounds of the 1960s, the decade so seminal for late-20th-century history and so incredibly scarring for us as a people."[93]

The same magazine also claimed: "For many younger Americans, Kennedy represented their postmodern esthetic: informal, irreverent, adventurous."[94] Kurt Cobain, too, was seen as a symbol of the eighties, though a different side of that era, not the ambition of the youngest Boomers, but the alienation of Generation X. "Even his struggles—with fame, with drugs, with his identity—caught the generational drama of our time," wrote *Rolling Stone.* "For people who came of age amid the greed, the designer-drug indulgence and the image-driven celebrity of the '80s, anyone who could make an easy peace with success was fatally suspect." This article called Cobain a spokesman "for a new tribe of disaffected youth," while *People Weekly* wrote, "As a poster boy for today's lost generation, Kurt turned his torn jeans and grungy T-shirts into an anti-fashion of punk alienation."[95]

Time described Jacqueline Onassis's death in terms of its generational significance not to Jackie's peers, but rather to "those of us who were children when she was in the White House."[96] A female writer for *Newsweek* called her "the last woman we could idolize. . . . When we wanted to grow up to be princesses, she was our princess. And later, when we wanted to be independent, she was independent."[97] Yet Onassis was not the last woman a generation of women could idolize. The appeal of Princess Diana, thirty-two years younger than Jackie, was described in almost exactly the same language. A female writer for *U.S. News & World Report*, using the first-person plural as a generational and female "we," explained: "As long as Diana was out there, plying her glamorous, uncertain path to a full self, we could at least retain our ambivalence about the [princess] myth. . . . this drama *is* girlhood and young womanhood in America: a succession of choices between the possibilities of independence and the seductions of dependence."[98]

While Sinatra and Sammy Davis Jr. were close friends and actually had similar life—and career—trajectories, Davis was remembered differently, as a symbol not of the country but of the African American experience within that country. *People Weekly* assessed his significance:

> He was the heir to such tap dancers as Bill "Bojangles" Robinson and a contemporary of Louis Armstrong, Duke Ellington and Lena Horne. He was one of the first black entertainers to break the color barrier, the first to play mixed audiences in Vegas and Miami, and the first to have his own TV talk show. . . . It was only toward the end, when disease cruelly slowed him, when young black entertainers began openly to acknowledge how much they owed him. . . . Musician and record producer Quincy Jones noted, "Sammy Davis Jr. was a true pioneer who traveled a dirt road so others, later, could follow on the freeway. He helped remove the limitations on black entertainers. He made it possible for the Bill Cosbys, the Michael Jacksons and the Eddie Murphys to achieve their dreams."[99]

In these ways, magazines conflate departed celebrities with the social groups in which millions of people find their identities. When such an icon dies, then, something dies in "us," and news coverage moves out of the realm of obituary and into that of tragedy. That tragedy is heightened by the implication that the celebrity was unjustly and even ironically snatched away too soon. *Sports Illustrated* ended its cover story on Earnhardt by saying so directly: "One sentiment was shared by the fans who won't have the chance to see him chase that elusive eighth title, the rivals who won't have a chance to swap paint with him again and the drivers who won't have a chance to share one more Victory Lane hug with their boss: This definitely was not fair."[100]

Even older celebrities' passings are described in these terms. When Onassis died at sixty-five, *People Weekly* described her as "dying young" and wrote: "She looked forward to . . . a growing brood of grandchildren to play with. The greatest sorrow, finally, is that this was denied her."[101] The magazine noted of Sammy Davis Jr., who also died at sixty-five, that "his reputation and career had been on an upswing, thanks largely to the 1988–89 tour with Sinatra and Minnelli."[102] Although Sinatra was eighty-two, *Time* pointed out that he died just as "the Rat Pack came back into fashion."[103] And while the magazine noted that Elvis Presley had been "extremely overweight," it pointed out that he had died "the day before he was to go on tour" and "the month that he again had a record on the charts."[104]

Of course, this subtheme is more pronounced when a celebrity's death truly is untimely. Princess Diana had survived a loveless marriage and a public divorce from the royal family only to die when she found a new life. *People Weekly*'s lead story in its first week of coverage was titled "Taken Too Soon" and quoted a friend of the princess as saying, "She wasn't meant to go now; she had such an incredible amount to give still." The article further noted: "Ironically, Di's life had seemed full of promise at the time of her death. . . . That evening, Diana telephoned the *Daily Mail*'s Richard Kay, who reported that she 'was as happy as I have ever known her. For the first time in years, all was well with her world.'"[105] *TV Guide* quoted Barbara Walters as saying of the princess: "She was just beginning to have fun. This was her first relationship that she could publicly enjoy. . . . she was going to be honored at a dinner for her charity work. . . ."[106]

People Weekly wrote that, at the time of his death, John Belushi "wanted to back away from his grotesque, buffoonish image," he had embarked on a serious film career, and "when he talked to [director Robert] DeNiro the night before his death, he agreed to take off 40 pounds."[107] *Newsweek* noted that Jerry Garcia had "checked into the Betty Ford Center . . . he'd gotten married for a third time just last year, the oldest of his four daughters was getting married . . . [he] had turned the corner and 'wanted to live.'"[108] Lennon was described as "a man finally at peace with himself, the creative juices once again flowing. . . . He was, as he titled his most popular new song, 'Starting Over.'"[109] *U.S. News & World Report* reported of JFK Jr., "He'd had some rough patches of late. But things seemed to be going his way again"; in *Time*, historian Arthur Schlesinger revealed, "He seemed to be edging into politics. . . . He was destined, I came to feel, for political leadership."[110]

To compensate for this unfairness, media narratives provide a villain who is responsible. Doing so is part of the funeral drama: as anthropologist Jack Goody noted, "the funeral is often an inquest as well as an interment, a pointer to revenge against a supposed killer or to ways of warding off death in general."[111] After Princess Diana's death, *U.S. News & World Report* declared, "Tragedy demands explication."[112]

Sometimes there is an identifiable villain. Lennon was murdered; Princess Diana and Earnhardt were killed in car crashes (in one case, an occupational hazard; in another, a matter of speeding, a drunk driver, and/or the paparazzi); drugs most likely killed Monroe, Garland, Belushi, Garcia, and Presley; Harrison died of cancer; JFK Jr. was a victim of his flying inexperience and the weather. Sometimes "fate" is blamed, as in the many references to "the Kennedy Curse"[113] and in articles such as *Us Weekly*'s recap of "untimely deaths" of John Lennon and George Harrison and people associated with the Beatles (Stuart Sutcliffe, Brian Epstein, Linda McCartney).[114]

Yet even in such cases, the villain must be more complex for the death to have public meaning. The larger story of Lennon's death was that of war and peace: just as he was cast as a peace figure, *Time* noted that his assassin had been crouched in a "combat stance" and that mourners at the Lincoln Memorial sang "Give Peace a Chance" in a vigil "that recalled the sit-ins of the '6os."[115] Even the celebrities who overdosed died of something greater. Garland had been "sentenced to martyrdom and sainthood in a show-biz world that cries too easily," wrote *Life*.[116] *Newsweek* also used the word "martyr" to characterize Monroe, declaring her a victim "of the Hollywood glamour machine, and the burden of being a sex symbol."[117] Presley fell victim to what *Newsweek* called "the Memphis Mafia."[118] Counterculture guru Ken Kesey saw Garcia as a soldier who died for a cause, claiming, "You can't work that frontier without getting into some danger now and then. The dire wolf finally got him."[119]

For all of these figures—along with Cobain, JFK Jr., and Princesses Grace and Diana—the true villain was the cult of celebrity. The notion of cult was invoked anthropologically in *Time* columnist Lance Morrow's assessment of Diana's cause of death: "Fame tends to draw [celebrities'] spirits away from them in the way that some tribal people fear that being photographed will steal their souls. Fame distributes their souls to the masses as in Communion. The famous get ingested by the world in some primitive manner."[120] Creating a script paralleling that of Diana's car chase and crash, both *Time* and *U.S. News & World Report* speculated that JFK Jr. flew to escape the constant presence of paparazzi, to be in "a place where he could get away, off camera, out of the bubble, on his own"; for him, "flying offered something precious: privacy, anonymity, freedom."[121]

JFK Jr.'s final escape, the magazines explained, was his burial at sea. Ironically, as with Diana, that burial was the largest part of the media story. News coverage of a celebrity's funeral is a script for a national memorial service. Frequently the magazine's coverlines are eulogistic, as with *U.S. New & World Report*'s salute to JFK Jr.: "America's Farewell" (figure 3.4).[122] Yet journalists share this duty with nonjournalists, a mixture of the ordinary and the famous who come forward to say a word. *Newsweek* asked two Pulitzer Prize winners, historian Doris Kearns Goodwin and novelist William Kennedy, to make sense of the deaths of Jacqueline Onassis and Frank Sinatra, while *Time* called on Schlesinger and *U.S. News & World Report* on presidential biographer Richard Reeves to write about JFK Jr. *Newsweek* printed reminiscences of Princess Diana by former First Lady Nancy Reagan and *Washington Post* owner Katharine Graham; *Time* ran essays on the meaning of her celebrity by novelists Joyce Carol Oates and Martin Amis. No less than the U.S. president eulogized John Wayne: "In an age of few heroes," said Jimmy Carter, "he was the genuine article."[123]

Other speakers are celebrities themselves, though through their participation in this service, they become one of "us." Among the show-business stars to offer testimonials about Sammy Davis Jr. was Frank Sinatra; when he died eight years later, Sinatra was eulogized by musicians as diverse as Rosemary Clooney, Paul Anka, Dwight Yoakam, and U2's Bono.[124] Even more diverse were tribute quotes to John Lennon (ranging from Chuck Berry to Norman Mailer) and George Harrison (from Keith Richards to Mia Farrow). Many musicians spoke for the former Beatles, as they had for Elvis Presley—of whom Bruce Springsteen said, "When I heard the news it was like somebody took a piece out of me."[125] Bob Dylan commented on Sinatra, Harrison, Garcia, and Cash, saying of the latter: "Johnny was and is the North Star—you could guide your ship by him."[126] John Belushi was remembered by other comedians, including Chevy Chase and Steve Martin.[127]

Several magazines printed the funeral eulogies delivered by Princess Diana's brother (*Entertainment Weekly* also reprinted the lyrics of Sir Elton John's musical tribute, "Candle in the Wind") and by JFK Jr.'s uncle. One reader wrote to *Time* to thank the writer "who transported us to the service and allowed us to hear the moving eulogy that Senator Edward Kennedy delivered. Her report was a healing experience."[128]

The readers themselves are the final speakers. Readers send a huge number of letters to magazines after celebrities' deaths; *Time* received nearly 1,500 about Diana and more than 1,200 about JFK Jr. in the first

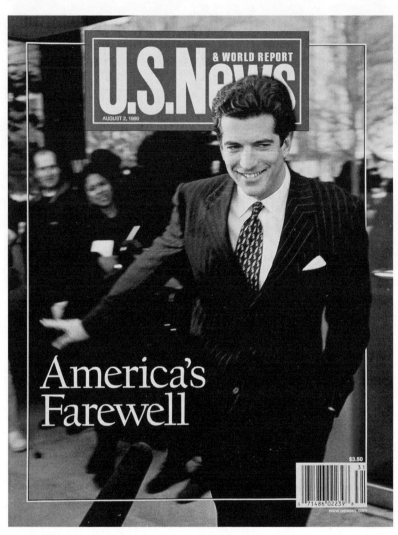

FIGURE 3.4
U.S. News & World Report *cover, August 2, 1999*
(Copyright 1999 U.S. News & World Report, L.P.
Reprinted with permission. Richard Ellis/Ellisphotos.com).

week after the death of each.[129] Although only a small portion of this mail is printed, all of the magazines devote an unusual amount of space in subsequent issues to readers who want to add to a celebrity's commemoration. With regard to reader letters sent about the celebrities discussed here, some were critical (generally of the press's excessive emotion), though most comments about the coverage were thankful. More significantly, most of the printed letters were not about the coverage at all; they were tributes to the deceased. Those quoted here are examples. The first three echoed the language of the magazines' reporters; the fourth was a response to journalists' criticism of the public's outpouring of grief over the death of JFK Jr.

> Our generation has just lost its greatest cosmic clown. . . . To think of facing the Eighties without him [Lennon], just when his light was once again in our lives, is the bleakest news yet. I mourn the passing of a great friend I never even met.

> Jacqueline Kennedy Onassis was the beautiful curator of silence. Perhaps her silence says more about us than her. Of her we clamored for more; of us she quietly waited for less. We wanted to know this shy woman who loved her family so. With delicate resistance, she let us know it was not to be. Her fawnlike eyes saw the grandiosity of the world but always refocused on the truly important, until they closed for the last time. Now the space she so graciously held will be filled with eternal time, and those of us who loved her shall cherish her memory forever.

> Like Icarus, Cobain flew too close. I will miss his grisly, grating melodies, his blond mask of hair, the crack of his voice and that perfect rise from tranquil desperation to uncontrolled bombast to which he gave his signature. Kurt, did it have to end so soon?

> Watching TV interviews at JFK's grave site in Arlington National Cemetery and outside John's apartment in New York City, I was struck by the derisive note of the commentary: "Who are they to grieve? They didn't know him." Yes, we should weep, and we should grieve, for our country has lost its finest son; it is our turn to salute.[130]

Such rhetoric from "ordinary" people is both a tribute to extraordinary people and an embracing of such stars as ordinary. Journalists do the same double construction: they make heroes, even mythic figures, of well-known people, conflating fame with newsworthiness and public significance, while at the same time they explain the famous in terms of the ordinary, uniting audience members with each other and with the celebrity through "basic" values. Leo Braudy calls celebrities "the large-screen projection of those human possibilities a culture believes are the most fascinating and perhaps useful for its survival . . . negotiated symbols in a human shorthand by which we process the world."[131]

When such icons die, the people to whom they were meaningful must make sense of a larger loss. They do so through the same forum in which they came to "know" the celebrity in life—the media, which take on the role of national healers. No matter who the deceased figure, the themes of coverage are essentially the same: the celebrity was "one of us" while also representing our greatest hopes; and though the death was tragic, it reminded us of societal ideals that temporarily had been forgotten. His or her death reminds us of the timeless emotions and values that constitute—and enfold us within—"the human condition."

4 The Voices of the Past Speak to Us, Calling Us by Name

Counter-Memory and Living History in Magazines for African Americans

History is to us what water is to fish. We are immersed in it up to our necks, and we cannot get out of it, no matter what we say or do.
—*Ebony*, 1982[1]

Negro folklore is not a thing of the past. It is still in the making. Its great variety shows the adaptability of the black man.—Zora Neale Hurston, quoted in *American Legacy*, 2003[2]

Implied in the notion that journalists construct national narratives is the assumption that Americans can be understood as a unified group based on nationality—a pluralistic, tolerant, and diverse nation (that is, in fact, one of the narratives), but a cohesive group nonetheless. Many challenges can be made to this assumption, but perhaps the strongest would come from African Americans, a group whose presence and experience in the United States are central to its history and yet whose stories only recently have become part of the broader historical narrative. Such integration has required not merely adding to that narrative, but rethinking it—and doing so has been largely the purview of African American authors, film makers, and journalists. Newspapers and magazines written by and for African Americans traditionally have been more historically conscious than the white press, and they have been active, especially during recent decades, in a reconfiguring of American memory. As Todd Vogel writes, over time they have "restaged race and nationhood, and reset the terms of public conversation."[3]

From the start of *Freedom's Journal* in 1827, the black press has been based on the premise that that African Americans[4] must have a way to "plead our own cause"[5] on issues of the day and to construct their own public identity within journalism. While several newspapers have received scholarly attention,[6] little has been written about the role of magazines within the mission of the black press. Yet since their own beginnings, with the 1837 launch of the *Mirror of Liberty*,[7] such magazines also have embraced the goal of self-representation. Writing in 1859, Thomas Hamilton, editor of the *Anglo-African Magazine*, insisted that its constituency "must speak for themselves" because mainstream journalism tended to "write down the Negro as something less than a man."[8]

Magazines for African Americans grew in number and nature during the nineteenth century, as did their circulation and presence in American life. The short-lived *Voice of the Negro* had a readership of 113,000 during the first decade of the twentieth century, and at the end of that decade, the National Association for the Advancement of Colored People launched the *Crisis*, which led circulation during the 1920s (and which survives today). Robert S. Abbott, Marcus Garvey, and A. Philip Randolph all published explicitly political magazines during this era, a time that saw innovation as well as growth in the field. Between 1910 and 1930, fifty-three new magazines for African Americans were launched, one of which was the highly regarded *Opportunity*, published from 1923 to 1949 by the National Urban League in cooperation with the Harlem

Writers' Guild.[9] Writing in 1928, that magazine's editor, Charles S. Johnson, claimed that in these new magazines "old shames and embarrassments are being displaced by new prides and the other essential elements of prestige."[10]

John H. Johnson used nearly the same language in describing his own enterprise, which would become the most commercially and culturally successful African American magazine empire of the twentieth century. After starting *Negro Digest*, which was similar to *Reader's Digest*, in 1942, Johnson imagined an African American version of the popular new photo-feature magazine, *Life*. In the oversized pages of *Ebony*, launched in 1945, readers could literally reenvision themselves through pictures. The concept was a success. The initial press run in November 1945 was 25,000; by the magazine's sixth month, circulation had grown to 250,000; ten years later, the paid readership was up to half a million.[11]

As Johnson originally had conceived it, *Ebony* was meant "to emphasize the positive aspects of Black life. We wanted to highlight achievements and make Blacks proud of themselves."[12] This mission has remained consistent in the magazine's six decades of publication, but by the 1960s, the civil rights movement forced the magazine to broaden its scope and mission.[13] Writing in the early 1970s, black press historian Roland Wolseley identified two stages in *Ebony*'s mission, first its presence in American culture as the "black *Life*" and then as a civil rights advocacy magazine after "the struggle for the righting of wrongs against the black race in America demanded its cooperation more heartily."[14] In their study of *Ebony* content from 1950 to 1979, Gloria Myers and A. V. Margavio found that during the 1950s the magazine displayed "minimal interest in black history" and that it was during the 1960s and 1970s that "racial group identification" shifted from "individualism" and toward "commonality" (which included "articles concerned with the black past").[15]

They attribute this change to the contemporary black pride movement, which Johnson himself acknowledges, along with the Afrocentric "Black Is Beautiful" movement, as a factor in the magazine's content during the 1970s.[16] Out of the same period came *Essence*, a women's magazine, and *Black Enterprise*, a business magazine, both of which were launched in 1970 and joined *Ebony* among the ranks of mass-circulation magazines for minorities. The birth and growth of Black Entertainment Television in the 1980s helped to transform African American audiences into a distinct market, leading to the launch in the

1990s of several new magazines for African Americans, including *Heart & Soul*, *Honey*, and *Savoy*, the latter named for the historic Harlem ball-room.[17]

In 1995 yet another new magazine called *American Legacy* was launched specifically as (according to its tagline) "A Celebration of African American History and Culture." Its success may be attributed to its initial distribution model, in which the magazine was given out free through a network of African American churches and relied primarily on revenue from advertisers interested in reaching middle- and upper-middle-class African Americans.[18] Publisher Rodney J. Reynolds promised readers of the inaugural issue that the magazine would "take you into the heart of black heritage, revealing the unbreakable will that runs throughout our history."[19] The readership of this glossy, quarterly publication now has passed half a million, and a growing portion of its revenue comes from paid circulation.[20]

This chapter explores the nature of historical content in *Ebony* and *American Legacy*, one relatively old magazine and one relatively new one, since the late-twentieth-century shift toward an emphasis on history in media targeting African Americans.[21] That shift grew out of the black pride movement of the 1960s and 1970s, taking hold in the early 1980s, during the decade between the naming of Black History Month in 1976[22] and the designation of Martin Luther King Jr. Day as a national holiday in 1986. These magazines' interest in history mirrored trends elsewhere in American media, from the growing interest in nostalgia in all types of journalism to a race-specific quest to recover the black past through productions such as Alex Haley's novel (and later television movie) *Roots*.

An additional factor in the increased attention to African American history has been the gradual realization by corporate America that middle- and upper-middle-class African Americans constitute a lucrative and relatively untapped consumer market. As the content of both magazines attests, media and public-education projects about African American history have drawn prominent corporate sponsors, and the language of advertisements frequently draws on history.

In *American Legacy*, Hallmark promotes its "Mahogany" card line for Kwanza, and the Bell South telephone company promotes its own diversity in an ad called "I am the Drum," with text: "My roots are grounded deep in the soil of Africa."[23] In *Ebony*, McDonald's pays biographical tribute to African American artists; it also offers customers booklets titled "Little Known Black History Facts." Budweiser salutes "Great Kings of

Africa," Miller High Life offers "Portraits in Pride," and Coors celebrates Sojourner Truth. Kodak film proclaims: "We're proud to have been a part of chronicling your family history for the past century." Pontiac tells readers, "We can make history together," while Chevrolet publishes a multipage advertising section titled "Classic American Faces," assuring readers, "When you look into [the] mirror, know that on your face our story is proudly displayed—past, present and future."[24] Another Chevrolet ad that has appeared more than once in both magazines is a double-page photograph depicting individuals—an African tribesman, a Civil War soldier, a jazz trumpeter, a civil rights protester, and a college graduate—marching through a field, with the title "Once Upon a Time in America" and a long text on the history and dignity of the African American experience.[25]

Some of the ads seem as informative and activist as the editorial pages. Philip Morris has purchased ad space in *American Legacy* to promote not its cigarettes but its "Black History Month radio documentary series" titled "Pass It On: Voices from Black America's Past."[26] The New York Life insurance company underwrote an art exhibit titled "Rising above Jim Crow."[27] General Motors sponsored a national tour of an exhibit called "A Slaveship Speaks," and the text of its special advertising section (appearing repeatedly in *American Legacy* issues) was meant to be the ship itself "speaking": "Listen, and I will tell you about the route I plied. The people I carried. Their lives. Their culture. See their artifacts. Feel their pain. Celebrate their nobility. I am the slave ship *Henrietta Marie*. My story must be told."[28]

Such approaches blur the distinction between advertising and editorial messages, co-opting editorial themes for the purpose of selling products and gaining "goodwill" for brand names, several of them alcohol and cigarettes. Yet the ubiquity of this kind of rhetoric in advertising in media that target African American audiences testifies to the effectiveness of those magazines' editorial uses of history and memory. The commercial dimension of this phenomenon also suggests that interest in the African American past now has staying power in American media culture.

For the past two decades, *Ebony* has contained a significant amount of historical material, including an annual special section on history published in every February issue (to mark Black History Month), its January-issue revisitations of the life of the Reverend Martin Luther King Jr. (to mark the national holiday of his birthday), occasional departments titled Chronicles of Black Courage and Great Moments in Black

History, and a regular department titled Memorable Photos from the *Ebony* Files.[29] From its start, nearly every article in *American Legacy* has showcased history, though the magazine defines history broadly to include present-day cultural phenomena—clothing, family reunions, art —that build on, or even create, "tradition." This combination underscores the two words in its tagline: *American Legacy* informs readers about history, the facts of the past, but it also involves them in culture, a social process of weaving the past, present, and future together, an act that constructs collective memory and anticipates the participation of modern-day readers. In this view of the present, explains editor Audrey Peterson, "living people . . . are making history."[30]

Both magazines acknowledge the relationship between the past and the present and convey the activist claim that African Americans can thrive in the present only with an understanding of the past. In another letter to readers, *American Legacy's* publisher summed up the point and tone of this message: "Telling our history to our children is our responsibility. It is our trust not only for them but for those not yet born. . . . The baton is in your hands. Be careful not to drop it."[31]

In this sense, history is a living presence in the lives of African Americans in ways that it is perhaps not as true for other kinds of reader communities discussed in this book. And while other chapters in this book draw on discourse theory—imagining the relationship between magazine editors and readers as an ongoing conversation—this intellectual notion is especially useful in understanding the nature, content, and evolution of magazines for African Americans. *Ebony* has taken the metaphor of conversation a step further, applying it not just to the editorial process but to the past itself. Lerone Bennett Jr., the magazine's resident historian, wrote in the February 1985 issue:

> In and through Black history, the voices of the past speak to us personally, calling us by name. . . . Black history is a perpetual conversation in which men and women speak to one another across the centuries, correcting one another, echoing one another, blending together into a mighty chorus which contrasts and combines different themes. Not only is there a dialogue between the living and the dead in this chorus but there is also a dialogue of the dead. . . . This living history, which goes on at all levels in the speech of everyday life, is embodied in the calling and responding of succeeding generations who communicate with each other as they pass and repass the baton in that endless relay race which began with the first revolt

on the first slave ships and will not end until America deals with the total challenge of Blackness.[32]

The notion of history as conversation is combined here with a reference to "call and response," a communication form that "originated in Africa and survived in North America in work songs and in responsive singing in churches," writes George Lipsitz. "Historically," he notes, "Afro-Americans have treasured African retentions in speech, music, and art both as a means of preserving collective memory about a continent where they were free and as a way of shielding themselves against the hegemony of white racism."[33] Moreover, such ritual is a part of a long tradition of resistance through music, of expressing anger and protest in what seems to be merely song, one of the African American "folklore traditions [that] enabled them to encode social messages in metaphorical form . . . preserv[ing] their dignity and self-worth by asserting faith in some kind of ultimate justice."[34]

To imagine history as call-and-response, therefore, is to imagine its conveyance as a political act, a form not just of memory, but also of "counter-memory." Borrowing this term from Michel Foucault's criticism of formal history,[35] Lipsitz explains that it "starts with the particular and the specific and then builds outward toward a total story. . . . Counter-memory focuses on localized experiences with oppression, using them to reframe and refocus dominant narratives purporting to represent universal experience."[36] He adds that "counter-memory is not a rejection of history, but a reconstitution of it."[37]

That reconstitution is accomplished through a simultaneous (and at first seemingly contradictory) process of documenting the past while challenging public memory of that past. Sometimes this is a matter simply of emphasis and interpretation, a recounting of known history in a way that points out racism, as in one Great Moments in Black History column in *Ebony* chronicling "Jesse Owens' Triumph over Hitlerism." Its subject was, the writer explained, "the story of an incredible moment of truth when the son of a sharecropper and the grandson of slaves temporarily derailed the Nazi juggernaut and gave the lie to Hitler's theories on Aryan (read White) supremacy. . . . this story, which will be told as long as men and women celebrate grace and courage, was more than a sports story. It was politics, history even, played out on an international stage."[38] An *American Legacy* article titled "All Blood Runs Red" opened its profile of "America's first black aviator" with this explanation of his military affiliation during World War I: "Gene Bullard wore fifteen French medals and decorations, and although he was buried in the United States, it was in a French military cemetery and in a French uniform. He served France not because he did not wish to serve his own nation, but because to the French the color of his skin did not matter. To the leaders of his own nation, it did."[39]

American Legacy editor Audrey Peterson explains that "what we are trying to do is put in that which was left out of recorded history," especially "information about the people of color who have contributed greatly to American society."[40] Some articles do so through discovery (or uncovering) of new information, while others are a matter of recovery. One issue of *American Legacy* reprinted photographs that had themselves been recovered from storage "on someone's patio in rotting wooden boxes," a collection of the work of three photographers that depicted one hundred years of life in the black community of Natchez, Mississippi.[41]

Both magazines recount great events from the African American past by assessing their relevance in the present. January-issue articles in *Ebony* frequently take this approach, with titles such as "King Speaks to the 21st Century."[42] So do articles marking the anniversaries of milestone civil rights events, such as "Montgomery 40 Years Later," which told the story of the bus boycotts through personal recollections, showing the now-older protagonists of that story standing once again in front of a 1955-style bus in Montgomery, Alabama (and testifying to their sheer survival as well as their past deeds).[43] When, like many other American magazines, *American Legacy* published a special issue in the year 2000, it reviewed its cover theme, "African-Americans in the 20th Century," in terms of their present-day legacy, featuring a "millennium panel" that "debate[d] 100 years of change."[44] The magazine's cover stories have included documentary articles on civil rights marches, public demonstrations challenging segregation, and African American "pioneer" accomplishments such as Jackie Robinson's integration of Major League Baseball. While this sort of theme pays tribute to past accomplishments, it also implies that civil rights is ongoing, a matter as much of today as of yesterday.

The most common type of historical articles—profiles of people—take the form of tribute as well as documentation. *American Legacy* devotes its Pathfinders department to notables or firsts in their fields.[45] *Ebony* has published several tribute-style photo-features, with individuals shown in full-page photographs and identified merely by name under titles such as "Giants of the Century" and "Living Legends."[46] Within its twenty-seven pages, the special history section of its February 1990 issue alone profiled historian John Hope Franklin, General Colin Powell, Virginia governor L. Douglas Wilder, seven black mayors, forty "martyrs of the movement," ten "most unforgettable women," and ten black inventors.

The past is personalized most often by famous individuals, but honor also is bestowed on those who achieved in groups, in articles such as "Blacks in Aviation History" and "Brotherhood of Sleeping Car Porters Honored," as well as a tribute to the Colored Intercollegiate Athletic Association.[47] Both publications have run articles on the unsung heroism of African American soldiers in the Civil War and World War II. The magazines' extensive use of portraits and profiles of accomplished people echoes historian Lerone Bennett's definition of African American history as "the scaffold upon which personal and group identities are constructed . . . a living library which provides a script of roles, and models."[48]

In addition to constructing that scaffold—documenting what audiences may not know about the past—these magazines also sometimes dismantle, challenging what audiences think they do know about history, another act of counter-memory. The author of the *Ebony* feature titled "Did Lincoln Really Free the Slaves?" contended that the president was "forced by circumstances" to become "the great emancipator" and claimed of the schoolroom mythology: "No other American story is so enduring. No other American story is so comforting. No other American story is so false."[49] An *American Legacy* article on Indian ancestry noted, "The very notion of a black Indian has most whites shaking their heads in disbelief or smiling at what sounds like a joke, a myth, or an unlikely play on words. No one remembers any such person appearing in a textbook, a Western novel, or a Hollywood movie."[50]

History is used to challenge present-day wisdom as well. For instance, one *Ebony* feature noted parallels between the political and rhetorical climate of the post–civil rights era and the post–Civil War era, both periods when blacks seemed to have won freedom that would be protected by law. The article's blurb asked: "Will history repeat itself and rob Blacks of the gains of the 1960s?"[51] Some articles correct African American history itself. In an *American Legacy* piece on a World War II Navy warship with an all-black crew, the author notes that, during the course of her research, an African American historian asked her: "'Aren't you confusing this story with that of the Tuskegee airmen or that tank division?'"[52]

An especially provocative act of counter-memory occurs in articles that put African Americans into what in public memory seem to be white histories and settings. This was the initial goal of *Ebony*: to show black faces beneath Fifth Avenue Easter hats and Ivy League mortar boards, black families vacationing in California and at Niagara Falls, and black performers getting the star treatment in Hollywood (the white visual mix of *Life*). Founder John Johnson believed that it was impor- tant to take note—in a way that made a public statement—of the fact that "Black people, in addition to being members of the NAACP and Na- tional Urban League, were also members of sororities and fraternities and lodges. They marched and raised hell but they also raised children and gave debutante balls and watched baseball and football games."[53]

Numerous *American Legacy* articles place African Americans into predominantly white historical narratives, with perhaps the most ex- treme example being a piece on antebellum black slaveowners.[54] One cover story profiled summer resorts that have been patronized for more than a century by the African American elite; others detailed the lives and work of African Americans who were colonial governors, western settlers, New England whalers, circus performers, fashion models, race- car drivers, and western settlers (figure 4.1). Editor Audrey Peterson confirms that "readers respond to stories about blacks who excel in areas that have been traditionally underrepresented by them."[55] A particularly interesting example was a feature on the dominance of black jockeys in nineteenth-century horse racing, which contained an extra counter- memory twist: "Homeowners across the country have painted black lawn jockeys white, not realizing they are tributes to triumphant black riders of the last century."[56] Another issue reprinted an advertising poster for a 1923 film featuring "the colored hero" steer-wrestler of a Wild West Show, with this caption: "Most Americans who grew up with movies and books celebrating the West knew nothing of black cowboys like Bill Pickett."[57]

An *American Legacy* article titled "Completing the Picture" was about the book *The Face of Our Past*, which "fill[ed] a gap in America's visual history" by reprinting historical pictures of nonfamous women. The article quoted historian Darlene Clark Hine's introduction to the book: "America's perceptions of black women are suffused with a host of de- rogatory images and assumptions that proliferated in the aftermath of slavery and, with some permutations, exist even today. What we have not seen is the simple truth of their complex and multidimensional lives."[58] Another example from the same magazine, and one that chal-

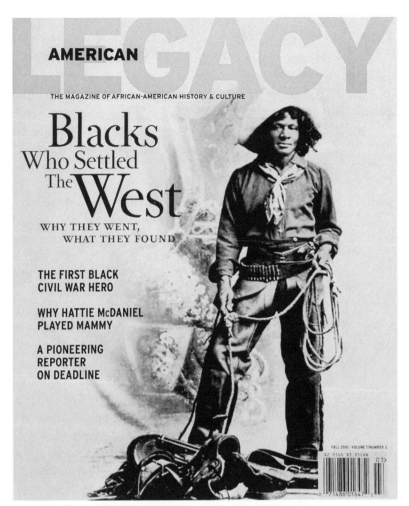

FIGURE 4.1
American Legacy *cover, Fall 2001*
(Reprinted by permission of American Heritage Inc.).

lenged conventional wisdom about black as well as white history, was "I Saw a Foreign Town," a cover story on the work of a Mississippi photographer who documented middle-class blacks during the 1950s and 1960s. The article described his work as "a visual record of Southern black life that, although segregated, was comfortable and wonderfully at odds with the typical image of sharecroppers toiling in fields, raggedy children on sagging porches, and African-American lives harassed by Jim Crow. . . . 'It looked like Andy Griffith's Mayberry but with an all-black cast'" (figure 4.2).[59]

As these examples suggest, visual images play a crucial role in counter-memory.[60] In one sense, photographs are a means of "bearing witness," which Barbie Zelizer classifies as "a specific form of collective remembering that interprets an event as significant and deserving of critical attention." She writes: "Bearing witness calls for truth telling at the same time as it sanctions an interpretation of what is being witnessed."[61] In another sense, photographic images are, in themselves, valuable as objects, especially in media such as magazines, which are durable and frequently are saved by readers. "No object is more equated with memory than the camera image, in particular the photograph," writes Marita Sturken. "Memory appears to reside within the photographic image, to tell its story in response to our gaze."[62]

Photographs also play a role, at any time, in present-day cultural identity, especially for minority groups. In his memoir, John Johnson remembered the impetus for Ebony's launch in 1945: "People wanted to see themselves in photographs. . . . We wanted to see Dr. Charles Drew and Ralph Bunche and Jackie Robinson. . . . We needed, in addition to traditional weapons, a medium to make Blacks believe in themselves, in their skin color, in their noses, in their lips, so they could hang on and fight for another day."[63] Photojournalism historian Maren Stange describes Johnson's vision in these terms: "Ebony's images would detach, or disarticulate, racialized icons—that is, the recognizable black face and body—from the familiar markers of degradation, spectacle, and victimization to which they had always been linked if represented at all; the pictures would, instead, reproduce iconic blackness articulated to equally naturalized and sanctioned symbols of class respectability, achievements, and American national identity. As had earlier reformers [sic] of popular visual discourse, Ebony relied on the presumed 'transparency' of photography's indexical representation of its 'real life' referents—the medium's 'special status with regard to the real'—to uphold its discursive interventions."[64] In other words, photographs can

FIGURE 4.2
American Legacy *cover, Winter 2004*
(Reprinted by permission of American Heritage Inc./Anderson LLC).

constitute a political statement simply because their very ordinariness contradicts stereotypes.

Such a visual counter-memory process begins with documentation of the present, but it gains strength, and acquires new levels of meaning, over time. What we think of as historic photographs began as works of photojournalism documenting accomplishment or trouble or daily life being lived. But it is their repetition and reuse and recaptioning and reviewing that have given them lasting meaning, extending the act of witnessing from journalism to history. That shift occurs with the audience's cooperation (depending on our individual and collective knowledge of the past and the present) and in "conversation" with other photographs of the era and published since. The resulting historical narrative then may convey larger truths even while the images themselves seem only to document specific people in specific circumstances.

Perhaps the best case study of this phenomenon is the *Ebony* department titled Memorable Photos from the *Ebony* Files,[65] which has appeared in most issues since the early 1980s and since 1988 almost always has featured a single photograph.[66] Some of the images published in this department are truly old—for instance, photos of the 1888 graduating class of Fisk University, of 1908 heavyweight boxing champion Jack Johnson, and of explorer Matthew Henson, who in 1909 reached the North Pole with Admiral Peary[67]—though most date back only as far as the magazine itself does, to the mid-twentieth century, and therefore are potentially within the memory of readers.

These images appear with text that is somewhat more than a caption, not just an identification of the person, but also some comment on why his or her accomplishment was significant in a larger sense—a short history lesson. For example, one page showed Bill (Bojangles) Robinson dancing with Lena Horne on the set of the 1943 film *Stormy Weather*, with this text: "The movie provided Horne with a starring role in which she sang and acted, and it also highlighted the fact that there were no Black leading men who weren't 'characters,' prompting such pairings as the 65-year-old Robinson with the 26-year-old Horne."

Three types of accomplishment have been particularly celebrated in this department: entertainment, political activism, and sports.[68] Appearing most often—twenty-four times during the two-decade period considered in this chapter—was Dr. Martin Luther King Jr.[69] Second was education pioneer Mary McLeod Bethune, who appeared nine times with text stressing the importance of education. Other figures to appear four or more times were: Coretta Scott King, Supreme Court Justice Thurgood Marshall, singer Nat King Cole, diplomat Ralph Bunche, Congressman Adam Clayton Powell, baseball player Jackie Robinson, singer-actress Lena Horne, singer Marian Anderson, Urban League head Whitney Young, Black Muslim leader Malcolm X, singer Mahalia Jackson, boxer Muhammad Ali, bandleader Duke Ellington, and historian Carter G. Woodson.

Famous people often were shown with props or backgrounds that signified their achievements. Baseball player Jackie Robinson was shown fielding a ball in his Brooklyn Dodgers uniform; Dr. Percy Julian stood working in his chemistry lab; bandleader Cab Calloway leapt into the air during a performance.[70] An elderly Mary McLeod Bethune smiled proudly at the camera, with young adults in the background, and the text explained that she was "the recipient of admiring glances from students as she walks the campus" of Bethune-Cookman College, which she founded in 1904.[71] These images told stories and conveyed feelings—courage, jubilation, dignity—in addition to providing portraits of their subjects.

White people are largely absent from these *Ebony* images of accomplishment,[72] and when they do appear, their most common role is to honor African American accomplishments. For instance, white military officers were shown awarding the French Legion of Honor to entertainer Josephine Baker for her work in the French resistance during World War II and promoting Brigadier General Benjamin O. Davis Jr. to his position as the first African American general in the U.S. Air Force.[73] First Lady Eleanor Roosevelt was shown presenting an award to singer Marian Anderson (figure 4.3). In other "witnessing" photographs, white cameramen zoomed in on a performing Nat King Cole, who had his own television show for two years in the mid-1950s, and tennis player Althea Gibson was accompanied by a white competitor and a mixed-race crowd of smiling supporters as she became the first black to compete in the U.S. Open Tennis championship.[74] Whites also have appeared in Memorable Photos as witnesses to, and often perpetrators of, injustices against African Americans. For instance, photos depicting the "Little Rock Nine" students integrating Central High School in Little Rock, Arkansas, showed white federal troopers with rifles standing guard outside the school, and a white student shouting angrily at the back of one of the nine students.

That image is one of a number of civil rights photographs that we now recognize as iconic. According to photojournalism historian Vicki Goldberg, iconic images "seem to summarize such complex phenomena as

FIGURE 4.3
*Eleanor Roosevelt with Marian Anderson
(National Archives and Records Administration,
Washington, D.C./Annenberg Rare Book & Manuscript Library,
University of Pennsylvania, Philadelphia).*

the power of the human spirit or of universal destruction" and provide for viewers a "connection to some deeply meaningful moment in history."[75] Such connection is possible because their composition casts their subjects as simultaneously dignified and ordinary, normal people caught up in the sweep of history, in circumstances that could have happened to anyone. This is true even of identifiable individuals who became famous because of their involvement in the movement: Rosa Parks seated on a Montgomery, Alabama, bus in front of a white man was potentially any rider after the boycotts; Linda Brown, the schoolchild at the center of the 1954 Supreme Court case on integration, shown posed at a classroom desk with a pencil in her hand, smiling and looking forward, was a future vision of every black child.[76]

Moreover, the injustice photos have a dialogic relationship with the previous category of images, the celebration portraits that certify black success. They create a negative[77] context against which to view and review the images of black accomplishment, so that the latter take on new meaning—especially since we now know the bigger story. To use Stuart Hall's term, the injustice photos offer a "preferred meaning"[78] for the accomplishment photos, which also become civil rights photos. Jackie Robinson, fielding a ball, was therefore not just a great baseball player, but a survivor-pioneer; Shirley Chisholm's two-fingered "V" gesture stood for a victory broader than her election as the first black woman in the U.S. House of Representatives; Florence Griffith Joyner's uppraised arms and shout of joy linked her 1988 Olympic victory not only to the triumph of other black athletes but also to the uppraised voices of Martin Luther King Jr. and the jubilant leap of Cab Calloway.[79]

Another bridge between the protest images and the celebration images has been the appearance of famous people in civil rights images. Memorable Photos of the Selma-to-Montgomery march and other protest events showed political leaders and celebrities blending into large crowds. Although she appeared three other times as an entertainer-celebrity in Memorable Photos, the text with one picture of gospel singer Mahalia Jackson anchored her in the world of social protest: "At the March on Washington, . . . Jackson delivers a stirring rendition of the spiritual 'I've Been 'Buked and I've Been Scorned.'"[80]

Yet in these pictures, famous people were not stars; they were African Americans testifying to injustice and pain. Thus they made rhetorical sense alongside photos that simply showed groups of people without identifying individuals: mourners at the 1955 funeral of Emmett Till;

southern blacks lining up to register to vote in 1960; civil rights workers surveying the bombed Baptist church in Birmingham, Alabama, where four little girls were killed in 1963; and striking Memphis sanitation workers in 1968, holding signs reading "I am a Man."[81] One photo of a woman standing in the rain, stoically facing the camera, identified its subject as "a foot soldier in the movement . . . [who] joined hundreds of Black protesters in 1955 who refused to ride segregated buses in Montgomery, Ala."[82]

Especially when seen in similar images repeated over time, ordinary people testify to the presence of African Americans in the country's social life—its national identity—as well as its political life. Much as an *American Legacy* cover story documented the black middle class in the 1950s South, the Memorable Photos department in *Ebony* has included nonfamous people among its portraits: an elderly woman playing with a kitten, a college "coed," a fashion model, soldiers, a farmer, western ranchers, a "prototype marine," and "a little girl in Easter finery." In these cases, the subjects' anonymity empowers them as proof that African Americans are part of the tapestry of idealized American life, not only of protest and unrest, but also of ordinary existence. Although this seems to be a simple, unprovocative statement, it actually is a counter-memory claim that African Americans are mainstream, not marginal, participants in the country's "good life" rather than outsiders who challenge it.

Photographs of unidentified but "typical" African Americans weave people of different eras into a temporal narrative, offering a history lesson while personalizing the historical black experience in a way that blends past, present, and future. One Memorable Photo in *Ebony* showed an unnamed family dressed in traveling clothes and solemnly posing for the camera:

> The indomitable spirit of the Black family is reflected in the eyes of a family who arrived in Chicago during the 1920s when thousands of Blacks left the rural South in search of new opportunities in Northern cities. Often squeezed into shabby and segregated neighborhoods, these Black men and women endured and prevailed over hardships to gain a better life. . . . the Great Migration and subsequent urbanization did not destroy the Black family. The truth is that the extended family has been an enduring institution in both urban and rural America and, despite much adversity, has remained the backbone of the Black community.[83]

The second part of that text positioned the magazine's readers, who tend to be middle- and upper-middle-class African Americans, as the direct (and proud) descendants of this poor but dignified 1920s migrant family. It also connected with another Memorable Photo in which a woman, child, and man were shown in silhouette, holding hands and walking toward the sun, with this brief text: "A new generation family looks confidently toward the future, secure in the knowledge that the family unit is the greatest source of strength available to Black Americans."[84] Though this was a contemporary image, this symbolic gesture had been made by *Ebony* forty-five years earlier, when its tenth-anniversary issue opened with the prototypical-black-family image as a full-page photo and this caption: "Marching forward into future of unlimited possibilities, typical Negro family beams with hope and confidence."[85]

The verbal and visual rhetoric linking these two photographs is an ongoing strategy, in both magazines, by which history is made relevant and the very limited circumstances of the past are interpreted as a foundation for a limitless future. What's more, the use of family to represent the race implies that shared experience extends forward as well as backward through time and that counter-memory narratives will continue to be remembered in the future (perhaps in new versions of such stories that incorporate today's present into history).

Conversely, the anonymity of African Americans in photographs can be a call to action, proof that specificity in historical research and racial memory remains important. One image published in the Flashback department of *American Legacy*—this magazine's back-page counterpart to Memorable Photos in *Ebony*—was a black-and-white photograph of a formally dressed couple, with this text: "Here's what we don't know about this picture: the subjects' names, the date they posed, the photographer who took the powerful image. That information, like so much of African-American history, remains to be unearthed." This text went on to explain that the image was one of many in a museum collection being studied by researchers as part of "the Black Dignity" project.[86] In this case, the subjects' distinct blackness—*not* their ability to blend in—was justification for historical consciousness, and for the recovery of the details of their identity and experience.

Similarly, the magazines use some photographic subjects to document a unique black experience, one separate from the white world and worth preserving as such. *American Legacy* Flashback pages have shown items in an exhibition of African American folk art and directed readers to a registry–oral history web site for former Pullman Porters.

One article in that magazine reprinted movie posters for black films of the mid-twentieth century, from well-known pictures such as *Cabin in the Sky* and *The Emperor Jones* to a singing-cowboy movie titled *The Bronze Buckaroo*.[87] *Ebony* Memorable Photos have shown participants in a New Orleans jazz funeral, people dancing at the World Black and African Festival of Arts and Culture, a black college marching band performing a distinctive strut, and "a Harlem society couple about to take an afternoon ride."[88]

Text, too, documents an "African-American America" that differs from what most people think they know about the country. *American Legacy* approaches the subject of travel in terms of cities and regions with historically black populations, with black historic landmarks, and with race-specific cultural events.[89] African as well as African American cultural tourism—or what one advertisement calls "heritage travel"[90]— is the theme of many advertisements and articles in the magazine.

African American material culture is a particularly fluid meeting point between the past and the present, a conversation in which yesterday's role models and ancestors speak to today's readers. As a collector of African American memorabilia explained in *American Legacy*, "The artifacts, documents, and photographs in my possession tell of people who cannot talk now about what it felt like to be enslaved or lynched. I don't want them to have died in vain. I feel I can serve as a sort of mouthpiece for those who have passed on."[91]

Such conversations occur across not just time but also space. Bridging a geographical divide is the goal of an *American Legacy* department titled Cultural Crossroads, which is dedicated to "the traditions and folkways of Africa, the Caribbean, Latin America, and any place on earth where black men and women have made an impact."[92] The magazine shows African traditions being enacted in the United States, displaying collections of quilts, cloths, and baskets, showcasing sculpture and painting, discussing fashions such as headwraps, and explaining festivals and other social rituals such as drumming or "stepping."[93] This department allows *American Legacy* to celebrate African practices while blending them into an existing national narrative of American freedom:

> Here in the fields of cotton and grain, hard by hog pens and horse sheds, black fife and drum music still thrives in its native habitat, a living link between Africa and the jazz, blues, and rhythm and blues that define American popular music. African-American fife and drum ensembles go back to the colonial era. Slave masters often

banned drumming, fearing it as a means of secret communication, but West African slaves found an outlet in military bands. Until the late seventeenth and early eighteenth centuries, many slaves were required to undergo military training but were allowed to enroll only as drummers, fifers, or trumpeters.[94]

In such articles, "history" reclaims items and rituals of the seemingly dead past as objects of inheritance, potentially alive in the present if they are understood and used. Such a rhetorical shift creates counter-memory in the sense that it denies that the past is past. Old texts as well as material culture are offered to readers as new resources for their present-day lives. During its first five years, *American Legacy* ran an Anthology department reprinting African American prayers and religious poetry, letters written to black press newspapers about the northern-migration experience, slave traders' journal entries, recipes from the Tuskegee Institute, works of black WPA (Works Progress Administration) writers during the Depression, and excerpts from a Harlem Renaissance children's magazine. In the current version of the magazine, a Readings department spotlights black writers and books and offers excerpts from certain types of texts, such as abolitionist or civil rights speeches.

Through words and images, magazines for African Americans reconstruct the past—or a set of possible pasts—on their pages. Referring to a Manhattan art gallery holding an auction of African Americana, an *American Legacy* writer noted, "This magazine and the gallery have both, each in its own way, been dedicated to putting black history—large pieces of which had been lost or forgotten—back together."[95] This is a process not merely of rebuilding, but also of reassembling those "pieces" of history in new ways that serve present needs and that enable current readers to use them to form a living sense of cultural and racial identity.

Such identity is, to again use the words of George Lipsitz, "the product of an ongoing historical conversation in which no one has the first or the last word."[96] The articulation of the past in African American media is a dual process of documentation and disputation, of telling truth and challenging truth at the same time. These magazines invoke memory so that past successes and outrages are not forgotten. They also create "new" memory, showing us black faces in what we thought were historically white places and eras, gathering and reconnecting fragments of historical evidence, and asking readers to use the past in order to question the politics of the present. "The past is not something back there; it is happening now," wrote *Ebony*'s Lerone Bennett in 1982, as the magazine was turning its attention to history. "It is the bet your fathers placed which you must now cover. . . . It is the web of relationships into which you were born and for which you must now answer. . . . By telling us who we are, history tells us where we can go."[97]

5 The Celebrated Tribe
Generational Memory and the
Reinterpretation of Youth

By comparison with the Flaming Youth of their
fathers and mothers, today's young generation is a
still, small flame. . . . The one new movement that has
begun in the younger generation is . . . the revolt
against revolt—an attempt . . . to stand up against
the bankrupt but lingering political radicalism of the
'20s and '30s. . . . today's youth is really the lost
generation. . . . [It] has no living heroes.—*Time*, 1951[1]

There was a time when teenagers believed themselves to be part of a conquering army. Through
much of the 1960s and 1970s, . . . what made the
young insurgents invincible was the conviction that
they were right: from the crusade of the children,
grown-ups believed, they must learn to trust their
feelings, to shun materialism, to make love, not
money. In 1990 . . . teens seem to be more interested
in getting ahead in the world than in clearing up its
injustices.—*Newsweek*, 1990[2]

Today most Americans are familiar with terms such as the Baby Boom, the Greatest Generation, Generation X, and Generation Y. This chapter examines the role of American newsmagazines—journalistic media that specialize in identifying social trends—in articulating these constructions.[3] In particular, it considers how such labels are created and perpetuated through nostalgia (a longing for lost youth) and through a narrative construction that requires a kind of collective *amnesia* in order to make sense over time.

Independent of mass-media influences, Americans have long defined their own identities with regard to people their own age, with whom they travel through life stages and weather special moments of social and political change. Such a cohort perceives itself to have, in Karl Mannheim's words, "a common location in the historical dimension of the social process."[4] He explained: "One is old primarily in so far as he comes to live within a specific, individually acquired, framework of useable past experience, so that every new experience has its form and its place largely marked out for it in advance. In youth, on the other hand, where life is new, formative forces are just coming into being, and basic attitudes in the process of development can take advantage of the molding power of new situations. Thus a human race living on for ever would have to learn to forget to compensate for the lack of new generations."[5]

Indeed, although generational identity can be determined by shared experiences such as war or depression, it tends to be most directly related to the experiences of young adulthood. Howard Schuman and Jacqueline Scott report that when people are asked to name the most important historical events of their own lifetimes, they "refer back disproportionately to a time when the respondents were in their teens or early 20s," confirming the theory "that adolescence and early adulthood is the primary period for generational imprinting."[6] Youth is an idea as well as a life stage. Joe Austin and Michael Nevin Willard note: "The public debates surrounding 'youth' are important forums where new understandings about the past, present, and future of public life are encoded, articulated, and contested. 'Youth' becomes a metaphor for perceived social change and its projected consequences."[7]

The belief in generational distinctiveness, especially with regard to youth, is part of human nature, though it is a temporary and elastic distinctiveness, as sociologist Maurice Halbwachs confirmed nearly a century ago:

Our parents marched in front of us and guided us into the future. The moment comes when they stop and we pass them by. Then we must turn back to see them, and now they seem in the grip of the past and woven into the shadows of bygone times. . . . A time will come when I will understand . . . that new generations have pushed ahead of my own. . . . And my children, having changed point of view, will be astonished to suddenly discover that I am so distant from them and so close to my parents in interests, ideas, memories. They and I will then be, doubtless, under the influence of a converse illusion: I am really not so distant from them because my parents were not really so distant from me. Depending on age and also circumstance . . . we are especially struck either by the differences between generations . . . or by the similarities.[8]

William Strauss and Neil Howe identified eighteen American generations over a 400-year period, arguing that there are "four generational archetypes" that recur cyclically, according to political and social conditions over time.[9] Morton Keller similarly has traced the nation's political history in terms of generations.[10] Generational identity has long been a theme of popular fiction, from F. Scott Fitzgerald's short stories in *Flappers and Philosophers* (1920) to Douglas Coupland's novel *Generation X* (1991), and of reminiscent films such as *American Graffiti* (1973), *The Big Chill* (1983), and *Saving Private Ryan* (1998).

Like these films, however, generational characterizations in news media are phenomena primarily of the last quarter of the twentieth century, and these reports have been closely linked to a labeling trend that emerged simultaneously in marketing. Though advertisers began to target youth in the 1920s and 1930s,[11] the strategy of marketing to generations dates largely to the 1970s. The Yankelovich firm has led market research in this field, and its president believes that a broad public awareness of a "generation gap" emerged during the socially tumultuous 1960s. His recent report on generational marketing claims that, since then, "each generation is driven by unique ideas about the lifestyle to which it aspires. . . . This is very different from the relatively homogeneous consumer marketplace of the immediate post–World War II era, a time when values and motivations were stable and centered around a shared vision of the American Dream."[12] While this characterization of a cohesive American identity prior to World War II is debatable, marketers have created and used generational labels in earnest only in the closing decades of the century.

As the Yankelovich research suggests, of course, marketers carve up the American population into generations less for cultural reasons than for commercial ones. For them, the concept of generation is a way to combine audience demographics (such as age, gender, and race) and psychographics (beliefs and opinions) in order to create what seem to be distinct and identifiable groups within the broader consumer population and then to "sell" those groups to advertisers and publishers. Even though demographics seem to define who falls within a given generation, advertisers (and publishers) actually stress psychographics, from social ideals to brand consciousness, when they appeal to a generational group. Cultural theorist Dick Hebdige likens this kind of marketing to "a social map of desire which can be used to determine where exactly which products should be 'pitched' and 'niched.'" In this way, he believes, audiences become "aspirational clusters," people who see themselves as belonging to a group that nevertheless is somehow better than they are, full of other, similar people they wish to become.[13]

Two recent magazine launches serve as examples of both the cultural and commercial aspects of generational identity. In 2001, when the American Association of Retired Persons realized that it had two generations among its membership — the Greatest Generation and the Baby Boomers, who began to turn fifty in the mid-1990s — it launched a new publication (in addition to its existing magazine, *Modern Maturity*) called *My Generation*. Addressing potential advertisers in its media kit, the magazine presented its audience in commercial and aspirational terms: "Born into the prosperity of postwar America, the first baby boomers grew up with a sense of limitless possibility. And they're not about to give up their high expectations. Now they're challenging our idea about what it means to be over 50. Committed to originality and to reinventing their lives, they are actively pursuing their lifelong dreams. Well-informed and media savvy, they are smart, avid consumers of ideas and information. *My Generation* is their guide to resources for living a better, fuller life. . . . *My Generation* is a catalog for living."[14]

Yet despite its $5 million launch and 3.1 million circulation, touted in the media trade press as "the biggest launch of all time,"[15] advertisers did not take the bait, and the magazine folded after less than two years of publication. One reason why may have been revealed in the editor's letter to readers in the very first issue: "This generation of ours refuses to believe it's getting older. How could we be old if we're still out there rollerblading and listening to Radiohead? 'I'm not fifty like my parents were,' was the refrain we heard from people across the country."[16] A magazine that identified Boomers as old while assuring them that they were not old was perhaps too much of a mixed message.

New magazines for the Boomers' children and grandchildren have been a different matter. *Teen People*, a spinoff of *People* created in 1998 to target Generation Y, has been one of the most successful launches in history. While it most likely has thrived thanks to the amount of money today's upper-middle-class teens have to spend—the magazine's marketing staff uses some 12,000 of its total 7.2 million readers as "trend-spotters," primarily of retail trends[17]—it also seems to have found a voice that addresses this generation. Its success has spawned imitators including *Teen Vogue, Teen Movieline, Elle Girl, CosmoGirl!,* and *MH-18* (a teen spinoff of *Men's Health*).[18]

These recent launches confirm the media tendency to think of readers in generational terms. In writing specifically for particular age groups, magazines define their identity as it has been formed over time, and this editorial content is distinctly nostalgic. *My Generation*, for instance, celebrated its one-year anniversary by "salut[ing] the people and ideas that have made us who we are. What made Bobby Riggs think he could clobber Billie Jean King at the height of her game? Why did Muhammad Ali capture the imagination of the whole world? Do you remember where you were when you first heard the pulsating twang of the electric guitar? And how many nights did you fall asleep with a transistor radio under your pillow while listening to a baseball game in a faraway city?"[19] Generational themes also have filled *People Weekly*'s special issues "celebrating" the 1970s and the 1980s and *Life*'s issues marking anniversaries of milestone 1960s events (such as the assassination of President John F. Kennedy, the arrival of the Beatles in America, the Woodstock music festival, and the moon landing).

Magazines do more than market *to* generations; they also write *about* generations, characterizing their places in American culture and in history. Indeed, magazines specialize in such trend reporting. This has been particularly true of newsmagazines, which underwent a shift in their own identity at the same time that generational marketing began in earnest. During the late 1960s and early 1970s, newsmagazines faced significant competition from color television for audiences as well as for advertisers hoping to reach a national audience.[20] One response was that they began running cover stories, and more coverage in general, of popular culture and life-style trends. While their editorial focus moved away from hard news,[21] the newsmagazines avoided the fate of other general-interest titles that folded during this era. And precisely because of their new emphasis on life-style, they took center stage in journalistic discussions of social identity.

The rest of this chapter focuses on these editorial aspects of magazines' role in creating and conveying generational identity and memory over time. It provides a study of twenty years of cover stories about generations published in the two leading American newsmagazines, *Time* and *Newsweek*, which by 2003 together reached 7.23 million Americans each week.[22] These stories claimed to "explain" the four generations most visible in current marketing terminology: the Greatest Generation, who were young adults during World War II (the 1940s); their children, the Baby Boom, who were young adults in the 1960s; Generation X, who were young adults in the 1980s; and Generation Y, the children of Boomers, who are young adults today.[23] (Even these brief descriptions make it clear that some Americans—notably those who were young adults in the intervening decades of the fifties, seventies, and nineties—do not fit neatly into these categories, instead falling into the margins between groups. But, on the whole, these groups correspond with the newsweeklies' definitions of living American generations.)[24]

Time's first such study appeared more than half a century ago, in a six-page article titled "The Younger Generation"—which it defined as ages eighteen to twenty-eight and described as puzzling, noting, "*Time's* correspondents across the U.S. have tried to find out about this younger generation by talking to young people." This 1951 article labeled this group "the silent generation" and provided the explanation quoted at the start of this chapter.[25] That passage is significant not only because it provides evidence of journalistic labeling of two additional generations ("Flaming Youth" and "the silent generation," presumably those groups born before and after what would much later become "the Greatest Generation"), but also because its tone and content foreshadow the magazine's more recent articles—most strikingly, their descriptions forty years later of both Generations X and Y. By the mid-1960s, "the silent generation" had given way to another, more exciting generation when *Time* announced that its "Man of the Year" for 1966 was a group it called "Twenty-five and Under." This article claimed that "today's young people are the most intensely discussed and dissected generation in history."[26]

Despite this early treatment, generational cover stories did not become a common subject in the newsweeklies until the 1980s, as a survey of the *Reader's Guide to Periodical Literature* confirms. It contained just one listing for "Baby Boom" (and it was a cross-reference to "Population Statistics") in 1982 but had eleven such listings by 1986 and thirty-four by 1998. The next label to emerge in periodical literature made its first appearance in 1990, when "Generation X" had one cross-listed reference to "Baby Bust" (which itself had four article listings); by 1998, there were thirty-three listings under "Generation X," which was by then its own category.

The newsweeklies followed the generational marketing trend that began in the 1970s, not devoting cover stories in any consistent way to generational labeling until the 1980s. Yet when they began to run those stories, they handled them in ways consistent with journalistic frames long in place in newsrooms. When he studied the operations of news organizations including *Time* and *Newsweek* during the 1960s and 1970s, sociologist Herbert Gans found that "novelty" was an important criterion in determining what gets covered, yet he maintained that "journalists create novelty. Unlike sociologists, who divide external reality into social processes, and historians, who look at these processes over long periods, journalists see external reality as a set of disparate and independent events, each of which is new and can therefore be reported as news. They increase the supply of novelty further by being ahistorical; in the 1960s, for example, they 'rediscovered' American poverty and hunger."[27] By the 1990s the media-industry trade magazine *Adweek* had come to the same conclusion about generational labeling, referring to a *Newsweek* cover story on Generation X, which it saw as evidence of "a growing tendency to treat new cultural fads as vastly more important than ongoing patterns of behavior." The article concluded that businesses, including the media, "have a vested interest in revving up the pace at which trends come and go. Think of it as planned cultural obsolescence. In that environment, the invention of a generational stereotype (and, then, quick abandonment of it) is business as usual."[28]

When they began covering generational identity as an ongoing set of trend stories, the newsweeklies continued this practice of explaining social groups as individual phenomena, each as surprising as the one before it. Yet the ways in which the newsweeklies characterized the various generations were fairly uniform. The novelty of these stories was as much a creation of journalism as it was a new, external aspect of American culture (indeed, its comprehension required journalists and audiences alike to forget what had been reported before). Read collectively, the reports reveal some remarkable similarities among the groups in terms of how labels emerge and in terms of what kinds of themes shape and later reshape the media identity of a generational cohort.

These threads are woven through a blend of current-trend reporting and reminiscent retrospectives, a mixture of "news" with rose-colored social memory.

Such similarities can be seen across generational descriptions. Even so, it is not insignificant that, of the twenty cover stories examined in this chapter, more are about the Baby Boom than any other generation, and that, to a great extent, the newsweeklies have discussed the other three generational groups in terms of their relation to the Baby Boom (as their parents, their unmotivated younger siblings, or their children). It was a Baby Boom milestone that was the occasion for the newsweeklies' first major generational-identity issue, *Time*'s 1986 cover story titled "The Baby Boomers Turn 40." The following discussion begins with that article, and with the Baby Boom, and then examines the journalistic portrayal of generations in the order in which they have appeared on newsweekly magazine covers.

Time's cover marking the Boomers' (first) entry into middle age bore an image of a blazing birthday cake and symbolic generational media paraphernalia (including the *Whole Earth Catalog*, the book *All the President's Men*, the album *Meet the Beatles*, and a poster for the film *The Big Chill*). Its cover story began by summarizing the less-than-successful life of a man who, as a college graduate, had been on *Time*'s cover in 1968, and explained, "The generation that wanted to stay forever young is entering middle age." This article labeled them while also blaming them for the labels: "The Baby Boomers were the Spock generation, the Now generation, the Woodstock generation, the Me generation. . . . Through high times and hard times, no other group of Americans has ever been quite so noisily self-conscious." The article noted, "Demographers somewhat inelegantly refer to the Baby Boom generation as 'the pig in the python,' a moving bulge that distorts and distends everything around it as it rumbles through the stages of life."[29]

This early portrait of Baby Boom adults combined present-day description with a summary of the group's past, and, although it called them "idealistic and assertive," it was mainly unflattering: "Bored? Just change the channel. Hopping from one instant fad to another—from Davy Crockett coonskin caps to Hula-Hoops—they moved as a single mass, conditioned to think alike and do alike . . . they embraced the In thing of the moment then quickly chucked it for another." The article cast Boomers as selfish and incapable of commitment, comparing them with their parents, who had "fought World War II to save the possibilities of freedom."[30]

When *Time* had portrayed the "Twenty-five and Under" group in the mid-1960s, its editors' social distance from young people was clear in their inclusion of an editorial called "Not Losing One's Cool about the Young."[31] Even two decades later, both magazines asked Boomers to explain themselves through polls and first-person essays. It published one account by a thirty-seven-year-old Boomer who admitted "I thought if I didn't settle down, I could stay young forever. I was wrong."[32] *Newsweek* took a similar approach by conducting its own polls of Boomers, printing one writer's six-page account of being young in the 1960s, and publishing the "Confessions of an Ex-Radical," who explained what went "wrong" with sixties political activism.[33]

At the same time, though, Boomer coverage was already nostalgic, as the magazine simultaneously tried to explain the generation to older people and to draw them in as new readers. Both magazines published backward-looking cover stories in 1988, offering possibilities, all from the 1960s, of the defining moment or figure in generational identity. *Time*'s cover montage included photographs of Bobby Kennedy, Janis Joplin, the widowed Coretta Scott King, and soldiers in Vietnam behind the sole coverline "1968: The Year That Shaped a Generation." Its cover story described that year as one in which "the air of public fire singed the private self. Revolutionary bombast gusted across the wake of elegy for something in America that had got lost, some sense of national innocence and virtue."[34]

A *Newsweek* cover also published in 1988 showed photos of a nude couple and an injured Vietnam soldier under the sole coverline "Will We Ever Get over the '60s?"; its cover story inside claimed, "Like the baby-boom generation itself, memories of the decade form an undigested lump in the national experience." Later in the story, the writers used nostalgic phrases such as "goodbye, John Wayne" and noted that the ideals of "peace, love and community [were] qualities that have sadly proven as ephemeral as flower power."[35] Just one year later, *Newsweek* examined (as its coverline put it) "The Summer of '69 and How It Still Plays in '89." Its writers commented, "it's hard to believe it all happened two decades ago" and offered "a look at the legacy those events have left us."[36]

Two early-1990s *Newsweek* cover stories continued this reminiscent treatment, as well as the metonymic use of popular culture to stand for the entire generational experience. A 1993 cover (with the coverline "Rock On") reported on the continuing careers of 1960s musicians and reassured Boomers—who now were described not as "they," but as "we" in journalistic text—that "it's immensely comforting to cast one's lot with one's peers, something that transcends the sweet, gentle notion of nostalgia."[37] And a 1994 *Newsweek* cover showed ecstatic hippies behind the sole coverline "Woodstock: The Way We Were: How It Looks from Middle Age."

Although the onset of middle age was the "news" of *Time*'s 1986 cover story on the Boomers, it remained a major theme in journalism about this generation for another fifteen years. In 1997, *Time* put Boomer First Lady Hillary Clinton on its cover in the issue it examined "Turning 50." As early as 1992, *Newsweek* anticipated Boomers' dread of the half-century milestone, predicting that "it can be a lot better than you think" in a cover story called "The New Middle Age."[38] Eight years later the same magazine ran precisely the same phrase on its cover, with the subline "A Boomer's Guide to Health, Wealth & Happiness" next to the Boomer cartoon character Mike Doonesbury (figure 5.1). The accompanying article reported, "The baby boom has always made its own rules, and now it's redefining growing old."[39] Indeed, the overall package portrayed Boomers as continually "new": graphics provided "a look at the stats that define this trendsetting generation,"[40] while another article offered a revised label for the group (drawing on the thesis of a new book), "Bourgeois Bohemians," or "Bobos." The magazine explained that "bohemian attitudes from the hippie 1960s have merged with the bourgeois attitudes of the Yuppie 1980s to form a new culture, which is a synthesis of the two. . . . this Bobo culture is the final resting spot for the baby-boomer generation. All their lives the boomers have been on a journey to find some sense of balance, and a set of rules and standards to live by that would be both liberating and yet rooted."[41]

As unlikely as it seems that the Boomers have reached a resting spot in public generational identity, throughout the 1990s they shared the journalistic spotlight with their younger brothers and sisters and with their own children—the groups that became known as Generations X and Y. Those groups had meaning primarily with reference to the Baby Boom, however. When Generation X made its first appearance on a *Time* cover in 1990, it was introduced in already-nostalgic terms: "The new generation pines for a romanticized past when the issues were clear and the troops were committed," the writers claimed.[42]

That first cover spotlighting Generation X, with the main coverline "twentysomething," was a photograph of anonymous young people with glazed eyes, walking aimlessly in different directions, and the cover blurb below them summed up the newsweeklies' initial attitude toward

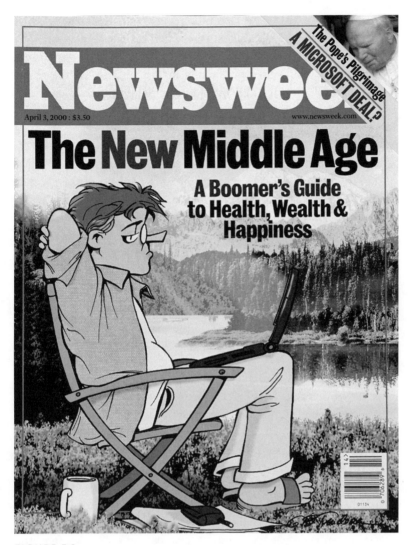

FIGURE 5.1
Newsweek *cover, April 3, 2000*
(© 2000 Newsweek, Inc. All rights reserved.
Reprinted by permission/Doonesbury © G. B. Trudeau).

this group: "Laid back, late blooming or just lost? Overshadowed by the baby boomers, America's next generation has a hard act to follow." (The blurb on the table-of-contents page had a similar tone, beginning: "What's the matter with young adults today?")[43] Defining the group demographically (in 1990) as "the twentysomething generation, those 48 million young Americans ages 18 through 29 who fall between the famous baby boomers and the boomlet of children the baby boomers are producing," the cover story called them "baby busters," "an unsung generation, hardly recognized as a social force or even noticed much at all" (an ironic statement, given that they were on the cover of *Time*). It offered this psychographic description: "They have trouble making decisions. . . . They have few heroes, no anthems, no style to call their own. They crave entertainment, but their attention span is as short as one zap of a TV dial. They hate yuppies, hippies and druggies. They postpone marriage because they dread divorce. They sneer at Range Rovers, Rolexes and red suspenders. What they hold dear are family life, local activism, national parks, penny loafers and mountain bikes. They possess only a hazy sense of their own identity but a monumental preoccupation with all the problems the preceding generation will leave for them to fix."[44]

While noting that this group was committed to "fixing" social problems, the writers added, "What worries parents, teachers and employers is that the latest crop of adults wants to postpone growing up." The article quoted an *American Demographics* editor who called them "the New Petulants because 'they can often end up sounding like whiners.' Their anxious indecision creates a kind of ominous fog around them."[45] Elsewhere, the writers noted that "down deep, what frustrates today's young people—and those who observe them—is their failure to create an original youth culture. . . . People in their 20s have been handed down everyone else's music, clothes and styles, leaving little room for their own imaginations."[46] The article provided (presumably for older folks) "a guide for understanding the puzzling twentysomething crowd"[47] by explaining the themes that defined their lives. Yet even as the magazine asked Gen Xers to define themselves, it did so in ways that referred to Boomers (for instance, among the questions of the issue's *Time*/CNN poll was "Which of these aspects of the 60s do you find attractive?").

Just as initial stories on the Boomers had called them self-centered, lost, and unwilling to grow up, the "baby busters" suffered an unflattering portrayal—but, also like the Boomers, they suffered only briefly, acquiring a better media image within just a few years. In 1994 *News-week* claimed, "The images baby boomers have of 20somethings [*sic*] are mostly unfair and untrue. It's the stereotyping of Generation X, not the reality, that bites."[48] Noting that Gen Xers were so sick of being insulted by older people that they had "taken to calling baby boomers 'baboos,'"[49] the article included sidebars profiling accomplished young people who proved that the group was "already leaving its mark on American culture,"[50] and its format debunked a numbered list of Gen X myths in order to "peel off" the label.

Seven years after its own first derogatory cover story, *Time* followed *Newsweek*'s lead with a cover that showed the closely cropped face of a young man looking out at readers behind a statement designed in a modern, chaotic typeface: "You called us slackers. You dismissed us as Generation X. Well, move over. We are not what you thought" (figure 5.2). The cover story admitted that this group "turns out to be full of go-getters who are just doing it—but their way," and claimed, "Slapped with the label Generation X, they've turned the tag into a badge of honor. They are X-citing, X-igent, X-pansive. They're the next big thing. Boomers, beware! It's payback time."[51] Though claiming to reveal the uniqueness of Generation X, the cover story placed them within an existing popular-culture framework in which generations were compared by such markers as hairstyle and favorite TV shows—an editorial technique that the newsweeklies employed in order to quickly (and visually) "explain" the Baby Boom and Generation Y as well.

As though it had not itself been involved in the earlier labeling of the group, *Time* asked: "If twentysomethings entered the decade floundering in the job market, did they deserve to be labeled dazed and confused?"[52] The writers quoted a pollster as blaming Gen Xers' negative portrayal not on the media but on "Boomers" in general: "Boomers entered the marketplace years ago with high expectations. And when they were disappointed, they thought the future looked bleak for Xers. So they portrayed them as a loser generation."[53] Like *Newsweek*, *Time* used sidebars to showcase young people who had become business successes, including one who claimed that "my generation believes we can do almost anything."[54] Its main story concluded: "For all their ironic detachment, today's young adults embrace an American Dream—albeit one different from the vision their parents or grandparents had."[55]

Although it was introduced to newsweekly audiences in exactly the same year Generation X debuted, Generation Y also was described as "different" and was compared with the Boomers. In 1990 *Newsweek* pub-

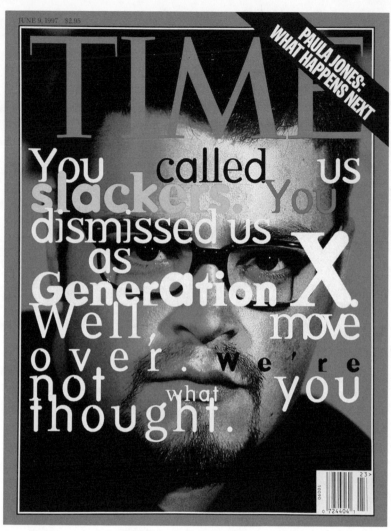

FIGURE 5.2
Time *cover, June 9, 1997*
(Credit: Time, *June 9, 1997).*

lished not just a cover story, but an entire special issue on "The New Teens," explaining: "Today's teenagers are different. No longer the celebrated tribe of the '60s and '70s."[56] In rhetoric similar to the magazines' coverage of Generation X, the special issue offered a left-handed compliment ("Not all teens are spoiled and self-consumed"),[57] and its lead article (quoted at the start of this chapter) looked back wistfully on an earlier era of youth: "There was a time when teenagers believed themselves to be part of a conquering army. Through much of the 1960s and 1970s, the legions of adolescence [sic] appeared to command the center of American culture like a victorious occupying force, imposing their singular tastes in clothing, music and recreational drugs on a good many of the rest of us. . . . what made the young insurgents invincible was the conviction that they were right: from the crusade of the children, grown-ups believed, they must learn to trust their feelings, to shun materialism, to make love, not money. In 1990 . . . teens seem to be more interested in getting ahead in the world than in clearing up its injustices."[58]

This is a fascinating passage for a number of reasons. It referred back, glowingly, to the Boomers' teenage years while also seeming to speak for older Americans ("us") forced to accept the Boomers' "rebellion" and "singular tastes." Even more striking is what was left out of this comparison between Boomers and their children: no mention was made of the teenage years of Generation X, and there was no acknowledgment that the Boomers themselves (the "new" teenagers' parents, who presumably set an example for them) became interested in "getting ahead in the world" during their thirties. In other words, the 1980s were erased from the chronological story that allowed this nostalgic vision.

By the years around the turn of the century, Generation Y had come to include a new group called "Tweens," preadolescents described in another *Newsweek* cover story as "a generation on fast forward"[59] who were multicultural, prematurely sexual, and technologically savvy. They also were described in terms of their popular culture and consumer behavior—their clothing, music idols, "gear," computer software and other technology they used—that made them "a retailer's dream."[60] This early coverage was condescending in what was by then a familiar sort of statement in the newsweeklies: "Psychologists worry that in their rush to *act* like grown-ups, these kids will never really learn to *be* grown-up, confusing the appearance of maturity with the real thing."[61]

Meanwhile, however, the magazine's assessment of the older members of Generation Y, now in their early twenties, had improved. Calling them "the millennial generation,"[62] it described the group as "spiritual, optimistic and ambitious." Though this 2000 cover story's perspective was still that of the parents, and though its writer closed the "special report" by comparing Generation Y to the generation that fought World War II, the conclusion was optimistic: "Teens today, with the tattoos and baggy shorts, could not seem more different from their grandparents. But every generation has a chance at greatness. Let this one take its shot."[63]

That conclusion and comparison now seem ominous, given the most recent characterization of this young group as "Generation 9-11," after the 2001 terrorist attacks on America. *Newsweek*'s writers declared that "the generation that once had it all—peace, prosperity, even the dot-com dream of retiring at 30—faces its defining moment. . . . Where they once dreamed of earning huge bonuses on Wall Street, they're now thinking of working for the government."[64] This article contained a quote from a twenty-four-year-old who said: "'We had no crisis, no Vietnam, no Martin Luther King, no JFK. We've got it now.'"[65] Here again was a remarkable rhetorical choice on the part of the writers and editors, since this quote, too, erased the history of the 1980s (and Generation X). Instead, much in the style of *Time*'s 1951 story on "the silent generation" who were the children of the "Flaming Youth" of the 1920s, the 2001 story linked Generation Y directly to the 1960s and 1970s radicalism of their parents. It held out hope for them, however, in also linking them to the heroism of their grandparents.

This oldest of all the generations was, ironically, the last of the groups discussed in this article to receive a media label. Though demographers had labeled them "the Matures" since the 1980s, they did not become the "Greatest Generation" until the publication of journalist Tom Brokaw's book of the same name in 1998.

Sure enough, early coverage of them was unflattering. A 1988 *Time* cover showed smiling, senior-citizen models wearing warmup suits and had the main coverline "And Now for the Fun Years!" Despite the seemingly enthusiastic cover, its blurb—"Americans are living longer and enjoying it more—but who will foot the bill?"—forecast the tone of the article inside, a report full of anecdotes about rich senior citizens gleefully cashing their Social Security checks while their adult children struggled to afford housing and child care.[66]

This tone continued even as the newsweeklies began to celebrate the fiftieth anniversaries of various milestones of World War II. A "cover package" on "The World War II Generation and How It Changed America," published by *Newsweek* in January 1993, explained that "the men and women who saved America also nearly bankrupted it. First were the entitlements: they'd won the war, right? . . . [Today] the long-living World War II generation consumes a huge share of the economic pie, burdening their children with debt."[67]

Yet the visual aspects of this cover story suggested that the "story" of this generation was changing from economic burden to patriotic heroism, especially as the century was drawing to an end and the newsweeklies began to assess its meaning. The photographs accompanying the article were black-and-white portraits of former presidents John F. Kennedy and George H. W. Bush, the latter of whom had left office that very month, replaced by the incoming Baby Boomer Bill Clinton. These images inside the magazine echoed the reminiscent feel of the cover, which contained a black-and-white photograph of an anonymous World War II sailor, smiling as he looked back over his shoulder, under the coverline, "So Long, Soldier" (figure 5.3). The article noted a "passing of the flame" from one generation to another, and concluded:

> Yet something connected to the success of a nation has been lost, or at least misplaced. Citizens of other countries have often respected the nobler values of the World War II veterans—shared sacrifice, hard work, old-fashioned pluck—better than have their own heirs. . . . The challenge, before the World War II generation dies off, is to transmit those values within the United States, to make the odds they overcame in winning the war and preserving peace a source of some inspiration.
>
> Recall that wartime song: "There'll be bluebirds over / The white cliffs of Dover / tomorrow . . . when the world is free." The world is, in most places, free—freer than ever, thanks in part to this historic generation. But the bluebirds are barely in sight. The soldiers can't bring them back; now it's up to their children.[68]

Following this introductory article was a series of essays by distinguished authors (including James Michener, David Halberstam, and Arthur Schlesinger Jr.) whom *Newsweek* had asked "to reflect on the legacy of the World War II generation."[69] This 1993 "cover package" can be seen as the beginning of what, within half a decade, became a full-blown World War II nostalgia industry, a generational image-enhancement campaign led by high-profile figures in American mass media.

In 1998, when *Newsweek* published a cover story on the phenomenon of movies and books about the experience of American soldiers in World

With Essays by: James A. Michener • Gore Vidal • Arthur M. Schlesinger Jr.
William Styron • Diana Trilling • Kenneth B. Clark • David Halberstam

Newsweek

January 11, 1993 : $2.95

SO LONG, SOLDIER

The World War II Generation and How It Changed America

FIGURE 5.3
Newsweek *cover, January 11, 1993*
(© 1993 Newsweek, Inc. All rights reserved.
Reprinted by permission/U.S. Navy).

War II (an article that focused on Steven Spielberg's film *Saving Private Ryan*), it compared them with the younger generation who had fought (or had not fought) in Vietnam: "One of the unique things about war is the way it thrusts ultimate responsibility on the very young. In World War II, on the American side, the kids accepted it, endured and prevailed. They were the sons of democracy, and they saved democracy. We owe them a debt we can never repay."[70] In the year 2000, *Time*'s "Memorial Day Special" closed with a tribute by Tom Brokaw to the group he had labeled "the Greatest Generation." Praising their "strong sense of loyalty and service, modesty and achievement," Brokaw concluded that, by the turn of the twenty-first century, "Baby boomers who were distanced from the values of their parents during the '60s now have a new appreciation for the sacrifices and deprivations of their mothers and fathers."[71]

As this final example suggests (and as other examples suggest), recent journalistic explanations of any generation tend to lead back to the Baby Boom. Boomers are present in every story about generations, either as the subject of the story or in opposition to the subject of the story. In *Time*'s first cover story on Generation X, the writers admitted, "The boomer group is so huge that it tends to define every era it passes through, forcing society to accommodate its moods and dimensions."[72] So too have the newsweeklies accommodated Boomers' moods and dimensions. One possible reason is that, during the twenty-year period surveyed in this article, Boomers moved into positions of power at newsmagazines (and in other industries) when they were relatively young, and they are still there; certainly this institutional change helps to explain the switch from "they" to "we" in journalistic language about this group.

Despite the Boomers' presence in every story, the newsweeklies have devoted significant attention to other generations. They have done so in seemingly historically specific explanations that confirm David Morgan's claim that "when we slice out a particular set of birth cohorts . . . and label them a generation, this requires us to locate 'watersheds' — those events and patterns that mark this generation as distinctly different from the ones that precede and follow it."[73] Yet these distinctions are blurred by similarities in the stories told about the various generations.

Paradoxically, while "watersheds" seem to mark boundaries between generations, the need to identify such events is one common device in generational reporting. The magazines have attempted to define each social group by pinpointing a defining moment that united it, whether that "moment" was a multiyear war (World War II or Vietnam), a cultural event such as Woodstock, or a disaster such as the September 11th attacks. This practice of assigning specific events to particular groups of people actually gives the events a social rather than historical definition, ignoring this broader truth according to Mannheim: "Every moment of time is . . . in reality more than a pointlike event—it is a temporal volume having more than one dimension, because it is always experienced by several generations at various stages of development."[74] Yet in retrospective journalism, a news event is seen as a defining moment that "belongs" to the generation that was *young* (in their teens or young adulthood) when it occurred.

Similarly, in a second typical device, generations are defined by the life-style items (such as clothing, hairstyles, and consumer products) that were popular during their adolescence or young adulthood. Although these symbols are chosen by the magazine writers, they also seem to come from the story's subjects and audience, presented in the forms of polls, lists, and trend graphics. In this sense, the magazines' references to brand names seem to be more than merely commercial shorthand; they are acknowledgments of material culture with social meaning to the audience. At the same time, though, the life-style-identity markers invoked in journalism are frequently self-referential, given that many are themselves media products or slogans.

Third, each generational story, even in the earliest coverage of a group, has been to some extent nostalgic, comparing the present with a happier previous era. Either memories of a shared generational past are overtly invoked in the coverage, or current phenomena are compared wistfully with lost values. Such nostalgia is a process of forgetting as well as remembering and can be seen in the only-recent emergence of the label for the Greatest Generation, suggesting Boomers' need to pay tribute to their dying parents and/or late-twentieth-century nostalgia for the idea of a "good" war. It also can be seen in the explanation of Generation Y's optimism as an echo of Boomers' idealism, based on logic that erases Generation X and the 1980s.

A fourth common aspect of each generational narrative is the progression of its tone from negative to positive. This has nothing to do with whether a group is actually new in American culture when it is first named: the Greatest Generation was hardly a new phenomenon as a cohesive social group, nor was the Baby Boom by the time it turned forty.

Each generation has been portrayed first as problematic (part of the journalistic "surprise" at its discovery) and then as increasingly acceptable and admirable. This common story line begins with each group's selfishness or irresponsibility and its seeming inexplicability to other generations. Then its image improves, as subsequent coverage discusses the generation's achievements, character, and merit. Those positive qualities, however, are described as somehow distinct from the qualities of the immediately preceding generation.

The move from positive to negative may have to do with issues of readership—the targeted generation grows older and moves into the target audience for the magazines covering them—or with the broader commercial concerns of publishers and advertisers (as John Hsu, the editor of *Inside Edge*, a magazine launched in the mid-1990s to appeal to the male members of Gen X, put it, "Who would want to market to a group that is lazy, apathetic, unmotivated, and alienated from mainstream society?").[75] Yet primarily this last aspect of generational reporting serves editorial needs, allowing the magazines to create a cohesive narrative that nevertheless has some plot twists and that satisfies the journalistic need for novelty. The "differences" of a "new" generation in the headlines are explained in terms of previous coverage of the preceding one; then the improvement of its image over time is presented as a correction of the interim coverage (or as the news media's discovery that "Americans" have been wrong). In just a few years, these layers of coverage create a sense of nostalgia for a generation that may not even be that old.

The progressive narrative that allows an originally objectionable group to redeem itself through "change" also is an example of the way in which journalists create cultural stereotypes—defining groups, events, and phenomena with labels—in ways that allow them to later (sometimes even just a few years later) knock down those stereotypes, revealing the "truth" underneath. This sleight of hand has characterized newsweeklies' coverage not only of generations, but also of other American social-group phenomena, including the civil rights movement and the women's movement.[76] At the same time, however, the reportorial devices consistently used in the generational cover stories—statistics and poll results, profiles of and interviews with members of each generation, who are allowed to speak for themselves—create an impression that the magazines are merely "reflecting" social identities, not creating them.

The stories the newsweeklies tell about various generations are simultaneously different and the same. These trend stories create definitions of seemingly distinct groups set in particular historical moments while also using timeless ideas about youth in order to blend those groups into a larger story about the progression of American culture. Over time, we come to understand, generations will continue to "emerge" and to surprise us; yet, once we begin to forget as well as remember, they will enfold us (or some of us) in comforting nostalgia.

6 Once upon a Time in America

Nostalgia Magazines and Reader Recollections

There were days, frankly, when life seemed a whole lot simpler. People were kinder, gentler, and showed more respect and concern for one another. What it came down to, basically, is that they trusted each other. Hardly anyone ever locked their doors in those days. . . . It was a time when the doctor made house calls. . . . When you made a deal, you didn't need a lawyer, you just shook hands, and that was enough.
—*Reminisce*, 1991[1]

Everyone worked together and shared what they had. Life sure was hard in those days, but looking back, I wouldn't trade my memories for anything. I grew up knowing that folks are good and that when you busy yourself with the needs of others, you don't have time to worry about your own troubles.—*Good Old Days*, 2001[2]

One consequence of the generational-memory trend, in marketing as well as journalism, is that nostalgic media have proliferated during the past twenty years. Whether fictional or fact-based, these media products are not souvenirs or artifacts from the past; they are items of the present that allow us to "recapture" the past (if a new version of it).[3] This chapter examines two such offerings, magazines called *Good Old Days* (which carries the tagline "The Magazine That Remembers the Best") and *Reminisce* ("The Magazine That Brings Back the Good Times") that are read primarily by senior citizens and that wistfully recall a "lost" America of the 1930s and 1940s.

Their reminiscences take the form of a generalized longing for a purer era when life presumably was more meaningful. Sociologists Scott Lash and John Urry describe this phenomenon as "the belief that social life in the present is profoundly disappointing and that in important ways the past was preferable to the present—there really was a golden age; the increased aesthetic sensibility to old places, crafts, houses, countryside and so on, so that almost everything that is old is thought to be valuable whether it is an old master or an old cake tin; the need nevertheless for a certain re-presentation of the past—to construct a cleaned-up heritage."[4] *Good Old Days* captures this idea on every cover with the phrase "Happy Days Gone By," while the *Reminisce* web site puts it this way: "Nostalgia is like a grammar lesson . . . you find the present tense and the past perfect."[5]

Ironically, the "simpler" past often is recalled in commercial terms. In 1998 *Business Week* magazine announced: "Old is new again, from Volkswagen Beetles to Burma Shave signs to ballparks in which your grandfather would have felt comfortable. In these anxiety-ridden times, it seems a lot of people yearn for the good old days. And that's what marketers are giving them." Its cover story listed products that had read-opted their original logos, designs, or campaigns, including Cracker Jack and Coca-Cola, both of which debuted in the late nineteenth century.[6] These examples suggest that people may wish for a past that they never experienced.

Nevertheless, reminiscence is not merely a matter of wishful thinking, nor is its practice simply the response of gullible old folks to commercial tricks played on them by media producers. Writing nearly a century ago, Maurice Halbwachs noted the natural and active nature of memory among the elderly: "Old people ordinarily are not content to wait passively for memories to revive. They attempt to make them more precise, ask other old people, go through old papers, old letters; above all, they tell what they remember, when they do not try to write it down. . . . Why should old people not then be passionately interested in the past, in the common treasure of which they are the guardians? Why should they not try quite consciously to fulfill the function which gives them the only prestige to which they can now lay claim?"[7]

Current theorists continue to maintain that reminiscence is part of the social conversation and individual life-review process common to old age, and that it is a constructive act on the part of those who look back. Anthropologist Janet Hoskins notes: "Through 'telling their lives,' people not only provide information about themselves but also fashion their identities in a particular way, constructing a 'self' for public consumption."[8] Gerontologists explain that "reminiscences may offer what no historical text can: an enhanced sense of how an individual life is part of a larger historical and cultural process; and hence, they may be the source of a deepened sense of identity and a more profound knowledge of our interconnectedness with the world."[9] Moreover, especially "during times of stress," reminiscence provides these positive psychological benefits not only for the elderly, but also for middle-aged people, for whom looking back may be "a means of preparing for future crisis."[10]

While life review may be, at least in part, distinct to the individual, nostalgia is by definition a social experience, a form of recollection based on shared ideas about the past and present and on cultural definitions of better and worse. Nostalgic media products anticipate an ongoing dialogue between the producers and the audience, as well as shared values and wishes. This sense of mutual understanding is an editorial quality of most magazines, which speak conversationally to their readers about topics of common interest. Indeed, magazines, more so than other media, have long dealt in nostalgia. Today, the *Saturday Evening Post* is full of wistful articles about better days gone by, and its covers showcase the reprinted artwork of its most famous illustrator, Norman Rockwell. Yet Rockwell's visions of family happiness were already nostalgic (for nineteenth-century small-town life) when they began to appear on the magazine's cover in 1916.[11] Like the *Post*, *Reader's Digest* and *Life* regularly have included reminiscent articles since they debuted in the 1920s and 1930s. More recently, both magazines also have published nostalgic "magabooks" on specific themes — in *Life*'s case, for instance, on Elvis Presley and on the Macy's Thanksgiving Day Parade, and in *Reader's Digest*'s case, *America in the '40s*.[12]

Nostalgia itself was the central theme of *Memories*, a short-lived magazine launched in 1988 with a tie-in network television show. Pronounced by the industry trade press as "the industry's hottest new consumer book," this magazine was characterized as "a sort of *Reader's Digest* of world history during the last 50 years" and was targeted toward "the immense over-40 population." Starting with a rate base of 500,000 and an ad-campaign slogan "Everything old is news again," *Memories* was credited with "creating a new media category" of nostalgia media, including another television show called *Only Yesterday*, along with the cable-television Nostalgia Network, which "show[ed] big band music videos and, unlike most of these other properties, target[ed] senior citizens."[13]

Memories did not last (perhaps because, like *My Generation* [see chapter 5], it targeted the "young old"), but another title launched at the same time, *Reminisce*, survived and thrived, becoming the primary competitor of the already-existing *Good Old Days*. These two magazines provide an illuminating case study in nostalgia for two reasons: nostalgia is the core of their editorial identity; and they involve readers in the reminiscence process to an unusual extent. This chapter, based on a survey of more than thirty consecutive issues of each magazine,[14] considers the narrative and dialogic nature of their content.

These publications focus on memories from the first half of the twentieth century, with the majority of their editorial matter contributed by readers (albeit heavily edited by the staff). Both magazines present themselves to readers as "family," and in the case of *Good Old Days*, the editors are a husband-wife team; editor Ken Tate says of his audience, "Janice and I view them as our extended family and I think they sense our loyalty to them and our genuine affection."[15] *Good Old Days* is published by an Indiana-based company called the House of White Birches (which originally was in New England), though its editors are in Arkansas; *Reminisce*, published bimonthly from an address on "Memory Lane," comes from Wisconsin-based Reiman Publications, which was acquired by the Reader's Digest Association in 2002.[16] The two companies have been in business since the mid-1960s, though *Reminisce* did not debut until 1991. *Good Old Days* dates back to 1964 and began as a spinoff of a magazine called *Women's Household*; it was named for a column in that publication that "gave readers a forum to write their memories of growing up and ask about old-time books, poetry and songs."[17] *Reminisce* has the broader reach, with more than a million readers, compared with *Good Old Days'* circulation of 200,000.[18]

Both magazines have supplemental titles—*Good Old Days Specials* and *Reminisce Extra*—that provide additional memories. And, while only *Good Old Days* contains advertising,[19] both magazines promote ancillary products with similar themes. The "*Good Old Days* Audio Collection" includes titles such as "Down on the Farm" and "The Little Country Schoolhouse" and books including *We Survived and Thrived* and *Country Wisdom*; these tapes' content is described as "just like the great stories you used to share on your front porch after chores on those warm summer evenings so long ago."[20] Every issue of *Reminisce* is polybagged (bound together in plastic) with an insert offering subscriptions to the other Reiman magazines and highlighting items the company sells in its mail-order catalog and its online "Country Store." Such products include, for instance, coin banks made to look like old gas pumps, model cars, a family-tree "Memory Book," an "authentic-looking replica" of an old telephone, "limited edition replicas" of old radios, and a video titled "Classic Commercials from the 50's and 60's."[21]

Reminisce is just one part of a company that more broadly markets an American life-style based on ideas about the past. While it is the only publication of Reiman's eleven magazines devoted specifically to memory, the editorial theme of all of the company's titles is a nostalgic idea of country life.[22] According to founder Roy Reiman, the company has "an unusually close relationship with our customers."[23] Its representatives go out to visit readers across the country through special events including cooking schools and a "hitchwagon" pulled by Belgian horses that stops at nursing homes, malls, and county fairs. Thousands of readers have visited the company's visitor center in Greendale, Wisconsin, often coming in bus tour groups,[24] where they can shop at the Country Store Outlet and eat at the Taste of Home Restaurant (named for another of the magazines). The center has "a fully operating test kitchen . . . a small theater where you'll learn how each magazine started . . . an editor's office staffed with someone to greet you . . . a variety of crafts and exhibits sent by subscribers . . . [and] the wagon pulled cross-country by our Belgian Hitch."[25] "It's a cozy scene," reports an article in *Reminisce*, with "subscribers from Texas and New Mexico sipping coffee and nibbling cookies while chatting with subscribers from Vermont and Pennsylvania."[26]

Editorially, *Reminisce* and *Good Old Days* convey a generalized sense that the past was "better" and include some "remembrances" that no living person today could remember, such as pictures of pioneer schoolhouses in the nineteenth century and articles with titles such as "Horse and Buggy Days" and "Life at the Turn of the Century." Their covers feature illustrations and hand-colored photographs that are reminiscent of unspecified bygone eras (see, for instance, figure 6.1).

Nearly three-quarters of *Good Old Days* readers are over age sixty-five, and more than 40 percent are over age seventy-five,[27] the latter group perhaps accounting for the magazine's strong editorial focus on Depression-era memories. According to a survey of *Reminisce* readers, the 1940s are the most popular decade for reader memories, with the 1930s and 1950s nearly tied for second place. Given that the median reader age is seventy-two, these results (along with the *Good Old Days* age demographics) correspond with sociological theory about memory, echoed in *Reminisce* editor Bettina Miller's comment that "people most want to read about memories from the time of their childhood, then their young adulthood, and then they like to remember stories that their parents told them."[28]

Even so, notes Miller, the magazine has readers who are in their twenties and thirties. "They're not contributors—they're not old enough to have memories in the time periods we cover—but they're just a certain kind of people, people who feel like they wish they had lived in that [an earlier] time."[29] That secondary audience explains a reader letter printed in a 2002 issue of *Good Old Days*: "'We want to raise our children in an old-fashioned country atmosphere that you always read about in magazines. Would love to hear from others who are living in these wonderful places.'"[30] Such wishfulness may explain the modern feeling of the nostalgia image shown in figure 6.2.

Both magazines publish readers' personal reminiscences, though only *Reminisce* systematically solicits contributions, assuring readers of "the satisfaction you'll derive from *sharing* some of those great memories and then saying to your family or friends, 'Hey, look here, they used *my* piece in this issue!'"[31] The editors write: "Basically, this is your magazine, not ours. Our editors simply serve as a 'receiving and distribution station' for all the great memories and pictures our subscribers want to share with each other. . . . So, if you'd like to join our staff, send us your favorite memory."[32] The magazine includes a map of the United States pinpointing the residences of reader contributors to the issue. The accompanying text explains: "As one *Reminisce* reader told us a while back, 'Your magazine makes me feel like I'm sitting at the table with a cup of coffee or visiting over the back fence with people across the country— it's like having a chat!'"[33]

FIGURE 6.1
Good Old Days *cover, February 2001*
(Courtesy of Good Old Days/The House of White Birches*).*

FIGURE 6.2
Good Old Days *cover, May 2001*
(Courtesy of Good Old Days/*The House of White Birches).*

Good Old Days also "chats" with readers, though in different ways. Each issue contains an editor's letter that often is a personal story tying the husband-wife team in with the themes of the magazine. For instance: "Decades ago when Janice and I were courting, I liked to take her to a Saturday night picture show in the nearest town. Like so many other young folks, we always liked to stop off at the soda fountain. . . . There was nothing quite like sharing a soda with your best girl on a Saturday night—the only night we farm kids had even a slight chance of getting into town."[34]

The magazine publishes a multipage Wanted department full of fifty-word notices, running, on average, a hundred of them in the back of each issue. Free for subscribers, these pleas come from people searching for old friends, relatives, neighbors, co-workers, or war buddies; seeking pen pals; wanting advice on medical problems; asking for recipes, needlework patterns, or words to old songs or poems; and looking for items to add to collections (of dolls, books, teapots, records, etc.). Editor Ken Tate discusses what he thinks is the real appeal of this exchange process: "I have received letters saying, 'Why do people ask for a poem or song that they could easily find at their local library or through the Internet?' The answer is, of course, that the reader wants more than an answer to a query. He or she wants human contact. Many times a Wanted generates hundreds of responses. How often does a person get that many letters, particularly an elderly person? Often these contacts turn into pen pals and more."[35] A reader letter printed in one issue attested to such a result: "I truly consider you all at *Good Old Days* friends. I asked you to place a Wanted for an old Army buddy of mine. I had tried for several years to find him with no luck. . . . Let me tell you my great surprise when my phone rang and a voice said, 'A lady came over and said she read in a magazine that you were looking for me.' We talked for over an hour and are exchanging letters now and making plans to get together. . . . I thank you for helping me find him."[36]

Similarly, the *Reminisce* departments that receive a high amount of reader mail are ones that promote reader interaction outside the magazine's pages.[37] They include Can You Give Me a Hand? in which readers ask each other for information about people, phenomena, or things (listing their own addresses for direct responses). Many of the magazine's articles and photographs are sent in response to topic-specific solicitations, which have included summer fairs, military memories, parades, family doctors, marching bands, large families, diners, railroads, old-wives' tales, hairstyles, swing bands, quilting, and Saturday night dances. Readers may contribute articles on subjects of their own choice as well. These narrative recollections often run with photographs of their contributors, because "people like to make a connection with a real person, to know what that person looks like today."[38]

Such interactive texts, while ostensibly about particular topics, allow for ongoing discussion of broader issues and ideas. Psychologists David Middleton and Derek Edwards explain: "It is not only that conversation affords examination of the micro-processes of collective remembering, as these unfold with talk. Larger, societal themes are also available for examination, including historical, ideological and political ones. . . . It is a feature of conversation that these themes are not merely available in the discourse for the analyst to discover, available like pebbles on a beach, to be picked up and examined, but rather, are worked on by the participants themselves. . . . cultural and ideological themes (even though they may not be named as such) are worked up, illustrated, used and commemorated."[39]

Although the scenes nostalgia magazines paint are sepia-toned, it is not hard to understand their appeal in a post–September 11th America, and their language seems familiar in current political rhetoric. A reader wrote in the January 2002 issue of *Good Old Days*: "Once upon a time in America, particularly in the small towns and villages, there was a sense of neighborliness that even national calamities—like the Depression and two world wars—and local disasters—like fires and tornadoes—could not quell. In fact, if anything, such events drew people together."[40]

Anthropologist Grant McCracken notes that the gap between the real and the ideal is a feature of every culture, and most societies cope with this problem through "displacing" ideals to another place or time, "transport[ing] them to another cultural universe, there to be kept within reach but out of danger. . . . When they are transported to a distant cultural domain, ideals are made to seem practicable realities. The destination for displacement is often the past, a 'golden age' that is a historical period for which documentation and evidence exists in reassuring abundance. In fact, the period is a largely fictional moment in which social life is imagined to have conformed perfectly to cultural ideals."[41]

In reminiscence magazines, the "other cultural universe" is not just a past time, but a type of place as well: rural areas, small towns, or close-knit neighborhoods that contain old-fashioned schoolhouses or corner drugstores (see figure 6.3). In all of these settings, the community's ideals are defined in terms of traditional "family values," altruism, and ingenuity born of necessity. One article, about growing up in Westby,

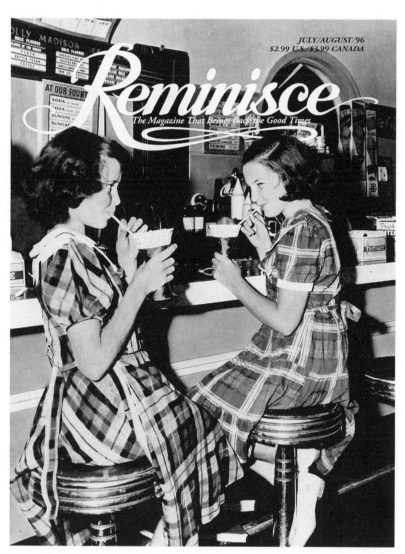

FIGURE 6.3
Reminisce *cover, July–August 1996*
(Courtesy of Reminisce).

Montana, in the 1930s, opened: "Dad not only owned the Westby meat and Grocery Store, he was also the fire chief *and* the local mortician. As you can imagine, the fact that the town butcher was also the town undertaker become a prime subject of humor."[42] These reader contributions have appeared in *Reminisce's* Short Memories department:

> When I was a child, nothing tasted better than licking the paddles of our hand-cranked ice cream maker (Vermont).

> My proudest moment came when I was able to hand Granny a blue ribbon I'd won at the Winnebago County Fair for a jar of bread-and-butter pickles (Wisconsin).

> I not only attended a one-room school, I taught in one! . . . I carried a half-gallon tin bucket with my lunch in it—a biscuit and a slice of sausage . . . (Texas).

> Making and giving May baskets was popular with kids in the small town of Calumet, Oklahoma, during the 1920s.

> Our favorite place to play as kids was the haymow in my uncle Clyde Rouser's barn on his farm near Mt. Hope, Kansas.

> The Kresge five-and-dime in Burlington, Iowa, was my favorite downtown destination in the early '40s.[43]

In this section of the magazine, specific and personal anecdotes are woven together to form an ideal, collective memory of a better place and time in the past. *Reminisce* articles have the same effect. One reader recalled his sixth birthday party in 1942, in Blakely, Georgia, as "a peaceful time when we never locked our doors. . . . Mom called when the homemade ice cream was ready. . . . Dad always gave it the last few tough cranks."[44] Even articles with urban settings contain similar images and language. One woman remembered that in her Philadelphia neighborhood of the 1940s, "late on summer afternoons, when supper was simmering on the stove," homemakers would "sit on the front porch chatting with each other and waiting for their husbands to come home from work. Those front porches served as second living rooms, the place where a man could sit and read the evening paper until daylight faded while his wife cleaned up the kitchen and got the children ready for bed."[45] Such anecdotal glimpses of particular pasts extend the creation of the imaginary ideal, as do these reader memories from *Good Old Days*:

On an early spring day in 1926, snow still lay on the northern side of the house and barn, but Burpee's seed catalogue had long since come in the mail. Now Mama was making out her order.

In the 1930s, my sister Fern and I attended Clover Hill grade school. Clover Hill was a four-room brick school heated with big coal stoves. The playground, covered with loose dirt, rocks, cinders and ashes from the stoves, must have been the roughest in Rockingham County, Va.

I lived with my grandparents in southwestern Oklahoma from 1939–1946. My granddad farmed two quarter sections, mostly in cotton, and that first summer I quickly found out there were four things you had to do to a cotton field: plant, cultivate, chop and pick.

On a summer morning in the 1930s, I waited with my mother and two cousins where the wagon-rutted lane from our little farm joined the graveled road that ran through our mountain community.

In the mid-1950s, when I was growing up on our small farm in rural Ridge, Md., my brother Sonny and I had the chore of hand-picking corn at harvest time.

In 1944 I lived on a farm near the small town of Hull, Iowa. Dad, my two sisters and I traveled the graveled road once weekly by Model-A to sell crated eggs and cans of whole cream, and to purchase groceries and other necessities.

As a small child growing up in the Ozarks where there was no electricity, I didn't know what a movie was. Then, one August night back in 1924, my parents, five brothers and two sisters and I got in our Model-T truck and went to our school for a program.

I grew up right in the middle of 11 children. The Depression was happening all around me in the 1920s and 1930s. . . . We lived in the small coal-mining town of Cunard, W. Va., also known as Coal Run. When I think of hometown America, that was it. Everyone knew everyone else, and they bonded together to form a family community.[46]

It may seem strange that so many memories are of difficult times, and that older people would want to recall the struggles of the past. Yet for today's elderly, depression and world war were the backdrops for their youths and young adulthood. What's more, their inclination is natural. Halbwachs offered this characterization of memory later in life: "When it comes to the most somber aspects of our existence . . . it seems they are enveloped by clouds that half cover them. That faraway world where we remember that we suffered nevertheless exercises an incomprehensible attraction on the person who has survived it and who seems to think he has left there the best part of himself, which he tries to recapture."[47]

The hardship stories told in the magazines are paradoxically full of images of plenty and kindness, typified by this sentence from an article in *Good Old Days*: "There was no electricity, no running water and no central heating, yet we were happy."[48] Several *Reminisce* features have been roundups about getting through difficult times, whether harsh winters or economic distress. A photo-essay showed "fashionable" dresses women made from feed sacks.[49] An article titled "Threshing Day Was Long, Hard . . . and Memorable" included these details: "Pies, cakes and bread were baked early in the forenoon before the huge, blue graniteware roaster of beef, pork or chicken went into the oven."[50] Other articles in the magazine have emphasized the close relationships among people experiencing difficulty:

> Times were tough in 1935, when my father, William, built a gas station on Quebec Road near our house in Cincinnati, Ohio so he and my three brothers would have jobs. . . . Besides all the service that customers received at my dad's station for the little money they spent, they could also come inside and visit with the owner while they paid. Today . . . there is no friendly attendant cleaning your windshield or checking your oil, tires and battery. Yes, the good old days of service stations like my dad's are over.[51]

> Father had died when I was three and my sister was nine. In order to make a living and keep her family close, Mom, Mary Gould, became a telephone operator. The switchboard office was the front room of our house. . . . The calls Mom made weren't the cordless or conference calls of today. But they had magic—the magic of a person who was interested in each call, knew everyone in town, would call you back when the line was free . . . and could keep a secret.[52]

As these examples reveal, stereotypical sex roles are frequent (and frequently celebrated) in these memories. What's striking, though, is the number of articles in which women, such as Mary Gould, are heroines. The many stories about admirable women surely are a reflection of the magazines' audience composition: two-thirds of *Reminisce* readers and four-fifths of *Good Old Days* readers are female.[53] Moreover, gerontologists have found that women look back on their lives differently than men do: "The process of life review seems to produce a more positive sense of a life career for women than for men. Failure is not a significant theme for women."[54] Researchers also have observed "greater continuity in values for women [which] reflects a greater continuity in their sense of the meaning of their lives," as well as a lower level of "bitterness revival."[55]

Women are recalled as the strength of the family in hard times, particularly during the Great Depression, as described in the following accounts from both magazines:

> Back in the 1930s, Granny's advice was the closest thing to psychotherapy. Many considered her a second mother. She was a teacher and friend, and many considered her "the lady with style." People from all over Nowata County would come to tell her their problems with marriage, money, cooking, etc. And Granny was loving and kind to all of them.

> I heard many familiar adages, like this favorite of my grandmother's: "Make it do or do without." My mother's was "Necessity is the mother of invention." I saw her put that notion to work as she concocted nourishing meals with what she had on hand. She also sewed and made over clothing to furnish us with a wardrobe that was ample and stylish.

> If it hadn't been for hard times, I might not have discovered the magic Aunt Annie could perform with her sewing machine.

> My grandparents had a secondhand store . . . and when Grandpa died, Grandma ran the store. She was spry for her age and thought nothing of climbing those high ladders to satisfy a customer's query. . . . Grandma was from the Old Country and spoke in broken English, but she had no trouble being understood.

> As an 18-year-old city girl in 1941, I took a teaching job at a country school near Omaha, Nebraska. Besides teaching 14 students in six grades, I had to start and bank a fire in the coal stove, pump water and carry it inside and make sure the outhouses were clean.

My sister was a baby, and I wasn't old enough to go to school. Dad had left us, and the Great Depression was at its worst. Mom took in washing to make a living.[56]

The last quotation is an example of an occasional theme that mars the pretty picture of the past presented in these magazines' reminiscences: the strength of women who were treated badly by men. One story in *Good Old Days* actually admitted that the writer's parents' marriage was unhappy and abusive. The author remembered how proud she was that her mother got a job at a time when the family needed money, even though it angered her father:

He told her she had no skills, that she was only good enough to be a wife and a mother. That did it! Mamma didn't just get angry, she got even. Soon Dad was taking the trolley east [from Hummelstown, Pennsylvania, to work in Hershey] and Mamma was taking it west, bound for Harrisburg, where she found a position as a piano player at Woolworth's five-and-dime. There she sat, bouncing around on the stool to the jouncing lilt of *Bye-Bye Blackbird*. She attracted a gathering who applauded her mightily. Dad was humiliated and was tempted to remove her bodily. But Mamma was ecstatic. She was loved, appreciated, and paid money for something she loved to do. When the manager offered her more money to stay, she was bloated with praise. She was a celebrity.[57]

These struggle narratives often underscore women's ambition and pride in notable accomplishments. In *Reminisce*, one woman who became an actress explained the price at which her dance and piano lessons came: "With no income and a mortgaged house, Ma rented out rooms in our home and bartered when the money didn't go far enough. . . . Although I had few worldly things while I was growing up, I had the love and encouragement of a great and unselfish lady. She was one of a kind and gave me an exciting life."[58] The following story is from the Depression-era memory of a Brooklyn girl printed in *Good Old Days*:

Aunt Peggy worked for Sinclair Oil and their office was in the Rockefeller Center. In my world, that made her very important. She was magical! . . . When I was about 10 years old, she took me to Radio City Music Hall. . . . A curved staircase with red padding on each step ascended to the mezzanine level. It was so big that I could hardly believe my eyes! Red velvet drapes hung over the windows. Glass chandeliers, more spectacular than any I had ever seen before, were suspended in the lobby that seemed three stories high. The gold-painted ceiling reflected the lights. It was so exciting that I wanted to dance. . . . I felt like a princess."[59]

Wonder and escape are elements in hardship-era stories about strong or admirable or lucky women. In these memories, women have one special moment or gift that gets them through hard times and that, in retrospect, is a reason why those times now seem so good. A *Reminisce* article titled "When Cinderella Went to Paris" began this way: "My mother, Katherine Bittner, was a quiet, modest girl who quit school in eighth grade so she could get a job and help her parents weather the tough economic times. By age 20, she was working in a factory in Milwaukee, Wisconsin. But she'd never given up her dreams of romance and adventure. That's why, in 1930, she entered a contest sponsored by the *Wisconsin News* and actress Gloria Swanson. The prize was a free trip to Paris." In this story, Mother won the trip and was dubbed a "Cinderella working girl" by her local newspaper. The writer noted that the story has been passed down through the years and that "one day, her great-grandchildren will hear that they're related to Cinderella, the factory worker whose fairy-tale dreams came true."[60]

In *Good Old Days*, another woman recounted her story as a travel adventure: "Our first trip to California! My friend Shirley and I were excited as we planned our summer of work at Douglas Aircraft Corporation. . . . On June 6, 1943, my friend and I boarded the Greyhound bus, bid farewell to our family, and took off for this great experience."[61] Articles about World War II, a common subject in both magazines, have described women's contributions as patriotic and self-sacrificing, but also revealed that the war gave them freedom and a feeling of satisfaction. A reader writing in *Good Old Days* recalled her service while making a sharper point: "While their sweethearts, brothers and fathers left home to fight on the battlefields, thousands of young ladies left their homes and families to fight the paper war in Washington, D.C. We might not have been worthy of mention in the best-selling book *The Greatest Generation*, but I can assure you that we did our part to help win the war. . . . I am proud to have been one of those young ladies referred to as 'the government girls.'"[62] Similar pride at having overcome societal sexism could be heard in this conversation between two women printed in *Reminisce*:

"I had an office job with Goodyear in Akron, Ohio but hated being behind a desk. It was hard to switch, but I finally managed to get transferred to Goodyear Aerospace, where Corsair fighter planes were being produced for the Navy."

"My dream was to fly airplanes someday, so the idea of helping build them was exciting."

"Did you ever get to fly?"

"By golly, I did! I trained in a Piper Cub and got my student pilot's license. . . ."[63]

The preceding exchange was part of one article in The Old Party Line, a recurring feature in *Reminisce* framed as a telephone chat between two readers who once had the same job or experience.[64] This feature also contained descriptive details that made the past come alive, as in this conversation between two readers who worked as clerks at a "General Store":

"We pumped gas, weighed up potatoes and nails, cut meat, sold penny candy, measured out yard goods, fitted the miners with boots and bought eggs from the farmers. . . ."

"Little kids would come with a dime and spend forever picking out root beer barrels and licorice whips. . . ."

"And nails were a nickel a pound, bolts were 10 cents, cold cereals were 10 or 12 cents a box, and oil was 10 cents a quart."[65]

To a great extent, both magazines are catalogs of physical objects of the past. Folklorist Barbara Kirschenblatt-Gimblett explains that the collection and display of treasured possessions is one communicative way in which older people "derive a sense of enlarged . . . significance through forging links between their individual lives and a larger whole . . . a lost way of life."[66] Each issue of *Reminisce* contains a photo-essay on some item such as cookie jars or model trains. Editor Bettina Miller notes that the magazine itself is a "collectible": "We've gotten letters from people who say they just bought a box of the magazines at a flea market, or people who say they have every issue we've published. I think that our core readers are packrat types—savers. They can't bear to throw things away."[67]

Certainly the same description applies to readers of *Good Old Days*, given the frequency of pleas for collectibles and other reminiscent items in the magazine's Wanted department. They have included, for instance, detective magazines from the 1930s and 1940s, a 1944 calendar plate, the original album of the "Beer Barrel Polka," "a mid-1950s pencil box," "old flapper-style beaded, mesh or tapestry purses of bags," "a set of wooden checks and a *Little Black Sambo* book," the "1930s pulp magazine *Doc Savage*," a shade for a Roy Rogers lamp, Nelson Eddy Club memorabilia, Shirley Temple memorabilia, and a "Pinocchio spoon with Pinocchio and donkey."

In *Reminisce*, feature after feature celebrates this world of things. Anecdotes and photographs sent in response to the magazine's topic-specific solicitations have included homemade toys, savings stamps, chewing gum, matchbooks, sheet music, jigsaw puzzles, hats, shoes, braided rugs, Victorian houses, baseball cards, and autograph books. Fashion-memory solicitations receive an especially high number of responses.[68] Readers' interest in old-time transportation is expressed in terms of details about the vehicles involved, including trains, streetcars, and, most of all, automobiles. Cars are remembered not only through photo-essays and quizzes about old models ("Name That Car!"), but also departments titled My First Car and Motoring Memories.

Items featured in a *Reminisce* department titled I've Kept It All These Years (with photos and descriptions sent by their owners) have included an army uniform, tea sets, dolls, teddy bears, buttons, Valentine's Day cards, a christening gown, a sewing machine, and a prom dress. One issue contained a four-page photo-essay on cookie jars.[69] In a department titled We Wish It Was Still Around, readers write about items from ball-bearing roller skates to buttermilk jugs, and these brief accounts include language like this: "Just once more, I'd like to take a stroll across a swinging rope bridge that would link me to my childhood."[70] In another department titled I'm Curious about This Antique, readers can ask an expert about the nature and value of their belongings.

Many of the possessions discussed in these magazines are themselves forms of media, from old radios and television sets to collections of Nancy Drew or Hardy Boys books. *Good Old Days* contains a department on memories of Big-Band-era performers (called Big Band Beat) and another recalling old movie stars (called Looking Hollywood Way); it also regularly reprints sheet music of favorite old songs inside the magazine. The magazine has run features on old radio shows such as *Ma Perkins* and Fanny Brice's *Baby Snooks Show* and television shows such as *The Lone Ranger* and *The Howdy Doody Show*.

Reminisce also has included articles on favorite radio and television shows of the past (as well as accounts of the *experience* of watching television when the medium was new), records, Sunday funnies (with certain comic strips reprinted), drive-in movie theaters, and advertising premiums (prizes children received in return for box tops, etc.). Each issue contains a department titled Ads from the Old Days, recalling and picturing items such as Kodak cameras, Campbell's Soup, and Colgate-Palmolive products. Such content supports sociologist Fred Davis's observation that "the very objects of collective nostalgia are in themselves media creations from the recent past. . . . the popular media have come increasingly to serve as their own repository for the nostalgic use of the past."[71] It also illustrates one of the several paradoxes of these magazines: that the "good old days" are a lost era of nonmaterialistic values that nevertheless is full of material culture, much of it commercial-media culture.

Yet in many of the possession-memories appearing in these magazines, the object in question is less significant as a possession than as a narrative device through which lessons are learned and values are passed across generations:

> Mama's sewing machine was given to her by her mother when Mama was 16 years old. Grandma, upon giving her such an expensive present, explained that she must treasure it because it would always provide her with a way to earn a living. And Mama did treasure it. She protected it with a homemade cotton cover and she oiled it lovingly so often that it gleamed. So, 84 years later, the sewing machine has a place of honor in my daughter's home. Its drawers no longer contain the treasures of my childhood, but it still serves as a warm reminder of the hours I spent listening to the beat of the treadle and Mama humming her favorite songs.[72]

Such physical items have a social function in the world of memory, becoming what anthropologist Janet Hoskins calls "biographical objects," things that "share our lives with us." She explains that even "ordinary utilitarian tools [can turn] into sometimes very significant possessions, which draw their power from biographical experiences and the stories told about these."[73] Russell Belk concurs that treasured objects can "symbolically extend self": "Our accumulation of possessions provides a sense of past and tells us who we are, where we have come from, and perhaps where we are going."[74]

In reminiscence magazines, readers recall treasured possessions and places in order to recall people who came before them, survived hard times, and took part in pivotal events, thus playing an important role in a broader American story. As the inheritors of their "legacy," the present-day recollectors affirm their own worth and historical importance, at a time in their lives when they may be less capable physically and mentally, or living alone or in nursing homes.

These publications are, of course, full of *good* memories, a "cleaned-up heritage" that ignores the political and social dissension of past eras and that celebrates even the most difficult periods of the American twentieth century as preferable to modern life. They are a form of "memory with the pain taken out," to quote geographer David Lowenthal's definition of nostalgia.[75] *Reminisce* editor Bettina Miller sees this result as logical and healthy: "People forget about the bad stuff because they let it go; otherwise they would go nuts. It's a kind of wisdom. They went through the horrible parts once. . . . What's interesting is that they now have good memories of hard times."[76] Psychologists David Middleton and Derek Edwards call this phenomenon the "rhetorical organization of remembering and forgetting," a matter of "telling the *right* kind of story, at the right time, to the right person, about what went on, or did not go on" in ways that make the past cohesive and that make the present a meaningful and positive result of that past.[77]

A number of traditional values are expressed consistently throughout the pages of both *Reminisce* and *Good Old Days*: family loyalty, rural simplicity, good service and quality work, heroism coupled with humility, resourcefulness and resilience (especially of women), and uncomplaining commitment to "getting the job done." These themes are naturalized because they emerge from the nonfiction experiences of real people who get to speak for themselves, as active participants in the storytelling process. Readers and the memory texts they create are involved in a conversation not only with the editors and with each other, but also across time. The many recollections of parents and grandparents (as well as, in a more general sense, all revisitations of earlier eras in these articles) constitute discursive connections between the past and the present and among generations. The fact that this dialogue takes place in the present means that current debates and events are woven into the mediated conversation as well—allowing senior citizens, who are so frequently ignored by commercial media, to "have their say" on those issues by offering parallels or contrasts from the past.

Indeed, these magazines illustrate the difference between history and memory, the latter of which has more to do with modern concerns and evolving social identity than it does with the representation of an actual past. That difference is underscored (ironically, given her word choice) in this reader letter printed in *Good Old Days*:

Thank you for bringing a bit of sanity and reality into this world of living in the fast lane and dependence on artificial intelligence, where values and a sense of belonging have somehow gotten lost in the shuffle. It is only through knowing where you have been that you can truly comprehend where you are, where you are going, and most importantly, who you are as a person. Thank you for keeping all us older folks grounded. Thank you, also, for keeping alive the treasured heritage and experiences that aren't reflected in the history books.[78]

Critics of media nostalgia tend to emphasize two aspects of the phenomenon. Many question the commercial motives of the producers, criticizing their co-optation of the past for profit.[79] While they are commercial enterprises extending beyond the magazines themselves in their marketing operations, the magazines discussed in this chapter suggest that reminiscent media also deserve attention as sites of cultural-identity construction and as texts that may help us to understand the narrativization of the past and the conversational aspects of reminiscence. Because of their dialogic nature, and because of the kinds of memory stories they consistently contain, senior-citizen nostalgia magazines offer evidence of the social, and not just commercial, functions of media.

It also is worth noting that the objects of readers' longing, their definitions of the lost and better past, tend to be places, circumstances, and feelings—big families, one-room schoolhouses, comforting foods, romantic courtship, patriotism—rather than consumer products (as is far more likely to be the case with, for instance, Baby Boom nostalgia).[80] What's more, the profits generated by these kinds of magazines are dwarfed by those of other media-memory productions, especially those considered the most "authentic" depictions of "important" American memory of the same eras (for instance, *Saving Private Ryan*).

The second common criticism of these kinds of media products is the "soft" nature of nostalgia itself, a view in which nostalgia (as opposed to history, the "truth" about the past) is defined as a wishful, lowbrow, and/or feminine response to both the past and the present. In a sense, this chapter confirms such a characterization: many older people are low-income, and perhaps, given the economic circumstances of their youth, not as well as educated as younger Americans; and most of them are women, who, as researchers have found, tend to recall the past as better than it actually was. Yet this study presents these circumstances in a far more positive light, revealing an interactive, female world of reminiscence held together by conversation and material culture, a world worth closer study by researchers from pop-culture scholars to gerontologists. Whether or not the past times and places of these magazines are "real," those visions meet some real need of many people, particularly older women, who have little say and virtually no other representation in media today.

Reminiscence magazines raise the question of why a certain vision of the past emerges, with clear and consistent symbols, themes, and narratives, in a reader-interactive medium. It may be that reminiscence is the territory of old folks, but the aging portion of the current American population is unprecedented in size, and, as the evidence presented here suggests, the idea of a "better" past has a hold on younger adults today as well. Media such as *Reminisce* and *Good Old Days* might prompt us to think more seriously about the pull of nostalgia—to consider *why*, at the start of the twenty-first century, we "find the present tense and the past perfect," and how we revise the past through recollection to ease that tension.

7 Snapshots in a Family Album
Anniversary Celebrations of a Shared Past

[These] collected notes and observations bear
comparison to the snapshots in a family album . . .
the distinguishing tone of voice is that of a practical
people interested in what they can see and make of
the world, the voice of travelers in an always new
country, optimistic and energetic, seeking to work
the soil of the American experience into a cash
crop, a grand hotel, a dream of heaven.
—*Harper's*, 2000 (150th-anniversary issue)[1]

As Jimi Hendrix importuned: Please, remember, got
to remember, yeah, got to remember, oh Lord. . . .
let's honor his advice and consider anew the things
of our past . . . the heroes and villains, feats and
blunders that have defined our world for the last
20 years.—*Outside*, 1997 (20th-anniversary issue)[2]

The preceding chapters have explored how pivotal historical events and iconic public figures are remembered in American journalism in ways that help to sort audiences into social groups, whether defined by nation, race, or generation. They also have explored the possibilities for the role of audiences in this process (a viewpoint from which one might reverse causality, theorizing instead that social-group identity prompts media memory). Media producers and receivers seem especially unified on anniversaries, when "we" look back together at personalities and events and when new layers are added to social memory. Today's mass media are full of anniversary observations: in 2004 alone, they ranged from the arrival of the Beatles in America (forty years) and the death of Kurt Cobain (ten years) to the D-Day landing (sixty years) and the landmark Supreme Court desegregation decision in *Brown v. Board of Education* (fifty years).

Media also celebrate their own longevity, making institutional anniversaries occasions to sum up history. When the television medium passed the fifty-year mark, networks aired nostalgic anniversary shows in which audiences were invited to join cast members in remembering characters and plots. Magazines have been putting out anniversary issues for an even longer time, counting on readers' urge to reminisce and save special issues, and they have marked them as such: when *Good Housekeeping* published a "Silver Anniversary" issue in 1910, those words appeared on its cover with an hourglass.[3] The midcentury years saw a succession of similar products from a broad range of publications: *Life* published a tenth-anniversary issue in 1946; *Esquire* published a twenty-fifth-anniversary issue in 1958; the *New Republic* published a fiftieth-anniversary issue in 1964. As with television specials, however, magazine anniversary issues proliferated close to the end of the twentieth century, as reminiscence became pervasive across media.

Anniversaries are reassuring, writes Susan Davis: "They assert the sense of time as passing and human life as ephemeral, but make a counter assertion: human institutions within the flow of time are permanent."[4] They are occasions to remind us—journalists and audiences alike—that we are part of something, in terms of place and time, greater than ourselves; they also are occasions to assess our cultural progress. Michael Kammen argues: "Any evaluation of the relative roles of memory and amnesia in American culture must ultimately acknowledge that we increasingly tend to measure how we are doing (in terms of collective knowledge) by how well we commemorate anniversaries."[5] They are among what Eviatar Zerubavel calls "manifestations of mnemonic synchronization," memory occasions when the past is jointly remembered by people who have been formed into a group by the event itself.[6] Even when it occurs in print and not face-to-face, such an event is a ritual celebration of those who willingly observe it, serving to strengthen their identity and values through remembrance. For a magazine's anniversary of its own founding, the community is its audience as well as its staff—although the event of the anniversary allows this group also to speak on behalf of society.

This chapter considers how thirty American magazines have celebrated their own anniversaries in ways that have allowed them to define national memory. It surveys national consumer magazines (excluding trade, regional, and specialist magazines,[7] which are not available to the entire public) that have chronicled various aspects of American life for as little as five years[8] or for longer than a century. Although several of the older magazines published earlier anniversary editions—and in some cases, more than one anniversary issue of a given magazine is discussed here—most of the issues examined are recent ones, providing evidence of how common this sort of journalism has become.[9]

In *Harper's*, the oldest magazine in this study,[10] editor Lewis Lapham summed up the techniques by which the reviewing process is accomplished: "The editorial pages run to nearly twice the normal number; the copy has been set in somewhat showier forms of the customary typefaces; and the authors assembled under the anniversary rubrics count among their company some of the most prominent figures to be found anywhere. . . . among the issue's several added attractions the reader will find not only a collection of dispatches from the year 1850 . . . but also . . . projections of the future."[11] The editor imagined the issue as a conversation among writers who together created a story spanning a century and a half: "The magazine owes its longevity to their collective sense of an historical narrative as closely bound to time future as to time past, the successive generations appearing on different stages but in the same repertory company, all of them caught up in the making of maps or metaphors with which to find the spirit of an age that they could recognize as their own."[12]

Such grand language was not limited to a literary magazine celebrating its sesquicentennial in the year 2000; it has characterized magazine anniversary issues of all types and all ages, from *Rolling Stone* to *Good Housekeeping*, from *Outside* to *Gourmet*, from *Glamour* to *Sports Illustrated*, from *House & Garden* to *Fast Company*. All of these magazines used similar language, article types, structures, and themes to tell more than just individual institutional stories. Despite their very different content and audiences, and despite the difference in their ages (and therefore the amount of time each one reviewed), these publications reveal striking similarities in how the past is presented in popular journalism. Based on these examples, this chapter identifies and discusses four ways in which anniversary media conflate their own past with the American past.

In her magazine's twentieth-century review issue, *Columbia Journalism Review* publisher Joan Konner claimed: "Journalism not only wrote the first draft of history, it played an ever larger role in defining history. . . . the words and images by which we came to know [events] are branded into our collective memories as the moments that defined our lives and times."[13] What Konner did not explicitly say was that such memories were made through the reuse of journalistic work of the past, a recycling process that has become part of the function of journalism itself. When an anniversary issue reprints the magazine's own content—the first editorial consistency in this kind of journalism—that content serves as historical "evidence" of the American past (and of the magazine's own importance in defining and explaining that past). Yet this earlier material is not merely revisited in documentary fashion; it is recombined in new ways to create a broader and grander narrative.

Most of the issues in this study reprinted previous covers, with the century-old *National Geographic* providing a twelve-page foldout section containing 360 of them (in thumbnail size) and with *Gourmet* and TV *Guide* reprinting their editors' favorite cover from each of their, respectively, sixty and forty-five years. A special issue published during the year-long celebration of *Sports Illustrated*'s fiftieth anniversary reprinted all of its 2,548 covers, noting who had appeared most often (among individuals, Michael Jordan; among teams, the New York Yankees).[14] The younger *People Weekly*, *Teen People*, *Fast Company*, *Out*, and *Vibe* also have reprinted all of their covers, while *Entertainment Weekly* listed all of its cover celebrities in order of how often they had appeared.[15] *Sports Illustrated* recreated its first cover by using the same baseball-action photograph on its fortieth anniversary cover.

These images provided textual and visual references that served as contrasts to the present, illustrating changes in American life. In *Good Housekeeping*, for instance, old covers with similar themes were inset into modern-day service features on subjects such as cooking, home decorating, sewing, and beauty. The same issue contained a feature titled "Pages from Our Past," which showed readers "how we used to be" by reprinting pages of articles and advertisements from the first five decades of the twentieth century (including the opening spread of the magazine's special section in its 1935 fiftieth-anniversary issue). On its fifth anniversary, ESPN *The Magazine* used dozens of the biweekly magazine's covers in a section that included "The Big Stories," offering "a look back at the plot lines that mattered most over the past five years—and how we covered them."[16]

More than half of the magazines in this study explained previous eras by reprinting or excerpting their own articles from those eras. Several presented the "best" of their past content as a way of defining the magazine: *Gourmet* chose not only recipes but also the editors' favorite food-related essays and fiction for each of its six decades; *Reader's Digest* filled its regular humor departments with favorite items from past years;[17] and throughout a previous anniversary year, *Sports Illustrated* reprinted "40 classic *Sports Illustrated* stories to be presented during 1994 as a special bonus to our readers in celebration of *SI*'s 40th anniversary."[18] For its thirtieth anniversary year, *Ms.* published a series of issues reprinting the best of its fiction, poetry, articles, and essays.[19]

In its fiftieth-anniversary issue, *Esquire* doubled the act of looking back through time by reprinting essays by distinguished writers about particular decades or phenomena of American life—articles that had themselves been reminiscent reflections in previous issues. For instance, it "remembered" the 1930s with pieces by historian Arthur Schlesinger Jr. and novelist John Steinbeck that first had been published in, respectively, the magazine's April 1957 and June 1960 issues. The *New Yorker* and *Life* drew on the authority of famous writers who had been published in those magazines over the years, presenting their work in sidebars titled "Takes" and "Voices from *Life*."

The latter magazine explained to its readers: "To pick up any copy of *Life* is to savor a bit of the world's history. In this issue we have tried to sample that history. . . . We have excerpted portions of memorable texts and presented here and there throughout the issue short pieces just as they originally appeared."[20] This recycling of material seems to turn an anniversary issue into a scrapbook in which the past is simply "recalled." It also redirects the focus from the magazine's history to history itself. In two anniversary issues occurring close to the turn of the century (its seventy-fifth in 1998 and its eightieth in 2003), *Time* presented its own content as documentation of the twentieth century, even though the magazine had not begun publishing until 1923. *Good Housekeeping* did the same—despite the fact that its centennial occurred fifteen years be-

fore the end of the century—by celebrating "100 Women of the Century." *Time*'s eightieth-anniversary issue extended its historical authority beyond America, naming "80 Days That Changed the World."[21]

Rolling Stone announced its twenty-fifth anniversary as a milestone in the history of rock: "Over the years, the *Rolling Stone* interviews have become . . . the most authoritative nonmusical communication between a performer and his audience. . . . *Rolling Stone*'s mission, from the outset, was to compile enough interviews with musicians—both seminal and contemporary—to create the primary oral record and historical archive of this art. The collection of excerpts presented here . . . is a small sample of a large historical treasure."[22]

In the text accompanying its pullout pages of reprinted covers, *National Geographic*'s editor explained that "these covers mark a century of holding up to the world our uniquely objective publishing mirror."[23] Yet what these magazines offered was a new picture, in which particular pieces of the past were resurrected and presented in a particular order and context—an example of Raymond Williams's definition of culture "as a continual selection and re-selection of ancestors."[24] This selective, narrative process was accomplished in many of the magazines by the organization of past material into themes that summed up aspects of American life. "These pictures of the champions and the villains, the news and the trends come straight from the pages of *Life*,"[25] that magazine explained as it used seven categories (with titles such as "Big Events," "Bad News," and "Heroes") to describe the news and popular culture of each of its fifty years of publication, arranging these lists into an evolutionary timeline.

Time and *Newsweek* have labeled slices of time in similar trajectories in their various anniversary issues, their grandest such productions being *Time*'s seventy-fifth in 1998 and *Newsweek*'s fiftieth in 1983.[26] The latter defined past eras in terms of Depression, war, prosperity, and disillusionment (with the editors unsure how to label the post-Vietnam period). *Time* divided its longer past into periods called "Exuberance" (1923–29), "Despair" (1929–39), "War" (1939–48), "Affluence" (1948–60), "Revolution" (1960–73), "Limits" (1973–80), "Comeback" (1980–89), and "Transformation" (1989–98). Such presentation corresponds with the way these same magazines characterize decades, as discussed in chapter 1, explaining them through "patterns of inversion, complementarity or negation" and creating "narrative linkages" in order to tell a larger story that is cohesive.[27]

In its fortieth-, forty-fifth-, and fiftieth-anniversary issues, *TV Guide* revisited the past decade by decade.[28] So did *Gourmet* and *Esquire*, with the latter titling its special issue "How We Lived, 1933–1983: An Extraordinary Chronicle of American Life" (figure 7.1). This "chronicle" opened with an essay on "Life in the Last Fifty Years" that was not a summary of *Esquire*'s past but rather a survey of American technological, political, and social change; it ended with a quotation from President John F. Kennedy, affirming his "unshakable faith in the future."[29] At just age ten, *Entertainment Weekly* "look[ed] back" at how the 1990s had "changed the way we talk, watch, listen and think"; it also included a humorous back page of illustrations showing covers the magazine might have run had it existed in previous decades.[30] *TV Guide* chose the "best" recordings and shows by genre, earnestly explaining its criteria ("We weighed such factors as the influence and impact of the series, both on the medium of television and on American culture; the show's quality; and whether it has held up over the years").[31]

Other magazines linked their own existence to historical and cultural currents. *Sports Illustrated* noted, "Sometime in the second half of this century, sports became an axis on which the world turns."[32] On its tenth anniversary, *Vibe* placed itself within a much longer historical trajectory—"African-American music is like a great river. . . . The past is really the foundation for the future"—while making a case that it, too, was a product of its time: "Urban culture has grown tremendously in the past 10 years, affecting the very warp and woof of our lives. Icons of hip hop and R&B have struggled with scandal and tragedy. Cataclysmic changes in geopolitics and historic shifts in domestic policy took place. A vision of conspicuous consumption arose, then was tempered by more sober realities. Yet hip hop kept growing. . . . across the VX Time Line, we recognize key artists, albums, songs, films, current events, sports highlights, books, slang, and styles that punctuated and symbolized these larger movements."[33]

The politically liberal *Utne Reader* called itself "a cultural artifact, the inevitable consequence of strange forces that were swirling around this country at the time of its founding in February 1984. Given what was going on when the magazine was started, *Utne Reader* seems fated to have happened—it was simply an idea that fit the times."[34] *Gourmet* offered a similar explanation: "Contrary to later opinion, January of 1941 —the tail end of the Great Depression, the eve of America's entry into World War II—was a fine moment to launch a magazine that celebrated civilized and even luxurious dining. Hardship (and later the war) fostered a taste for images of a happier past and perhaps a happier future.

FIGURE 7.1
Esquire *cover, June 1983*
(Courtesy of Esquire).

. . . The time was ripe for what *Gourmet* represented."[35] In its forty-fifth-anniversary issue, *GQ* noted that presidents John F. Kennedy and Bill Clinton both had appeared on its cover and declared: "Whereas the magazine once simply covered the nation's culture, now it has become a part of the culture itself. We often hear a man described as looking like he belongs on the cover of *GQ*."[36]

House & Garden—which claimed that "design is social history, telling us who we are and where we've been"[37]—made one of the heaviest historical gestures, linking the year 2001 with both World War II and the Civil War. On the final page of its centennial issue, it reprinted the magazine's February 1944 cover, containing a quote from Abraham Lincoln ("I like to see a man proud of the place in which he lives. I like to see a man live so that his place will be proud of him"), with this explanation: "No article accompanied this remarkable cover by Irving Penn: the editors of *House & Garden* simply found in Abraham Lincoln's straightforward statement an 'ideal slogan'—and we can proudly stand by it now."[38]

Such content was part of the magazines' implication that these were not merely regular installments to be discarded, but definitive documents that would serve as records of the readers' past and as treasured keepsakes. This second aspect of anniversary journalism is accomplished structurally through editorial themes and visually through consistent design choices.

Black Enterprise and *Time* announced their themed sections inside colored banners that ran across the tops of pages; in *Time*'s case, that color was its signature cover-border red, uniting not only the various eras with each other, but also the anniversary issue with all *Time* issues. *Newsweek*'s fiftieth-anniversary issue was actually golden, the color of the cover and of the borders around every page inside. Though it was the magazine's 100th anniversary, *Good Housekeeping* also used a gold cover; *Esquire*'s fiftieth anniversary cover was silver; and the background cover of *National Geographic*'s centennial issue was that magazine's border-signature yellow, behind the coverline "100 Years: Reporting on 'the world and all that is in it'" (figure 7.2).[39] Elsewhere in the magazine, "the yellow border" was used as a rectangular icon at the tops of pages, the opening page of every article was framed by yellow, and one feature, in which covers were reprinted, was titled "Within the Yellow Border."[40]

The sole coverline of *Harper's*—"Celebrating 150 Years of Literature, 1850–2000"—was backed by royal blue over photos of Mark Twain and Tom Wolfe (to represent the opposite ends of its literary timeline), with a gatefold "second cover" folding out to reveal the names of distin-

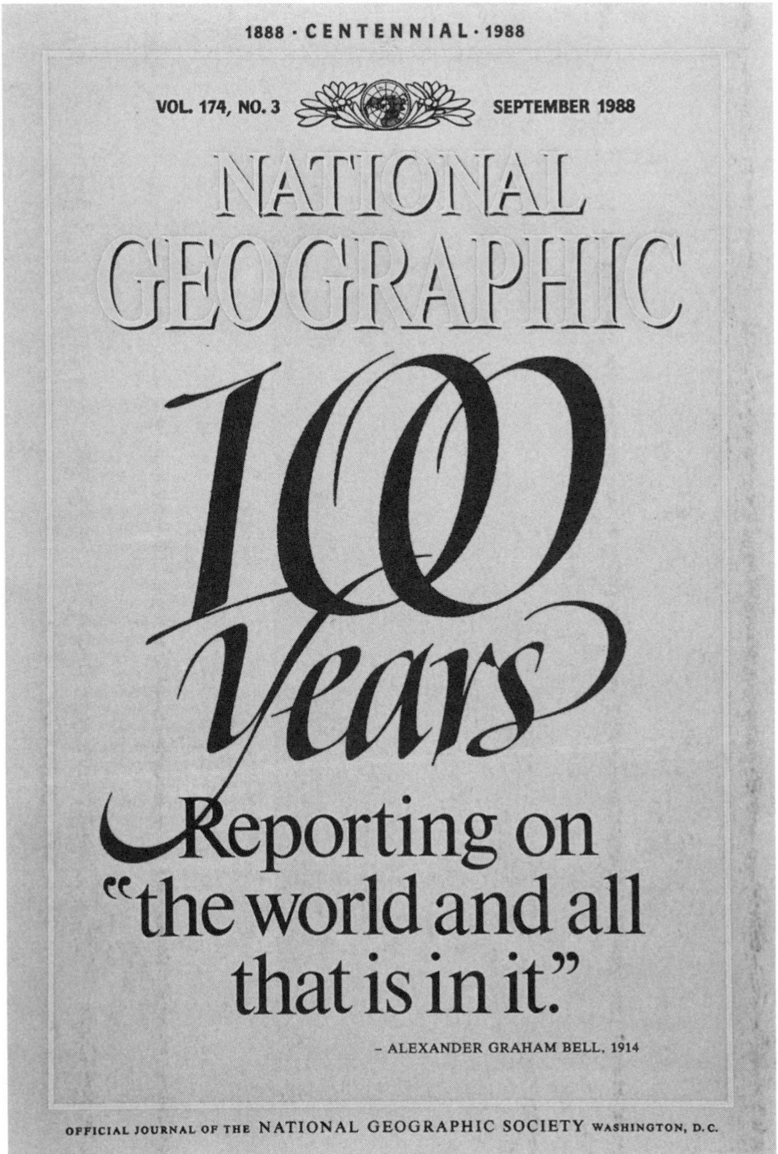

1888 · CENTENNIAL · 1988

VOL. 174, NO. 3   SEPTEMBER 1988

NATIONAL
GEOGRAPHIC

100
Years

Reporting on
"the world and all
that is in it."

– ALEXANDER GRAHAM BELL, 1914

OFFICIAL JOURNAL OF THE NATIONAL GEOGRAPHIC SOCIETY WASHINGTON, D.C.

FIGURE 7.2
National Geographic *cover, September 1988*
(Courtesy of the National Geographic Society).

guished contributors to the special issue. *House & Garden* used a cele-bratory background of multicolored balloons behind its large number "100" on its centennial anniversary cover. On *Jane*'s fifth-anniversary issue, the cover celebrity dangled a necklace from her hand that said, in gold letters, "Happy Birthday Jane," while two celebrities on the cover of *Out* magazine wore T-shirts with the numbers "1" and "0" under the sky-line, "10 Gloriously Gay Years."[41] And on the cover of the *New Yorker* was the image of "Eustace Tilley," the puffed-chested, high-hatted, society snob peering through his monocle who was drawn for the magazine's first cover in 1925 and has resurfaced in slightly altered illustrated forms every year since.[42] (Indeed, the cover of this seventy-fifth-anniversary issue contained no text at all, merely the Tilley figure, with a dog's face, a presumption that readers would understand the reference and simply *know* that this was a special issue.)[43]

Other consistent cover devices were the founding and current dates, the labels "Special Anniversary Issue" or "Collector's Edition," and a large use of the anniversary-year number. Such numbers often appeared over images that signaled the essence of the magazine's editorial mis-sion: for instance, a large number "25" appeared over the unidentified faces of women, representing feminism as a social and political force, on the cover of *Ms.* (which also used a large "30" on its anniversary series five years later); *Entertainment Weekly* surrounded its "10" with the faces of celebrities; *Time* framed its "75" with thumbnail-sized images of its own covers featuring newsmakers; and *Life*'s large "50" appeared over a montage of iconic twentieth-century photographs, from the Statue of Liberty and the moon landing to Shirley Temple and the Beatles. The plain, silver back cover of *Esquire* bore its fiftieth-anniversary logo and the magazine's ongoing tagline, "Man at His Best," with a statement de-claring that "*Esquire*'s original spirit thrives because its original vision remains intact. What it sought when it came into being half a century ago it seeks today: in a word, quality."[44] For its tenth anniversary, *Vibe* published ten different covers (over the same editorial content), one of which is shown in figure 7.3.[45]

If such cues did not make it clear that these magazines were meant to be saved, their sheer size did. The anniversary issues of *National Geo-graphic*, *Good Housekeeping*, *Life*, *Esquire*, and *GQ* each weighed in at more than 400 pages; the *New Yorker*, *House & Garden*, and *Vibe* each topped 300 pages. *Rolling Stone*, *Ms.*, and *People Weekly* (in its twenty-fifth year) published multiple anniversary issues. The number of pages devoted to anniversary issues is proof that these special issues are profit-

FIGURE 7.3
Vibe *cover, September 2003*
(*Courtesy of* Vibe).

able ventures: *Life*'s fiftieth-anniversary issue set a record for the magazine in advertising sales, with 199 of its 422 pages containing ads.[46]

Some of the magazines repackaged their anniversary material for presentation beyond the magazine itself. During their centennial years, both *National Geographic* and *House & Garden* mounted photography exhibitions, the former at the Corcoran Galley of Art in Washington, D.C., and the latter (whose show was titled "The Well-Lived Life: 100 Years of *House & Garden*") in New York and Los Angeles.[47] On its forty-fifth anniversary, *TV Guide* displayed its 2,340 past covers in a New York department store's window (claiming, "It's an incredible visual history of the past 45 years of pop culture") and staged "a serious retrospective on the cultural resonance of the *TV Guide* cover" at the Museum of Television & Radio in New York.[48]

Magazines also published anniversary books with different content than that of their anniversary issues. *Outside* issued a collection of the magazine's best photography, as did *Vibe*.[49] *Gourmet* anthologized favorite articles from past issues in a volume similar to *Sports Illustrated*'s *Fifty Years of Great Writing*.[50] *Esquire* profiled *The 50 Who Made the Difference: A Celebration of Fifty American Originals*, describing its subjects as "men and women who charted the course of American life over the last half-century."[51]

Over the years, *Time* and *Life* republished several of their various anniversary issues as books, as have some of the other magazines, and their milestones have been the subject of television specials.[52] For the book form of its 150th-anniversary issue, *Harper's* took on a different title, *An American Album*, and, with a new foreword by historian Arthur Schlesinger Jr., even weightier historical nature; an advertisement explained that the volume was meant to be "a window on life in this country and an essential heirloom addition to any library." *Harper's* also announced a web site containing the complete archives of the magazine's contents, a chance to "search and browse through 150 years of American culture. . . . It's a trip through America you won't want to miss."[53] The "heirloom" status of the sesquicentennial issue was underscored by its inclusion of facsimiles of congratulatory letters from New York City mayor Rudolph Giuliani and President Bill Clinton, with the latter writing:

> When its first issue appeared in June of 1850, *Harper's* was embraced by a young America—a restless, energetic, optimistic nation, still living in a predominantly rural society and years away from the hor-

rors of the Civil War and the upheaval of the Industrial Revolution. In the ensuing decades, our country experienced great challenges and changes—some tragic, some confounding, many exhilarating—and *Harper's* illuminated those years with invaluable information, perspective, insight, and analysis.

Now, at the beginning of a new millennium, we are still seeking to achieve American ideals and to make their meaning clear not only at home, but also around the world. I am confident that, in this new age, *Harper's Magazine* will continue to capture the American quest.[54]

Presidential proclamations appeared only in *Harper's* and *Good Housekeeping* (which ran a letter from President Ronald Reagan in its 1985 centennial issue), but each of the anniversary issues contained a message from the editor, publisher, or company president, often in personal language. In the 120th-anniversary issue of *McCall's*, its editor wrote: "We hope you enjoy this special issue (and save it as a keepsake for your grandchildren)."[55] Jane Pratt's editor's letter in *Jane's* tenth-anniversary issue traced where former staffers had gone, as if they were old high school classmates.[56] In the magazine's fiftieth-anniversary issue, *Life's* editors wrote: "Many of you can recollect the moment of discovering a special picture—when a teacher pinned *Life's* pages on a bulletin board; while sharing a copy in an Army barracks; during a quiet time at home. Several of *Life's* photographs have become a part of the national memory, and we hope that some of your own fondly remembered images appear here."[57]

The editors of *Reader's Digest* and the *Utne Reader*—which, though politically very different, are the same editorial concept—thanked their readers in similar ways. The former noted that founder DeWitt Wallace "never saw readers as some vast mass, but as distinct individuals with whom he wished to build a strong bond. That's why the apostrophe is before the 's' in our name"; founder Eric Utne wrote, "We'd like to thank you, our reader (the most important part of our name). . . . We've come to think of you as family."[58] Prefacing its "choices for TV's all-time best," *TV Guide* admitted, "We wouldn't be here at all if not for our readers. . . . Thanks—*you're* the Best."[59] *People Weekly's* president wrote in the magazine's thirtieth-anniversary issue that its success, "its special attainment, its predominant place in the fabric of American culture, lies in the intimate conversation that it has each week with you—our devoted readers. . . . I know I speak for everyone here at the magazine when I say thank you to all of you."[60]

Ms., Good Housekeeping, and *Reader's Digest* solicited letters on how the magazine had changed readers' lives and then printed them in their anniversary editions. *Gourmet, Vibe,* and *Time* reprinted reader letters that had run in the magazines in earlier decades, using them to sum up important events and phenomena of the past. The latter two magazines published lists of their best- and worst-selling issues; *Time* also reported on the cover stories that had drawn the most reader mail. *Esquire*'s seventieth-anniversary issue profiled "Our Longest Subscriber," an eighty-three-year-old who looked back on his own life as representative of the *Esquire* style and of American history itself.[61]

Including the readers—by addressing them directly, describing their lives, anticipating their opinions, and including their voices in the content—was one way the magazines personalized the past, the third characteristic of the anniversary issues. They also defined and celebrated their own identities in terms of representative individuals. *Life* closed its fiftieth-anniversary issue with a photograph of George Story, whose photo as a squalling newborn had opened its first issue in 1936, leaning over a cake adorned by flaming candles and the icing inscription "Happy 50th Birthday."[62]

In sidebars titled "Dramatis Personae" scattered throughout its twentieth-anniversary issue, *Outside* profiled activists and athletes of the past; five years later it published an "anniversary issue bonus map" that was "a worldwide guide to the greatest outdoor achievement of the past 25 years."[63] *Sports Illustrated*'s main essay in its fortieth-anniversary issue was a set of profiles of four individuals, each representing "an essential aspect of sports in America."[64] *TV Guide* profiled "45 People Who Made a Difference: Our salute to the legendary personalities, on-camera and off, who made television television."[65] *Black Enterprise* revisited businesspeople it had profiled in its thirty years and showcased "The 10 Most Important Black Business Luminaries"—chosen by readers—whose stories went well beyond the magazine's history (including, for instance, Booker T. Washington and Marcus Garvey).[66]

GQ's forty-fifth-anniversary issue included a photo-essay titled "Icons," whose blurb explained: "In every decade, there is one man who captures the era—who comes into his own and, in so doing, shapes the standards and sensibilities of the times." (The icons the magazine "saluted" included Paul Newman for the 1950s, Warren Beatty for the 1960s, Bruce Springsteen for the 1970s, Harrison Ford for the 1980s, and Michael Jordan for the 1990s.)[67] Similarly, the special section of *Rolling Stone*'s thirty-fifth-anniversary issue was a series of profiles with this explanation: "Instantly recognizable, venerated and inimitable, here are some of the icons that have transformed our world."[68] Ten years earlier, the magazine had taken a somewhat different approach, reviewing its greatest articles by asking the writers of those stories to create new pieces recalling what *their* lives had been like at the time (period photographs of the writers accompanied these essays) and recounting the reporting of the original work. The result was a collection its editor called "true tales of journalism—how it really happens, out on the road."[69]

In its twenty-fifth and thirtieth anniversaries, *People Weekly*, not surprisingly, reviewed the past through famous people. Yet so did *Ms.*, *Good Housekeeping*, and *McCall's*, explaining women's history by printing profiles of or quotations from accomplished American women. The latter magazine printed "a salute to women we've deemed rule breakers, influential role models who owe their success to not necessarily conforming to comfortable stereotypes" (these included First Ladies Eleanor Roosevelt and Hillary Clinton and actresses Whoopi Goldberg and Roseanne Barr).[70] The first two magazines also represented ordinary women. *Good Housekeeping* published a photo-essay titled "A Century of Great American Faces," showing ordinary women in various symbolic life situations (in wedding gowns, at work, with children, etc.), while an article in *Ms.* captured "the voices of our century" (despite the fact that it was only the magazine's twenty-fifth anniversary), featuring "women of all ages, from all walks of life . . . [who] offer vivid testimony of how our lives have, and have not, changed."[71] Another women's magazine took a similar approach, in language typical of the conversational nature of this type of journalism: "In honor of *Glamour*'s 60th anniversary," its editors wrote, "we asked 60-plus women to give you their inspiring, life-altering advice on love, looks, money, men, even mental health. You name it, they've seen it. We dare you not to listen."[72]

Indeed, it was ordinary people who most powerfully embodied the American past in anniversary issues. *Life* revisited individuals whose stories originally had been told in the magazine as emblematic of human nature, as suggested by the titles (of both the original and follow-up articles): "Country Doctor," "Steelworker," "Wounded Soldier," "Career Girl," "Nurse Midwife," "80-Hour-Week Housewife," "Adopted Boy," "Dropout Wife," "Runaway Kids."[73] The same issue included a photo-essay titled "American Anthem: A Recollection of the Way We Were," including present-day photographs inset into larger, nostalgic photos from "a bygone era" of "hometowns." The latter images showed a little boy joyfully running out of a rural New England schoolhouse on a winter afternoon, a Depression-era Iowa farm family eating dinner, a Saturday night on the main street of a 1940s Indiana small town, women on the World War II homefront hanging laundry, and two images from the 1950s, a mother reading to her children from the Bible and a teenagers' dance party.[74]

While small-town life has long been at the heart of *Life* magazine's nostalgic vision (even in regular issues),[75] the anniversary issue that most dramatically used the symbolic inhabitants of a prototypical American town was *Newsweek*. The cover blurb of its fiftieth-anniversary issue (figure 7.4)—set against the gold backdrop and underneath the title "The American Dream"—presented the theme: "For fifty years *Newsweek* has covered the people who make news. Our anniversary issue celebrates the men and women who live the news, the unsung people who make our country. This extraordinary saga of five heartland families is richer and more compelling than fiction. It is the true story of America."[76] Those families lived in Springfield, Ohio, and represented a range of identities and experiences: a prominent family descended from a nineteenth-century industrialist; an Italian immigrant family; an African American family who had come north out of slavery; a white working-class family; and a farm family. In a letter opening the issue, the editors wrote that Springfield "has been a town of tinkerers and inventors, of farmers and their ties to the land, of immigrants and black Americans with their visions of a better life, of entrepreneurs and executives and union men. . . . It is its own place, different from every other. But at another level it is every American town, and the people who come to life in this narrative are connected by circumstance and character to all of us. Their joys and pains, their fears and victories are ours."[77]

By explaining the historical climates of previous eras through the tensions and triumphs of family life, and by weaving together the individual stories into a larger narrative about America, this issue spoke for "us." Its opening article—titled "Our Town," borrowed from Thornton Wilder's play about small-town life—explained, of all of the families: "Their hometown is one of those American cities that grew almost at random from the wilderness, thriving because its people didn't know when they were licked. It was built on a dream of progress and the faith that inventiveness and industry were bound to succeed. . . . the dream and the faith still endure."[78] This idealistic vision was as forward-looking as it was reminiscent. Fittingly, the *Newsweek* special

FIGURE 7.4
Newsweek *cover, Spring 1983*
(© 1983 Newsweek, Inc. All rights reserved.
Reprinted by permission).

issue ended by introducing a sixth family of Cambodian refugees newly arrived in Springfield.

The other magazines also used their understanding of the past as a way of—and their anniversaries as an occasion for—imagining and assessing the future, the fourth common aspect of these issues. *Reader's Digest* "asked some prominent Americans to think about our country and its future" as a way of marking the magazine's seventy-fifth anniversary.[79] The editor of *National Geographic* wrote that "we're looking ahead to the next 100 years," noting that other issues published during the centennial year would "deal with the life-and-death environmental and population problems that will affect all of us in the century ahead, and introduce people who are doing something about them."[80]

As the last letter suggests, personalization was the editorial lens through which editors looked forward as well as backward. The twenty-fifth-anniversary issue of *Ms.* contained an essay in which founding editor Gloria Steinem listed the issues that would be important to women over the next twenty-five years and concluded with an article profiling "21 of the most accomplished, promising young feminists age 30 and under . . . women who will remain leaders in troublemaking and risk-taking and changing our world in the twenty-first century."[81] In its 100th-anniversary issue, *Good Housekeeping* profiled "100 Young Women of Promise" who "will change our world in the years to come," just as *Glamour* saluted rising stars in "Maverick Mamas for the Millennium" in its sixtieth-anniversary issue and *Outside* ran a piece on "young go-getters who'll soon be making headlines."[82]

Teen People did much the same in its fifth-anniversary issue, which recapped the progress of "past winners of our annual '20 Teens Who Will Change the World' awards" and summarized the results of a survey titled "What Will Your Future Look Like?" in which 13,000 teens provided "a vivid snapshot of your generation's vision for the future."[83] In addition to telling readers "What You'll Need to Know in Twenty Years That You Don't Know Now," *Discover* named "20 Young Scientists to Watch in the Next Twenty Years."[84] *Black Enterprise* profiled "30 for the Next 30," people it identified as "the movers, shakers, and decision makers poised to dominate the pages of *Black Enterprise* in the decades to come," and "Generation XCeptional," who were "30-and-under overachievers" providing "their take on the world they are poised to inherit."[85]

The idea of a future based on the past was the theme of *Black Enterprise's* entire anniversary issue, and the magazine presented its articles in three sections representing the past, present, and future of black American business. Its publisher's letter explained that the special issue "honors where we've been, and celebrates where we are. But the lasting message of this issue is our rededication and passionate commitment to where we're going—toward the creation of the better world to which you and your children are heir."[86] Such language makes *Black Enterprise* an example of the special importance of historical knowledge and continuity (and a broad, political definition of "family") in African American media memory, as discussed in chapter 4. Yet this same language appeared in scientific and business magazines' anniversary issues. *Discover's* editor's letter promised "to boldly look ahead and prepare you for what lies ahead during the next 20 years," while *Fast Company's* editors reaffirmed the magazine's original mission statement, declaring, "We will continue traveling into the future with you, making sense of this epic journey, charting the changes as they come."[87]

Time also characterized history as a trajectory in which the magazine played a pivotal role. In its seventy-fifth-anniversary issue, published in 1998, its managing editor noted that founder Henry Luce had wanted the magazine to celebrate independence, freedom, and opportunity, and that these themes would take the country—not just the magazine, but America—into the future. "As the American Century draws to an end, these values are now ascendant," he concluded. "The main, albeit unfinished, story line of the century is the triumph of freedom. . . . To the extent that America remains an avatar of freedom, the Global Century about to dawn will be, in Luce's terminology, another American Century."[88]

Much as the 150th-anniversary issue of *Harper's* offered "an historical narrative" reporting "the tumult of new fortunes coincident with the rise and fall of seven generations,"[89] *Time's* seventy-fifth-anniversary issue was a chronicle of American life. By reusing "documents" of the past and by packaging them as keepsakes and collector's items, anniversary issues not only invoke but reconstruct this "chronicle." By enlisting readers' participation in this process and showcasing real people, the magazines seem to speak for "everyone." And by explaining the country's history as the story of representative individuals profiled in their pages, the magazines identify American values that are presumably timeless.

Although the stories told in anniversary journalism are presented as a set of particular, historical truths, they actually constitute a narrative vision, a remarkably unified view that is prescriptive as well as descriptive, a matter of mythology as much as reporting. They are a convergence of the universal and the specific, illustrating film scholar Will Wright's contention that, even though "the structure of myth is assumed to be universal," it is in fact "embodied in a symbolic content that is socially specific. This content presents characters and events, telling a story that society's members understand and enjoy. Both consciously and unconsciously the myth relates to the individual's experience as a social and historical being. . . . myths organize and model experience."[90] We recognize mythic media narratives because we have heard them before—and yet (especially as they are conveyed in one magazine with a particular theme and a specialized audience) somehow they seem to apply uniquely to "us" in the here and now. In this vision, our present circumstances are the culmination of our convictions and hard work throughout the past, and our future is secured by ideals articulated collectively and yet confirmed through the work and faith of typical individuals.

The story of the American past in anniversary journalism is not correct in a verifiable sense. It is ideal in a way that the past itself was not; it is cohesive and orderly and progressive in a way that the past itself was not. Yet neither is it fiction; as Barry Schwartz notes, "The materials of the 'constructed' past, after all, include facts as well as biases and interests."[91] And because this tale is remembered by audiences and journalists together in a collaborative process resulting in a seemingly documentary product, it has collective meaning that is, as an ideal, in a sense real. As publications continue to mark anniversaries, that idea is reiterated and revised in ways that further naturalize it as the memory of the audience—as not just a wistful look back on one magazine's history, but "the true story of America."

Epilogue The Present and Future of Media Memory

During the months when this book was being completed, journalistic media were full of contradictions to the seemingly cohesive stories it presents: September 11th intelligence failures were revealed; photographs surfaced showing American soldiers torturing Iraqi prisoners, while casualties rose in a controversial war; American workers continued to be laid off from their jobs; and much of the rest of the world criticized and protested U.S. foreign policy rather than admiring America as a "moral counselor" to the world. Yet American media remained full of patriotic memory and nostalgia. This brief, closing essay offers a look at how social memory continues to emerge today in not just magazines but also other kinds of media, factual and fictional, and how their texts connect with the types of memory (and amnesia) discussed in the preceding chapters.

When George W. Bush won a second term as the U.S. president in November 2004, he swept the country's "heartland," having managed to cast himself, in political advertisements and in campaign rhetoric that was covered by news media, as just an ordinary guy, a typical citizen whose character was a combination of Texas candor and down-home simplicity. At a time of political conservatism and international isolationism, his vision of the ideal American—himself as well as the people he claimed to be his supporters—was nearly identical to *Time*'s mid-1960s tribute to "Mr. and Mrs. Middle America, the ones who . . . feel most threatened by the attacks on traditional values . . . [who] sing the national anthem at football games—and mean it," who are offended by "a movement in this country to discredit our nation," and who feel that "dissent is disgusting."[1]

His victory may have benefited from media coverage of Ronald Reagan's week-long funeral in June 2004, a remarkable misremembering of the 1980s—the height of Cold War military buildup, and a time of backlash against the women's and civil rights movements—as a golden age of peace, progress, and national pride, "morning in America." As the *Wall Street Journal* noted, that story was the creation not of journalists but of the former Republican president's public relations people, who had spent years planning this ceremonial pageant they called "Operation Serenade."[2] Yet most major news media portrayed the event as a

spontaneous national tribute (coming from "the people") to a historically great leader. The *New York Times* wrote that Reagan had "Old-Time
Values" and was "imbued with a youthful optimism rooted in the traditional virtues of a bygone era."[3]

It's not hard to see how his portrayal as a cowboy hero of the American past served present-day needs in terms of several aspects of memory. Given his long life-span, his story confirmed news media summaries of the meaning of whole twentieth century while conjuring up
the nostalgia magazines' fondness for self-reliant, Depression-era perseverance and strength. Reagan was portrayed as an all-American boy,
a football player and lifeguard, from a midwestern small town who was
just like any of "us" and yet, through his sunny good nature, rose to be
the two most admired types of people in America, a movie star and then
the president; and in the end, he was struck down by a villain (Alzheimer's disease) that robbed all of us of something greater than ourselves.
Ronald Reagan was placed by news media into the common-man and
Horatio Alger molds that, for decades, they had employed after other
celebrity deaths.

The same narrative template was used to explain the passing of another celebrity who died just four days after the former president—and
whose life really had been rags-to-riches in a more convincing, though
less sunny, way. "Five decades ago, a blind orphan sat at a piano and
belted out raw yet sophisticated songs that forever changed music,"
began one magazine tribute to Ray Charles.[4] Like Reagan, Charles was
praised in journalistic coverage for his "great humility," though in this
case the eulogy came from musician James Brown, not Vice President
Dick Cheney, and it appeared in *Rolling Stone*.[5] *Time*'s article on Charles's
death opened in a familiar way: "When Ray Charles could see, he saw
nothing but trouble. As an infant, he could see, if not understand, his
father walking out on him and his teenage mother Aretha. At 6 months,
he and his mother moved from his birthplace, Albany, Ga., to Green-
ville, Fla., where all he saw was poverty, with his family being even
poorer than most, 'nothing below us 'cept the ground,' as he put it."[6]
Entertainment Weekly, noting his subsequent blindness, the death of his
mother, and his seventeen-year drug addiction, wrote, "It's a wonder
that Charles didn't, to quote one of his best-loved songs, drown in his
own tears."[7] The same magazine called him "an American Hero" and
asked, "Really, does any artist better embody the great American dream
of success against overwhelming odds than Charles?"[8]

Ray Charles provided an instructive counter-memory to the Reagan mythology that the operators of "Operation Serenade" had not anticipated and could not manage. As with other forms of counter-memory, especially when race and poverty become elements in a telling of "the American story," his death coverage challenged conventional national mythology while also building on it. His biographical details seemed to create the negative image of the all-American-boy-made-good narrative of Ronald Reagan: if Reagan's life was a pep rally, Charles's life was a blues song. Yet his too was a Horatio Alger tale, and it reiterated the greatest of all national myths: that in America any talented and determined young man can do anything he hopes to do. The appearance of Ray Charles's face on newspaper front pages alongside the Reagan funeral coverage was a reminder of this former president's record on race and poverty issues, as well as a visual contrast that highlighted how few black faces were among the Reagan mourners shown on television and in news photos. Yet his death was another occasion for journalists to hail a successful, individual man as emblematic of the country's nature and strength, to explain the country through a portrait of "an American hero."[9]

The prototypical working-class white hero remains a prominent symbol in news and entertainment media today, despite the many complications of post–September 11th New York City and America and despite the enormous messiness of the real circumstances of the war on Iraq. As they did during Vietnam, news media have continued to pay tribute to ordinary soldiers who are "fallen heroes" in this war—the CBS Evening News began a nightly feature with that very title—profiling them as everyone's son or daughter, even while they may question the war itself. Such a comparison brings up one interesting narrative shift in this story that emerged during the 2004 presidential campaign, which featured debates about the patriotism of Democratic nominee John Kerry, who was a Vietnam veteran as well as former war protester.[10] In news media as well as political rhetoric, the Vietnam experience is now incorporated into (rather than contrasted with) the story of the valor of today's typical soldier, creating an uninterrupted memory trajectory of patriotic military actions, in service of "freedom," since the "good war" of World War II.

This heroic working-class character also starred in three fictional media texts that debuted in 2004. One was a film that was released three weeks after the three-year anniversary of the September 11th attacks and was promoted as "a gripping and very human story about America's heroes."[11] *Entertainment Weekly* summarized its plot: "*Ladder 49* is an upright, noble-minded World War II–type picture in search of an upright, noble-minded war. Finding none, it settles for honoring lives similar to those of so many who died on the homeland front lines not long ago. . . . a beefed-up [Joaquin] Phoenix and a reined-in [John] Travolta balance each other believably, playing men made interesting and poignant by their averageness."[12] Another new fireman story was told on cable television: the characters of the series *Rescue Me* were New York City firemen coping with the ghosts of September 11th. Sponsored by Miller Beer, this nighttime drama was described by *Time* when it began in July 2004 as a "post-9/11 M*A*S*H" and hailed as "more real, more unsparing" than network shows.[13] Opening with an essentially military scene in which the character played by writer and star Denis Leary chewed out a group of "probies," new firemen, this drama explained away its characters' open misogyny as proof that firemen are, after all, "just human."[14]

The third recent ordinary-hero story was the patriotically nostalgic Disney film *Miracle*, a fictional treatment of the true story of the American hockey team that won the Olympic gold medal in 1980, defeating the seemingly unbeatable Russians on their way to doing so.[15] This media text was a fascinating example of Maurice Halbwachs's definition of remembrance as "a reconstruction of the past achieved with data borrowed from the present."[16] In *Miracle*, the U.S. team was made up of young men who at first didn't get along and in many ways were ordinary; the coach intentionally cut better players in the process of picking the ones that he somehow knew were, as a group, destined for greatness. They were portrayed as working class (signified by their Irish and Italian names, even though in real life most of these players were in college), and initially they were anxious, obnoxious, and contentious. But, under the leadership of an older, disciplinarian man, they became "a family" (the toughest among them actually used that word when they finally stood up to their coach) through grueling punishment that killed their individual spirits while creating group solidarity. It was when they decided to play for the coach and for their fathers, when they stopped saying, "I play for Boston University" and started saying "I play for America," that they began winning.

What was particularly interesting about *Miracle* was its timing. This is the sort of event that usually is revisited through anniversary journalism (as, for instance, Woodstock was celebrated on its thirtieth anniversary in 1999). Instead, it was released twenty-four years after the original event, at a time when America had become involved in a controversial war. The movie also was released on video in the same month as the "D-Day 60th Anniversary Commemorative Edition" of *Saving Private Ryan*, which itself was timed to coincide with the D-Day anniversary and the World War II Memorial Dedication.[17] In this media climate, the 1980 Olympic hockey players were Ernie Pyle's "good boys" resurrected sixty years later.

That correspondence somewhat changed their meaning in the twentieth-century story as it had been told in century-summary journalism several years earlier. In the previous narrative, the 1980 "Miracle on Ice" was not a military echo of the ordinary heroes of World War II (who actually did not become the focus of nostalgia until then-president Ronald Reagan directed ceremonial attention to D-Day on its fortieth anniversary in 1984). Instead, they were seen as a recovery story from the narrative of Vietnam and the counterculture, a heroic tale in which strong, patriotic, young men defeated an "Evil Empire." Of course, that narrative also was useful in 2004. One might even say that the original account of the 1980s Olympic hockey team was the blueprint for the Reagan memorial nearly a quarter century later. Together, these two stories in 2004 media brought the 1980s back into national memory and made that era seem to lay the groundwork for the current "war on terrorism."

Indeed, the 1980s — the decade that had to be forgotten in order for Baby Boomers to claim cultural and political superiority over their Generation Y children — is the latest focus of much media nostalgia. Now, its memory has been improved by Boomers (who still remain largely in charge of America's newspapers and magazines and television networks and film studios) so that the eighties are retold in a way that eases their own transition from hippies to yuppies. In retrospective media depictions of that decade, it turns out that ambition in business, when embodied in the right kind of people, is admirable after all (or once again). Witness the overwhelming popularity of Donald Trump's "reality" show *The Apprentice*, in which dressed-for-success Gen-Yers compete to become a mogul like him in the Big Apple.[18]

The 1950s, too, received some complimentary re-remembrance, or at least acknowledgment, in coverage of the death in early July 2004 of actor Marlon Brando. News media had a difficult time fitting Brando into an American narrative, despite his popularity and sex appeal in his youth and the macho toughness of the working-class men he played in films such as *On the Waterfront* and *A Streetcar Named Desire*. The problem was that he had become an overweight, cynical recluse whose career had stalled without hope of recovery. One Op-Ed piece in the *New York Times* saw him as an unflattering metaphor for America, grown bloated with his own success and willfully out of touch.[19] There was a role for him to play in generational memory, though, and it resurrected a group neglected by conventional labels, albeit the very first generation *Time* magazine had expressed concern about. It is 2004 coverage of Brando's death, *Time* invoked this cohort again, though with approving wistfulness: "If you were young and impressionable in the '50s, he was forever Our Guy—a man whose inarticulate yearnings, whose needs and rages somehow spoke for a silent generation, privately nursing our grievances at the bourgeois serenity of our elders."[20]

Sixties nostalgia remains popular in shows such as the prime-time series *American Dreams*, though its plot has moved away from the "innocence" of that decade and toward Vietnam and the civil rights movement. And there is increasing evidence that the 1970s—the "dark" period out of which Ronald Reagan's "morning" presumably dawned—may be up for a memory overhaul. Media evidence for such a transformation ranges from current teenagers' resurrection of 1970s fashions, several current cable-television shows on that decade's popular culture, and the oddly simultaneous reemergence of disco and punk music.

Because the Baby Boom is involved in all of these eras and because, finally, some members of Generation X and even Y are moving into management positions in American media, we seem on the verge of simultaneous nostalgia for the 1960s, the 70s, the 80s, and even the 90s. In order to effect this trick, mass media, and especially journalism, will have to find some way to differentiate them so that there is a narrative thread holding it all together. Yet in the meantime, the new media-memory discoveries that, for instance, the eighties were a decade of world peace or that military heroism prevailed in Vietnam will create the novelty that makes memory revision "news." These shifts will, in other words, emerge in journalism as psychographic "trends" out there in the population, even if their evidence comes from media themselves—especially as American entertainment media productions increasingly are based on "real" life.

The examples mentioned in this brief essay deserve their own further critical attention, and they are offered here anecdotally more so than analytically, as food for thought. Their variety suggests that the American magazines that are the main subject of this book are only one part of a larger trend. And yet their consistency with the magazine-specific examples offered in the preceding chapters suggests that media memory has some distinct qualities.

Perhaps the most striking commonality of all of the stories discussed in this book is their main character: the common man who is ordinary, just like any of us, and yet has heroic potential. The figure of a typical and yet ideal person in media memory is a meeting ground for the individual and the collective, especially in times of turmoil, such as World War II, the civil rights movement, and the events of September 11th. That symbolic convergence allows media texts to characterize American life (and its problems) as a shared, continuous experience, a trajectory that anchors the present in past survival and future promise. It also enables media to present the values and identities of individual citizens as the values and identities of the nation. The common-man figure further blends fame and typicality into the same concept of an American ideal: if the dead celebrity is meaningful primarily because he is, at heart, ordinary, and if the fireman-soldier is heroic primarily because he is just doing what anyone would do, then we all are implicated in "the human condition."

Put to use in specific cultural and political circumstances, this common man does tend to function conservatively, as a wishful vision that looks backward instead of forward. Nearly all of the retrospective journalism discussed in this book expresses nostalgia for a prototypical American, stronger and wiser than those of us who live in the present day, who represents a better future—even if he never really existed in the past. That he should be such an appealing and recurring media character surely says something about American political life as well as American media imagery today.

The figure of the common American as a central memory device further connects media production with the work—or, at any rate, some of the expressed goals—of social historians and public historians. For comparison, consider Tamara Hareven's discussion of the late-twentieth-century change in the nature of genealogical research: "Whereas, in the past, formal family histories were limited primarily to the upper classes, the uniqueness of our time lies in the democratization of the process and in the inclusion of large segments of the population in the search. . . . the current populist mood encourages the search for one's origin, regardless of the social status of one's ancestry. The discovery of ancestors who were mere commoners, poor immigrants, or slaves is now considered as legitimate as linkage to nobility and great heroes."[21]

Paradoxically, therefore, media attention to a single, typical character who unifies the past also is a nod to the diversity and individuality of audience members: if everyone is (ostensibly) represented by the symbolic common man, then media seem to be telling a diverse story as well as a uniform one. Media memory negotiates the inherent American tension between the individual and society and between plurality and unity by conveying the idea that, when we look back over the past, we discover that we are all really a part of the same story—and yet also that it is a story that couldn't be told without all of us.

A "bottom up" version of social history underlies magazines' (and other media) retrospective characterizations of the American dream, as understood through the immigrant experience and the promise of upward economic mobility through hard work (albeit within a capitalist society, with the ideal of capitalism equated with technology and freedom). In these symbolic stories, to return to John Bodnar's terminology, official culture endures only because it takes shape around expressions of vernacular culture—the hopes and dreams and group identities of ordinary people.

If this rhetorical negotiation of national identity takes place publicly, it is, today, more likely to occur in and through mass media than in the town square, or in schools or churches, or in museums or at memorials. Some media scholars see the participation of journalists in this process as active but constructive: Donald Shriver argues that "both journalists and historians are obliged to redraft history in the interest of their mutual service to the building of democratic public culture."[22] Conversely, many historians and other academics greet this assertion with alarm, convinced that media memory is the antithesis of history, that it is a process of amnesia as much as recall and of sanitizing the past rather than revealing it.

Certainly media recall the past in particular ways. They personalize history, telling the stories of admirable and yet also representative individuals, whose actions and consequences give human form to historical events and eras. In some cases, representative people are imagined as representative groups, including generations as well as cohorts who faced common challenges such as the Great Depression, World War II, the civil rights movement, or a national disaster at the level of the September 11th attacks. In recalling individuals and groups who suffered profoundly from a shared historical experience, media memory includes—and is increasingly given to—commemoration and tribute as aspects of memory. All of these recollective media texts are structured through narrative explanation and are enhanced by visual imagery, which augments the symbolic value of representative actors and events in history.

Because of the "narrative paradigm" of the ongoing practice of journalism itself, certain details of the past are left out of media-memory texts, particularly those that represent unsolved problems that don't fold well into a story format. Over time in retrospective media productions, "a desire for coherence and continuity produces forgetting," notes Marita Sturken. This process of "forgetting" certain people and episodes of the past is not as much a matter of omission as it is a way to ensure the survival of a broader narrative "that substitutes for other memories that are too painful or disturbing to relive."[23] Beyond the evasion of narrative discrepancies or painful (socially fracturing rather than unifying) episodes in the story of the past, media memories also omit aspects of the American story that problematize the overarching nationalist themes of democracy and capitalism. This seems economically likely in that mainstream media in the United States are businesses that function within a country based on national ideals of success achieved through a certain life-style and work ethic; more broadly, it seems inevitable, in that media are part of the very culture on which they report. Media memory on the whole does indeed support the status quo. It has been the goal of this book not to challenge that assumption, but rather to explore it—to consider how it is that media, looking back through time, define "the American experience," and which aspects of that vision have the greatest staying power in cultural consciousness.

Given the decline of regional identities and civic participation in local politics, one could argue that, of all the institutions that today "tell history," media are the most dialogical, encompassing the identities and views of audiences, in part because they are so frequently engaged in conversation with those audiences, but for other reasons as well. The verbal and visual images used in retrospective or commemorative issues and programs are emotionally powerful because of their familiarity, because they already have appeared in media. The audience is therefore implicated in the recycled images, which are meaningful only if remembered and if understood as having some collective significance. In this sense, media memory is an interactive and evolving practice, rather than a static set of texts, and it is a cultural phenomenon that deserves serious consideration from historians as well as media scholars.

What most people know about the American past is encoded in stories, which today are told primarily through the media. When they are recycled and refined over time, and when they are ritualized in the inclusive language of reminiscence, such narratives themselves become part of cultural history. That popular version of history—as it is told and retold in journalism and other types of media—will increasingly shape Americans' future memory of the present, as well as of a national past.

Notes

INTRODUCTION

1 Halbwachs, *The Collective Memory*, 69.

2 Winfield and Hume, "Remembrances Past."

3 See Cohn, *Creating America*.

4 F. Davis, *Yearning for Yesterday*, 128–29.

5 Zelizer, *Remembering to Forget*; Zelizer, *Covering the Body*; Sturken, *Tangled Memories*; and Schudson, *Watergate in American Memory*.

6 For instance, Barkin, "The Journalist as Storyteller"; Berger, *Narratives in Popular Culture, Media, and Everyday Life*; Bird and Dardenne, "Myth, Chronicle, and Story"; Dahlgren, "Television News Narrative"; Darnton, "Writing News and Telling Stories"; Eason, "Telling Stories and Making Sense"; Fisher, "The Narrative Paradigm"; Lule, *Daily News, Eternal Stories*; Rock, "News as Eternal Recurrence"; R. Smith, "Mythic Elements in Television News"; and Zelizer, "Achieving Journalistic Authority through Narrative."

7 For example, Carey, *Media, Myths, and Narratives*; Edy, "Journalistic Uses of Collective Memory"; Lang and Lang, "Collective Memory and the News"; and Zelizer, "Reading the Past against the Grain."

8 For instance, Bodnar, *Remaking America*; Kammen, *Mystic Chords of Memory*; Lowenthal, *The Past Is a Foreign Country*; and White, "The Value of Narrativity."

9 For instance, Barthes, *Image—Music—Text*; Levi-Strauss, *Structural Anthropology*; Propp, *Morphology of the Folktale*; and Turner, *From Ritual to Theater*.

10 For instance, F. Davis, *Yearning for Yesterday*; Gans, *Deciding What's News*; Molotch and Lester, "News as Purposive Behavior"; and Tuchman, *Making News*.

11 Foss, *Rhetorical Criticism*, 6–8.

12 Bird and Dardenne, "Myth, Chronicle, and Story," 338–39, 346.

13 Barthes, *Image—Music—Text*; Propp, *Morphology of the Folktale*.

14 Carey, *Communication as Culture*, 43. Also see Dayan and Katz, *Media Events*.

15 Rothenbuhler, *Ritual Communication*, 25.

16 Bird, *The Audience in Everyday Life*, 30.

17 Bellah et al., *Habits of the Heart*, 153.

18 Fisher, "The Narrative Paradigm."

19 DeConcini, *Narrative Remembering*, 106.

20 Arendt, *The Human Condition*, 192.

21 White, "The Value of Narrativity," 3.

22 Manoff, "Writing the News (By Telling the 'Story')," 228–29.

23 Halbwachs, *The Collective Memory*, 72.

24 Bakhtin, *The Dialogic Imagination*, 19.

25 Bodnar, *Remaking America*, 13–14.

26 Grele, "Whose Public? Whose History?," 48.

27 Bodnar, *Remaking America*, 14, 16.

28 Britton, "Public History and Public Memory," 19.

29 I am referring here specifically to scholarship about the role of film in shaping public ideas about history; I am not including the much broader body of literature on the historical uses of film or on film history itself. Public historian Michael Frisch also has included "mass media and popular culture" along with historic sites in his explanation of how the public learns history ("What Public History Offers, and Why It Matters," 41–42).

30 See, for instance, Barta, *Screening the Past*; Carnes, *Past Imperfect*; Landy, *The Historical Film*; Rollins, *Hollywood as Historian*; Rosenstone, *Visions of the Past*; Toplin, *History by Hollywood*; and Toplin, *Reel History*. Recently, the role of film in telling history was the theme of an entire issue of the scholarly journal the *Public Historian* 25, no. 3 (Summer 2003).

31 Toplin, *Reel History*, 7.

32 Landy, introduction to *The Historical Film*, 13.

33 Kaes, "History and Film," 113.

34 Rose and Corley, "A Trademark Approach to the Past," 50. It is worth noting that this essay was about the work of Ken Burns; one can only imagine the extension of this attitude to other types of mass media.

35 Herman, "Creating the Twenty-First-Century 'Historian for All Seasons,'" 93–94.

36 The rare discussion of magazines in historical scholarship—that is, a scholarly acknowledgment of magazines as presenters of the past, rather than merely scholars' far more frequent use of magazines as sources of historical evidence from the past—is even more dismissive than historical scholarship about film. One example is Roy Rosenzweig's declaration that the popularity of *American Heritage* magazine "is a depressing commentary on the state of historical consciousness in post–World War II America" ("Marketing the Past," 47).

37 Zelizer, "Reading the Past against the Grain," 232–33.

38 Radley, "Artefacts, Memory and a Sense of the Past," 54.

39 For instance, the *Patriot-News* (Harrisburg, Pa.) marked the end of the century by reprinting its own front pages reporting on major events of the twentieth century, and it did the same in March 2004 in its twenty-fifth-anniversary coverage of the accident at the Three Mile Island nuclear power plant.

40 *Life: 40th Anniversary Reprint Edition: John F. Kennedy Memorial Edition,* Fall 2003, and *Life Commemorative: Woodstock: The 35th Anniversary: 1969 Special Edition Reprint,* n.d. 2004. Both of these appeared during a period when Time Inc. was no longer publishing regular, dated issues of *Life* but instead was issuing theme-specific retrospectives (such as these) under the *Life* logo. The new edition of the issue on the Kennedy assassination was cosponsored by the History Channel, which promoted its new program *JFK: A Presidency Revealed* on the back cover and a double-page-spread advertisement inside the magazine.

41 *Life: The American Immigrant: An Illustrated History,* foreword by Frank McCourt, September 20, 2004.

42 Robert E. Lee Tice, "Letters," *Sports Illustrated,* August 16, 1994, 4.

43 These items are promoted primarily on the company's web site, but also inside the magazines. "Own Your Moment in TIME" is the main line in an advertisement appearing in that magazine's issue for October 25, 2004 (p. 99), that urged readers to purchase *Time* covers coinciding with personal milestones such as their birthdays or wedding anniversaries. This is the language of another ad in *Time* (November 16, 2003, 15): "Now, a piece of history can be yours to enjoy in your home or office with these beautifully reproduced TIME magazine covers. Choose from among the more than 4,000 covers dating back to 1923 and let TIME, with its iconic red border, help you celebrate the most influential people and events of the past 80 years. . . . Makes the perfect gift for a special birthday or anniversary." The price is $15.95 without a frame. The company also sells prints of images by the famous photographers who worked for *Life,* starting at $99. During its fiftieth-anniversary year, *Sports Illustrated* gave readers the chance to buy one of "1,500 mint-condition inaugural issues from August 16, 1954" for "only $299" (subs.timeinc.net/SI/firstb.jhtm).

44 *TV Guide,* August 16–22, 1997; *Vibe,* September 2003.

45 The two best-selling issues were the magazine's two consecutive weeks of coverage of the death of Princess Diana; its cover story on John Lennon's murder was fourth (the resignation of President Richard Nixon was third). These rankings were calculated before the death of JFK Jr. ("75 Years of Miscellany," *Time: 75th Anniversary Issue,* March 9, 1998, 177).

46 See http://www/nytimes.com/nytstore/photos/americanexp/general/, accessed on April 14, 2003.

47 Carey, "Why and How?," 150.

48 Anderson, *Imagined Communities*.

49 "Celebrating a Half-Century of America's Life," *Life: Special Anniversary
Issue: 50 Years*, Fall 1986, 3.

50 Lance Morrow, "The *Time* of Our Lives," *Time: 75th Anniversary Issue*,
March 9, 1998, 86–87.

51 I am not counting the *Crisis*, the magazine of the National Association
for the Advancement of Colored People, which was launched in 1910, as
a consumer magazine.

52 Kammen, *Mystic Chords of Memory*, 667–68.

53 Time-Life Books, direct-mail solicitation for *Our American Century* book
series, December 1999, received in regular mail by the author.

CHAPTER 1

1 Daniel J. Boorstin, "The Luxury of Retrospect," *Life: Special Issue: The 80s*,
Fall 1989, 37.

2 Norman Pearlstine, "To Our Readers," *Time: Special Issue: Leaders & Revolutionaries of the 20th Century*, April 13, 1998, 4.

3 Walter Isaacson, "Luce's Values—Then and Now," *Time: 75th Anniversary
Issue*, March 9, 1998, 196.

4 Zerubavel, *Hidden Rhythms*, 86.

5 E. Hall, *The Silent Language*, 173; Sorokin, *Sociocultural Causality, Space,
Time*, 195.

6 Frank Rich, "Why the Best?," *New York Times Magazine*, April 18, 1999, 79.

7 Jennings and Brewster, *The Century*. Jennings incorporated parts of this
book into weekly segments on *ABC News*; it was promoted on ABC's web
site; and the network ran a twelve-part documentary based on it during
March and April 1999. The book also was the basis for a fifteen-hour series
on the History Channel, which is partly owned by ABC (which is in turn
owned by Disney). (Doreen Carvajal, "Cross-Media Deals Mean Bonanzas
for Publishers," *New York Times*, January 25, 1999, C1, C4.)

8 Newsmagazines were, of course, not the only kinds of magazines to summarize the century. Other examples ranged from *Business Week*'s "Collector's Edition" titled "100 Years of Innovation" (Summer 1999) to the
Ladies' Home Journal's special issue titled "100 Years of Great Women,"
which in 1999 was also the basis for a book, *The 100 Most Important Women
of the 20th Century*, and an ABC News television special hosted by Barbara
Walters (*A Celebration: 100 Years of Great Women*, air date April 30, 1999).

9 Walter Isaacson, "Thinkers vs. Tinkerers, and Other Debates," Editor's Page, *Time: Special Issue: Scientists & Thinkers of the 20th Century*, March 29, 1999, 6.

10 Audit Bureau of Circulations (Schaumburg, Ill.), June 30, 2000. There may, of course, have been some overlap in readership.

11 As a weekly, *Life* passed 2 million in circulation by 1940 and 8 million during the 1960s (Tebbel and Zuckerman, *The Magazine in America, 1741–1990*, 247). *Life* published as a weekly for thirty-six years, until 1972, when it suspended publication for six years (though Time Inc. published "special issues" of *Life* twice a year during that period); in 1978, it was revived as a monthly, folding again in 2000 but reemerging in 2004 as a Sunday newspaper supplement. Through the later periods, however, it has emphasized features with relatively timeless themes.

12 The very first issue of *Life*, dated November 23, 1936, was conceived as a keepsake, "an album jammed with snapshots the collector couldn't bear to throw away"; all 466,000 newsstand copies sold out on the first day (Wainwright, *The Great American Magazine*, 75; Kunhardt, *"Life": The First Fifty Years*, 6–7).

13 *U.S. News* was first a newspaper and then, by 1940, a magazine.

14 Among several sources that give fuller background on the birth and continuing genre of newsmagazines is Tebbel and Zuckerman, *The Magazine in America, 1741–1990*, and Elson, *Time Inc.*

15 Untitled advertisement, *News-week*, February 25, 1933, n.p.; "A Letter to News-Minded People" [advertisement], *News-week*, March 25, 1933, 33. The magazine's title was hyphenated during its first few years of existence.

16 *Life*, November 23, 1936, 3.

17 Quoted in Tebbel and Zuckerman, *The Magazine in America, 1741–1990*, 160.

18 Lance Morrow, "The Time of Our Lives," *Time: 75th Anniversary Issue*, 86–87. For an in-depth discussion of the founders' editorial philosophies, see Herzstein, *Henry R. Luce*.

19 "The Story of an Experiment," *Time*, March 8, 1948, 63. The former managing editor quoted here was Martin Gottfried.

20 See, for instance, Cohn, *Creating America*; Kitch, *The Girl on the Magazine Cover*; Ohmann, *Selling Culture*; and Schneirov, *The Dream of a New Social Order*.

21 Zelizer, *Remembering to Forget*.

22 It is important to note that specialized magazines continued to present diverse political views (at any rate, a wider range of diversity than the views of the newsmagazines) and different kinds of American life.

23 Morrow, "The Time of Our Lives," 86.

24 The first quotation is from *Life*'s publisher in the June 2, 1961, issue; the second, from Luce, is quoted in Kunhardt, *"Life": The First Fifty Years*, 134.

25 "Postwar Horizons," *Newsweek*, March 1, 1945, 24; *Newsweek: Special Issue: Ten Years That Shook America . . . Now, the '80s*, November 19, 1979, 85.

26 Wainwright, *The Great American Magazine*, 178.

27 *Life: Special Issue: American Life and Times, 1900–1950*, 3; "A Letter from the Publisher," *Time*, December 26, 1969, 5.

28 *Newsweek: Special Issue: Good-Bye to the 60s*, December 29, 1969, 12.

29 *Life: Special Issue: American Life and Times, 1900–1950*, 13; *Life: Special Double Issue: The '60s: Decade of Tumult and Change*, December 26, 1969, 39.

30 Isaacson, "Thinkers vs. Tinkerers, and Other Debates," 6.

31 *Life: Special Issue: The Decade in Pictures: The 70s*, December 1979, 4.

32 Even on the few occasions when *Time*'s "Man of the Year" (for which five women have been chosen) has not been a single person, the concept has been personalized: for instance, the "Man of the Year" for 1950 was "The American Fighting-Man"; in 1966, the choice was a generation, "Twenty-Five and Under"; in 1970, it was "The Middle Americans" (discussed in the main text of this chapter); and in 1975, it was "American Women." The two nonhuman exceptions were "The Computer" in 1982 and "Endangered Earth" in 1988 (*Time: Man of the Year: A Collector's Edition of the Men, Women and Ideas of the Year, 1927–1991* [New York: Time-Life Custom Publishing, 1992]).

33 Wainwright, *The Great American Magazine*, 173.

34 Carey, "Why and How?," 180.

35 Borman, "Symbolic Convergence Theory," 134–35.

36 Bird and Dardenne, "Myth, Chronicle, and Story," 345; Barkin, "The Journalist as Storyteller," 31.

37 Turner, *From Ritual to Theater*, 74, 76.

38 Steven Heller, "Photojournalism's Golden Age," *Print*, September–October 1984, 68–79, quoted in Tebbel and Zuckerman, *The Magazine in America, 1741–1990*, 230.

39 Untitled advertisement, *News-week*, February 25, 1933, n.p.

40 Henry Luce, "A Letter from the Publisher," *Time*, March 8, 1943, 9.

41 Jostein Gripsrud writes that melodrama "presents individuals representing certain moral values or forces, supposedly fighting underneath the surface of all of us, and underlying the developments of life and society at large." Like melodrama, he writes, journalism uses this type of universal characterization as a way to "teach the audience a lesson" by focusing on

"emotions, fundamental and strong: love, hate, grief, joy, lust and disgust. Such emotions are shared by all human beings, regardless of social positions, and so is 'general morality': crime does not pay, betrayal is betrayal, doing to others . . . etc." ("The Aesthetics and Politics of Melodrama," 87).

42 *Life: Special Issue: American Life and Times, 1900–1950*, 69.

43 *Time: Special Issue: Man of the Half-Century, with Half-Century Supplement*, January 2, 1950, 37.

44 Ibid., 40; *Time: Special Issue: Man of the Year: The American Fighting-Man*, January 3, 1951.

45 *Life: Special Double Issue: The '60s*, 61–65; *Newsweek: Special Issue: Good-Bye to the 60s*, 14.

46 *Life: Special Double Issue: The '60s*, 30.

47 *Newsweek: Special Issue: Ten Years That Shook America*, 98–111.

48 *Time: Special Issue: Man of the Decade*, January 1, 1990, 42–45.

49 *Time: Special Issue: Man of the Decade*, January 1, 1990; *Time: Special Issue: Man of the Half-Century*.

50 *Newsweek: Special Issue: 60 and the 60s*, December 14, 1959.

51 *Life: Special Issue: The 80s*, 52–53; *U.S. News & World Report: Special Double Issue: Outlook 1990s* [with "Epilogue: The Icons of the 1980s"], December 25, 1989-January 1, 1990, 92. This *Life* issue began by praising Ronald Reagan but quickly noted that "he was far from the only principal commanding the world's stage," that there were other "people, places and things making indelible entrances." It then switched to a movie metaphor—with a photo of Ronald and Nancy Reagan looking forward, toward a movie screen (not visible to the magazine readers) in the White House screening room—and invited readers to "freeze the frame and share our reflections on the past 10 years" (12–13).

52 *Life: Special Issue: American Life and Times, 1900–1950*, 86–87.

53 *Life: Special Issue: American Life and Times, 1900–1950*; *Newsweek: Special Issue: Ten Years That Shook America*; *Life: Special Issue: The 80s*; *U.S. News & World Report: Special Double Issue: Outlook 1990s*.

54 *Life: Special Issue: The 80s*; *Time: Special Issue: Man of the Decade* (1990); *U.S. News & World Report: Special Double Issue: Outlook 1990s*.

55 *U.S. News & World Report: Special Double Issue: Outlook 1990s*, 88.

56 *Life*, November 23, 1936; *Life: Special Anniversary Issue: 50 Years*.

57 *Life: Special Issue: American Life and Times, 1900–1950*, 13, 79; *Time: Special Issue: Man of the Half-Century*, 42.

58 Kozol, *Life's America*, 9.

59 *Life: Special Double Issue: The '60s*, 76, 10.

60 Turner, *From Ritual to Theater*, 69, 104, 11.

61 *Life: Special Double Issue: The '60s*, 10–11; *Time: Special Issue: Man and Woman of the Year: The Middle Americans*, January 5, 1970, 17; *Newsweek: Special Issue: Ten Years That Shook America*, 98–111.

62 *Life: Special Issue: The 80s*, 96–105.

63 *Time: Special Issue: Man and Woman of the Year*, 1, 10, 12, 13.

64 Ibid., 14–15.

65 *Life: Special Double Issue: The '60s*, 25.

66 I am borrowing this term from Paul Ricoeur, who used both it and "narrative time" to describe this social sense of time ("Narrative Time," 171).

67 *Life: Special Issue: American Life and Times, 1900–1950*, 5.

68 F. Davis, "Decade Labeling," 21.

69 Bennett and Edelman, "Toward a New Political Narrative," 169.

70 Larson and Bailey found a similar theme in their study of five years' worth of *ABC World News Tonight*'s "Person of the Week" segments, from 1989 to 1994 ("ABC's 'Person of the Week'").

71 *Life: Special Issue: The Decade in Pictures: The 70s*, 35–36.

72 *Life: Special Issue: The 80s; U.S. News & World Report: Special Double Issue: Outlook 1990s.*

73 *Time: Special Issue: Man of the Half-Century; Life: Special Issue: The 80s; U.S. News & World Report: Special Double Issue: Outlook 1990s.*

74 *Life: Special Issue: The Decade in Pictures: The 70s*, 9, 12.

75 *Life: Special Issue: American Life and Times, 1900–1950; Life: Special Issue: The 80s; Time: Special Issue: Man and Woman of the Year; U.S. News & World Report*, December 31, 1979, January 7, 1980.

76 *Life: Special Issue: American Life and Times, 1900–1950; Newsweek: Special Issue: Good-Bye to the 60s; Time: Special Issue: Man of the Decade* (1990).

77 Gans, *Deciding What's News*, 44, 46, 48, 50. Analyzing the "mythic formulas" that constituted the stories told in 1995 television newsmagazine shows, Krishnaiah found six similar story lines: "confronting evil and winning; transparency of the moral order; hope through science and technology; modernity as the resolution of contradictions; the infallibility of the work ethic; and the ideal of heroic individualism" ("Television News Magazines," 4–5). It is worth noting that most of these themes also can be seen in many midcentury films, such as westerns and the works of Frank Capra, even though that medium continued to offer a more varied view of American life.

78 F. Davis, "Decade Labeling," 16.

79 "Foreign News," *Time*, January 6, 1941, 23.

80 Tom Wolfe, "The Sexed-Up, Doped-Up, Hedonistic Heaven of the Boom-Boom '70s," *Life: Special Issue: The Decade in Pictures: The 70s*, 103–14.

81 *Newsweek: Special Issue: Ten Years That Shook America,* 84.

82 *Time: Special Section: Epitaph for a Decade,* January 5, 1970, 38–39.

83 Paul Fussell makes this argument about Time-Life Books as well, contending that they "can't overcome the limitations of the picture-magazine mind and format, which determines that contemporary history be diminished to moments of vivid 'human interest' and that what resists melodramatic form simply vanish" ("Time Life Goes to War!," 22).

84 *Time: Special Issue: Man of the Half-Century,* 29.

85 *Newsweek: Special Issue: Ten Years That Shook America,* 59.

86 For instance, *Life* reviewed the 1960s and previewed the 1970s in consecutive "special issues," *Newsweek* combined its 1970s review with a 1980s preview, and *U.S. News & World Report* reviewed the 1980s in the same issue it previewed the 1990s. The *Newsweek* issue included an article on the history of the "pseudoscience" of futurology, as if to justify the magazine's contribution to that field.

87 *Newsweek: Special Issue: 60 and the 60s.*

88 *Life: Special Double Issue: Into the '70s,* January 9, 1970.

89 *U.S. News & World Report: Special Double Issue: Outlook 1990s.*

90 *Time: Special Issue: Beyond the Year 2000,* Fall 1992; *Newsweek: Special Edition: The 21st Century Family,* Winter–Spring 1990, 20.

91 "The Face of the Future," *Newsweek: Special Issue: Beyond 2000: America in the 21st Century,* January 27, 1997, 58. Curiously, the same issue characterized the American life-style of the twenty-first century as "fun" (60).

92 "A New Section for the Millennium," *Newsweek: Special Issue: Beyond 2000,* 15.

93 Pearlstine, "To Our Readers," 4.

94 *U.S. News & World Report: Special Double Issue: Our Century,* August 28–September 4, 1995.

95 *U.S. News & World Report,* March 16, June 1, and August 17–24, 1998.

96 *U.S. News & World Report,* March 16, 1998, 52. Five years later, three years after the millennium, *U.S. News* continued to publish similar "special issues," including "Builders of Dreams: The Visionaries and the Creations That Changed Our World" (June 30–July 7, 2003) and "Secrets of Genius: Three Minds That Shaped the Twentieth Century" (Summer 2003). The latter special issue, which profiled Albert Einstein, Karl Marx, and Sigmund Freud, carried the skyline "Special Collector's Edition."

97 *U.S. News & World Report,* March 16, 1998, 54.

98 *U.S. News & World Report,* June 1, 1998, 64.

99 *U.S. News & World Report: Man of the Century,* December 27, 1999. The same issue also included twenty-five profiles from the "Makers" series.

100 *The "Time" 100* [special issues]: *Leaders & Revolutionaries of the 20th Century,* April 13, 1998; *Artists & Entertainers of the 20th Century,* June 8, 1998; *Builders & Titans of the 20th Century,* December 7, 1998; *Scientists & Thinkers of the 20th Century,* March 29, 1999; *Heroes & Icons of the 20th Century,* June 14, 1999; and *Person of the Century,* December 31, 1999.

101 *Newsweek Extra: 2000: A New Millennium,* Winter 1997–98.

102 David Ansen, "Our Movies, Ourselves," *Newsweek Extra: 2000: A New Millennium,* Summer 1998, 10–12.

103 "Americans Go to War," *Newsweek: Voices of the Century,* March 8, 1999, 30. The other installments in this series were titled "America Goes Hollywood," June 28, 1999, and "Sports," October 25, 1999.

104 "Americans Go to War," 32, 5.

105 *Time: Special Issue[s]: Leaders & Revolutionaries, Artists & Entertainers, Scientists & Thinkers,* and *Builders & Titans.*

106 *Time: Special Issue: Builders & Titans,* 70.

107 *Collector's Edition: The Life Millennium: The 100 Most Important Events & People of the Past 1,000 Years* (New York: Life Books, 1998). Although this is a book, its copyright page contains a magazine-style masthead.

108 *Life: Special Issue: The Millennium: 100 Events That Changed the World,* Fall 1997.

109 Lowenthal, *The Past Is a Foreign Country,* 216, 217.

110 *Time: Special Issue: Artists & Entertainers,* 204–5; *Life: Special Issue: The Millennium.*

111 Pearlstine, "To Our Readers," 4.

112 Walter Isaacson, "Our Century . . . and the Next One," *Time: Special Issue: Leaders & Revolutionaries,* 70, 73–74.

113 *Time: Special Issue: Beyond the Year 2000,* 29.

114 Isaacson, "Our Century . . . and the Next One," 75; *Life: Special Issue: The Millennium; Newsweek: Special Issue: Beyond 2000,* 52, 66. *Newsweek* also began its century-summary *New Millennium* series with the subject of inventions and discoveries—as its editors described the theme, "the technological heritage our century bequeaths to the next" (*Newsweek Extra: 2000: A New Millennium,* Winter 1997–98, 11). One of *Time*'s special issues (*Artists & Entertainers*) opened with an essay surveying twentieth-century American arts and entertainment as a story of technological advances, and closed with an essay on how technology will change entertainment in the twenty-first century.

115 Isaacson, "Our Century . . . and the Next One," 75.

116 *Time: Special Issue: The "Time" 100,* April 26, 2004.

117 *U.S. News & World Report: Special Issue: Builders of Dreams*, June 30–July 7, 2003.

CHAPTER 2

1 Hendrik Hertzberg, "Comment: Mine Shaft," *New Yorker*, August 19 and 26, 2002, 57–58. Though admiring of the miners, this article criticized the media's pursuit of the miners' story and the Bush administration's lack of commitment to mine safety.

2 Gloria Berger, "What Heroes Tell Us," *U.S. News & World Report: Special Commemorative Issue: Fallen Stars*, February 2003, 49.

3 Quoted in Silberstein, *War of Words*, 96.

4 It also reveals how strongly entrenched are the ongoing "news values" delineated thirty years ago by sociologist Herbert Gans (*Deciding What's News*) and illustrated by the summary journalism discussed in chapter 1.

5 Nancy Gibbs, "Life on the Home Front," *Time*, October 1, 2001, 14.

6 In media representation, this symbol has been almost exclusively male, and that is why the word "fireman" and not "firefighter" is used throughout this book (excluding direct quotes). One of the few notable exceptions was the cover and cover story of *Latina* magazine, featuring three Latina women, a paramedic, a Red Cross worker, and a police officer, who had been involved in the New York rescue effort (December 2001).

7 Notably *Third Watch* and *Law and Order*.

8 Rhetorician Silberstein makes the case that such productions—including a nonfiction episode of the television show *Third Watch*, on which real firemen and police officers told their stories in place of the usual fictional plot about the NYFD and NYPD—were extensions of a single narrative that began with news coverage and newsmagazine stories but moved seamlessly into other types of media. She says that together these kinds of media "served to provide a nation with a shared tale of September 11" (*War of Words*, 89).

9 Lule, *Daily News, Eternal Stories*, 15.

10 Schudson, *The Power of News*, 164.

11 Winfield, "The Press Response to the Corps of Discovery," 877.

12 Hume, "Changing Characteristics of Heroic Women," 10.

13 Drucker and Cathcart, "The Hero as a Communication Phenomenon," 2.

14 Ibid., 8.

15 Faludi, *Stiffed*, 16.

16 Linenthal, *Changing Images of the Warrior Hero in America*, 118–19.

17 Dubbert, *A Man's Place*, 235.

18 Fussell, "Images of Anonymity," 76.

19 Faludi, *Stiffed*, 16–18. The Pyle quotations are from Faludi, who cites (respectively): Ernie Pyle, *Here Is Your War* (Cleveland: World, 1943), 117; and Ernie Pyle, *Ernie's War: The Best of Ernie Pyle's World War II Dispatches*, ed. David Nichols (New York: Random House, 1986).

20 Sturken, *Tangled Memories*, 102.

21 Jeffords, *The Remasculinization of America*, 169.

22 Raphael, *The Men from the Boys*, 19–20. Other scholarly work on this "crisis" includes Kimmel and Kaufman, "Weekend Warriors," and Horrocks, *Masculinity in Crisis*.

23 Philip Caputo, "My Last War," *Esquire*, October 1991, 161–66; this quotation is from the description of the article on the issue's table-of-contents page, 7.

24 Kipnis, *Knights without Armor*; Betcher and Pollack, *In a Time of Fallen Heroes*. The most influential popular work on the 1990s "crisis of masculinity," credited with creating the men's movement, was Robert Bly's *Iron John*.

25 Kimmel and Kaufman, "Weekend Warriors," 286.

26 Beisecker, "Remembering World War II," 394.

27 Kimmel, *Manhood in America*, 6–7. He is quoting from General S. L. A. Marshall, *Men against Fire* (New York: Morrow, 1947), n.p.

28 Ernie Pyle, *Brave Men* (New York: Henry Holt, 1944), 197.

29 Schwartz, "Frame Images," 6.

30 Jerry Adler, "Hitting Home," *Newsweek*, October 1, 2001, 64–65.

31 Ibid., 67–68.

32 Myrna Blyth, "Editor's Journal: God Bless America," *Ladies' Home Journal*, December 2001, 6.

33 "Talking about the Unspeakable," *Talk*, November 2001, 104–5.

34 Adam Gopnik, "The City and the Pillars," *New Yorker*, September 24, 2001, 38.

35 Cover and Betsy Carter, "Going Forward," *My Generation*, December 2001, 4.

36 Jerry Useem, "Back to Work," *Business 2.0*, November 2001, 27.

37 "Lending a Hand," *People Weekly*, October 1, 2001, 38.

38 Kenneth Auchincloss, "Back on Our Feet," *Newsweek: Commemorative Issue*, n.d. 2001, 18.

39 Hume, "'Portraits of Grief,'" 177.

40 John Squires and James Seymore, "Local Heroes," *Entertainment Weekly*, September 24, 2001, 6–7.

41 Chris Smith, "Braving the Heat," *New York*, October 1, 2001, 24.

42 Cover and "The Fire Fighters," *Men's Journal*, November 2001, 66–90. In a somewhat stranger though equally masculine gesture, *This Old House* magazine used as its November 2001 cover a photo of eight men on the roof of a house, positioned so they appeared to be climbing it, with two of them installing an American flag, itself at an angle—a compositional re-creation of both the World Trade Center fireman-flag-raising photo and the World War II Iwo Jima soldier-flag-raising photo.

43 Keith Blanchard, "New York Forever," *Maxim*, November 2001, 20.

44 Cover, *ESPN The Magazine*, October 1, 2001.

45 Cover, *Savoy*, November 2001.

46 Tim Layden, "A Patriot's Tale," *Sports Illustrated*, September 24, 2001, 42–46.

47 Thomas George, "Top Prospects Putting the Day in Perspective," *New York Times*, April 20, 2002, D1.

48 Cover and Michael Bamberger, "True Heart," *Sports Illustrated*, December 24–31, 2001, 108.

49 "The Day That Changed America," *Newsweek*, December 31, 2001–January 7, 2002, 40–71.

50 Ibid., 71.

51 Cover and table-of-contents page, *Men's Health*, April 2002, 10.

52 ". . . And Our Flag Was Still There," *Newsweek*, September 11, 2002, 4.

53 Dennis Smith, "The Brotherhood Now," *Newsweek*, September 11, 2002, 66–70; the quotation is from p. 70.

54 "Filling His Brother's Boots," *People*, September 16, 2002, 57.

55 Jim Axelrod, reporter, *CBS Morning News*, July 30, 2002.

56 Elisabeth Bumiller, "Bush Meets Rescued Miners, Saying They Represent Spirit of America," *New York Times*, August 6, 2002, A10; *All Nine Alive: The Dramatic Mine Rescue That Inspired and Cheered a Nation, from the Pages of the "Pittsburgh Post-Gazette"* (Chicago: Triumph Books, 2002), 80.

57 Bob Meadows, "Never Give Up," *People*, August 12, 2002, 59.

58 Dirk Johnson, "Miraculously, 'All Nine Are Alive,'" *Newsweek*, August 5, 2002, 28–29.

59 Tamara Jones, "The Women Who Never Gave Up Hope," *Good Housekeeping*, December 2002, 46–53.

60 Stephen Fried, "A Miner's Miracle," *Ladies' Home Journal*, December 2002, 12–25; the quotation is from the article's blurb on p. 120.

61 Peter J. Boyer, "Rescue at Quecreek," *New Yorker*, November 18, 2002, 59.

62 Nancy Gibbs, "Seven Astronauts, One Fate," *Time*, February 10, 2003, 30–

35; "Seven Became One," *People*, February 17, 2003, 92–93; "The Magnificent Seven" and Gloria Berger, "What Heroes Tell Us," *U.S. News & World Report: Special Commemorative Issue: Fallen Stars*, February 2003, 33, 49.

63 "Farewell Columbia," *People*, February 17, 2003, 94, 100, 92.

64 Roger Simon, "To Dare Mighty Things," *U.S. News & World Report: Special Commemorative Issue: Fallen Stars*, 10.

65 Ordinary American soldiers were the cover subjects for three consecutive weeks (April 7, 14, and 21, 2003) in *Newsweek* and *U.S. News & World Report*, as well as for the April 7, 2003, issue of *Time*.

66 Kevin Peraino and Evan Thomas, "The Grunts' War," *Newsweek*, April 14, 2003, 32.

67 "The Face of Our Forces: A Demographic Profile," *Newsweek*, April 14, 2003, 33.

68 Cover, *Newsweek*, April 7, 2003; Peraino and Thomas, "The Grunts' War," 32.

69 Kurt Pitzer, "Into the Fray," *People*, April 7, 2003, 56.

70 Cover, *Newsweek*, April 14, 2003.

71 Jodie Morse, "Saving Private Jessica," *Time*, April 14, 2003, 67.

72 Patrick Rogers, "Saved from Danger," *People*, April 21, 2003, 56.

73 James Dao, "Private Lynch Comes Back Home to a Celebration Fit for a Hero," *New York Times*, July 23, 2003, A11.

74 This was the phrase used in coverage of one such visit in Pennsylvania: Yvonne M. Wenger, "Jessica Lynch Gives Comfort," *Reading Eagle*, June 16, 2004, A1–A2.

75 Kumar, "War Propaganda and the (Ab)uses of Women," 305, 310.

76 Jeff Goodell, "Who's a Hero Now?," *New York Times Magazine*, July 27, 2003, 28–35, 57–66; the quotation is from p. 31.

77 Will Langewiesche, "American Ground: Unbuilding the World Trade Center," *Atlantic Monthly*, July–August, September, and October 2002. This series was later published as a book with the same title.

78 Evan Thomas, "Groping in the Dark," *Newsweek*, September 1, 2003, 33.

79 *Parade: The Best & Worst of Everything*, December 28, 2003; *Time: Person of the Year*, December 29, 2003–January 5, 2004. Another report at the end of 2003 connecting the Iraq war with not only the events of September 11th but also the Quecreek Mine rescue appeared in the *New York Times*, which visited Shanksville, Pennsylvania, to get public reaction to the capture of Saddam Hussein. It began: "When news broadcasts showed a ragged Saddam Hussein being dragged out of a hole in Iraq, there was elation in the small mining town, where one of four airliners hijacked on Sept. 11

crashed" (Elisabeth Rosenthal, "In Small Town Scarred by 9/11, Voters Debate Bush's Iraq Strategy," *New York Times*, December 20, 2003, A11).

80 Nancy Gibbs, "Person of the Year: The American Soldier," *Time*, December 29, 2003–January 5, 2004, 32–41. Her *Time* cover stories on September 11th included: "If You Want to Humble an Empire," n.d. [special report on sale September 14,] 2001, n.p.; "Mourning in America," September 24, 2001, 14–27; "Life on the Home Front," October 1, 2001, 14–17; "What Comes Next?," October 8, 2001, 22–25; and "Person of the Year," December 31, 2001–January 7, 2002, 34–39.

81 Gibbs, "Person of the Year: The American Soldier," 34, 36. This gesture was made locally as well as nationally. For instance, the *Patriot-News* (Harrisburg, Pa.) named as its "Midstate People of the Year" the Harrisburg-based "Echo Company," Marines "representing all our local troops serving in Iraq and around the world." Although this article was published after the year-end issue of *Time* was on the newsstands, the newspaper claimed to have made its decision before knowing of *Time*'s choice. (Jim Lewis, "Midstate People of the Year: Echo Company," *Patriot-News*, December 28, 2003, A1, A16.)

82 Covers, *Time*, January 1, 1951, and December 29, 2003–January 5, 2004. The illustration opening the cover story inside was an illustration showing three soldiers, one a white male, one an African American male, and one a white female, all shown from the side as if seen marching forward. Curiously, the two men were drawn gazing steadily forward, while the woman looked directly at the viewer, with a lock of her curls escaping her helmet.

83 "Men at War," *Time*, January 1, 1951, 16–17.

84 Ibid., 23.

85 And once again this was the same *Time* staff writer: Nancy Gibbs, "The Greatest Day," *Time*, May 31, 2004, 40. *Time* also published a "magabook" special issue titled *D-Day: 24 Hours That Saved the World: 60th Anniversary Tribute* (New York: Time Inc. Specials, 2004), with an introduction by *Saving Private Ryan* star Tom Hanks.

86 Faludi, *Stiffed*, 607.

87 During his 2004 reelection campaign, President George W. Bush attempted to reinsert himself into the fireman-hero narrative, using footage of a flag-draped firefighter's body in his advertising campaign. This choice prompted immediate protests from survivors' families, as well as from the International Association of Fire Fighters, which endorsed Bush's Democratic opponent, Senator John Kerry. (Mark Memmott and Judy Keen, "Bush Accused of Exploiting 9/11," *USA Today*, March 5, 2004, 4A.)

88 Middleton and Edwards, introduction to *Collective Remembering*, 8.

89 Levi-Strauss, *Structural Anthropology*, 38–39.

CHAPTER 3

1 Greil Marcus, "Blue Hawaii," *Rolling Stone*, September 22, 1977, 56.

2 Barbara Grizzuti Harrison, "The Princess We Loved," *TV Guide*, September 20–26, 1997, 16.

3 For more on this ritual practice with regard to sites of tragedy, see Jorgensen-Earp and Lanzilotti, "Public Memory and Private Grief."

4 Anthony DeCurtis, "Johnny Cash, 1932–2003," *Rolling Stone*, October 16, 2003, 70.

5 Ellis Cose, "The Trouble with Virtual Grief," *Newsweek*, August 2, 1999, 30; Lance Morrow, "A View from the Shore," *Time*, July 26, 1999, 32.

6 Julie Suzanne Lantz, "Letters," *Time*, August 23, 1999, 13.

7 Roger Rosenblatt, "The Measure of a Life," *Time*, August 2, 1999, 56.

8 Diana is the only individual celebrity examined here whose death coverage has been the focus of a significant amount of scholarship. These are among the book-length treatments: Kear and Steinberg, *Mourning Diana*; Merck, *After Diana*; Re: Public, *Planet Diana*; and Walter, *The Mourning for Diana*. The Merck book is a collection of, as its title notes, irreverent perspectives of both academics and popular writers. Re: Public is a group of Australian scholars whose name is a reference to both "republic" and online communication. That and the other two books include scholarship from sociology, anthropology, and cultural studies and deal more with the reaction of mourners than with media coverage; because most of this work is by British or Australian scholars, a major focus is on Diana's role as a symbol of nation (the United Kingdom), though they also consider her symbolic significance in terms of gender and race. John Lennon's death was the subject of two dissertations, the first of which is now a book: Fogo, *"I Read the News Today"*; and Wolfe, "'I Read the News Today, Oh Boy.'"

9 Rushing, "Putting Away Childish Things," 164–65.

10 Those celebrities are, in order of their deaths: Marilyn Monroe (1962); Judy Garland (1969); Elvis Presley (1977); John Wayne (1979); John Lennon (1980); John Belushi (1982); Grace Kelly (Princess Grace) (1984); Lucille Ball (1989); Sammy Davis Jr. (1990); Jacqueline Onassis (1994); Kurt Cobain (1994); Jerry Garcia (1995); Princess Diana (1997); Frank Sinatra (1998); Joe DiMaggio (1999); John F. Kennedy Jr. (1999); Dale Earnhardt (2001); George Harrison (2001); Katharine Hepburn (2003); and Johnny Cash (2003). This study does not include coverage of the anniversaries of their deaths—which in a few cases, such as those of Elvis Pres-

ley and Kurt Cobain, has been considerable—but rather focuses on the death itself and the immediate "funeral."

11 Braudy, *The Frenzy of Renown*.

12 Kuhn, "Special Debate," 67–68.

13 Looking back on the history of news coverage, the *Columbia Journalism Review* dated this type of coverage to Elvis Presley's 1977 death: "The next morning, banner headlines and huge photos greeted newspaper readers around the country and the world. . . . U.S. papers that did not typically send their own reporters to big national stories sent them to Graceland. By week's end, an estimated 250 journalists were chronicling the mourning in Memphis. In the days and weeks to come, news outlets would produce special programs, editions, and supplements to feed the bottomless demand for Elvis" (Brent Cunningham, "The Elvis Obsession," November–December 2001, 83).

14 Brian Williams, "No. 3 and Me," *Time*, March 5, 2001, 67.

15 Carey, "Communication and Economics," 69; Carey, *Communication as Culture*, 43.

16 Ariès, "The Reversal of Death," 154.

17 Turner, *The Ritual Process*, 167.

18 Van Gennep, *The Rites of Passage*, 164–65.

19 Fogo, *"I Read the News Today."*

20 Mazzarella and Matyjewicz, "'The Day the Music Died'—Again."

21 Meyrowitz, "The Life and Death of Media Friends," 63.

22 Dyer, *Heavenly Bodies*, 2, 8–11.

23 Gamson, "The Assembly Line of Greatness," 12.

24 Marilyn Manson, "The Dead Rock Star," *Rolling Stone*, May 15, 2003, 77.

25 Caughey, *Imaginary Social Worlds*, 33–54.

26 Wills, *John Wayne's America*, 14.

27 Richard Stolley, "Journalistic Standards vs. Market Demand: The Future of Celebritude," presentation to the Magazine Division of the Association for Education in Journalism and Mass Communication, August 6, 2004, Toronto, Canada. These best-selling issues were cover stories on (in order of sales) Princess Diana, JFK Jr., John Lennon, and Princess Grace.

28 Rodden, *The Politics of Literary Reputation*, 400.

29 Roger Rosenblatt, "Look Homeward Angel, Once Again," *Time*, July 26, 1999, 88.

30 Dan Wakefield, "Forever Frank," *Frank Sinatra, 1915–1998, His Life in Words and Pictures, from the Editors of "TV Guide,"* n.d. 1998, 2, 5.

31 Meyrowitz, "The Life and Death of Media Friends," 76.

32 Scott Spencer, "John Lennon," *Rolling Stone*, January 22, 1980, 12–13.

33 Ezra Goodman, "Delirium over Dead Star," *Life*, September 24, 1956, 75; Hollis Alpert, "It's Dean, Dean, Dean," *Saturday Review*, October 13, 1956, 28; "Milestones," *Time*, October 10, 1955, 114; "Transition," *Newsweek*, October 10, 1955, 76.

34 For instance, Baughman, "The Transformation of *Time* Magazine."

35 Marshall, *Celebrity and Power*.

36 Gronbeck, "Character, Celebrity, and Sexual Innuendo in the Mass-Mediated Presidency."

37 Lumby, "Vanishing Point," 108.

38 Boer, "Iconic Death and the Question of Civil Religion," 86.

39 Bud Schulberg, "A Farewell to Judy," *Life*, July 11, 1969, 26.

40 Mikal Gilmore, "The Mystery Inside George," *Rolling Stone: Special Edition: George Harrison*, n.d. 2001, 20.

41 Richard Meryman, "A Last Long Talk with a Lonely Girl," *Life*, August 17, 1962, 32–33.

42 Paul Gray, "Left and Gone Away," *Time*, March 22, 1999, 93.

43 Tina Brown, "A Woman in Earnest," *New Yorker*, September 15, 1997, 59.

44 Karen Schoemer, "The Kid from Hoboken," *Newsweek*, May 25, 1998, 57–61.

45 Peggy Noonan, "America's First Lady," *Time*, May 30, 1994, 27.

46 Angie Cannon and David L. Marcus, "The Boy under the Desk," *U.S. News & World Report*, July 26, 1999, 24.

47 This similarity may be partly explained by the fact that these two stories not only ran in the same magazine, but also were by the same writer, Jay Cocks ("Last Stop on the Mystery Train," *Time*, August 29, 1977, 56; "Put Your Dreams Away," *Time*, May 25, 1998, 67).

48 Michael Elliott, "Death of a Princess," *Newsweek*, September 8, 1997, 36.

49 Paul Gray, "Farewell, Diana," *Time*, September 15, 1997, 37; "Portrait of a Lady," *Newsweek*, September 27, 1982, 38.

50 Schulberg, "A Farewell to Judy," 26.

51 "Over the Rainbow," *Newsweek*, July 7, 1969, 19.

52 Robert Sullivan, "The Last Lap," *Time*, March 5, 2001, 62, 65.

53 Wakefield, "Forever Frank," 5.

54 Rivers, *Slick Spins and Fractured Facts*, 186–87.

55 Mazzarella and Matyjewicz reported the same finding in their study of newspaper coverage of the deaths of popular musicians, noting that journalists, "while making icons of some of these men, referred to their reluctance to be designated as icons and role models" ("'The Day the Music Died'—Again," 222).

56 DeCurtis, "Johnny Cash, 1932–2003," 72.

57 Jack Kroll, "John Wayne: End as a Man," *Newsweek*, June 25, 1979, 76; Schoemer, "The Kid from Hoboken," 57; Maureen Orth, "All Shook Up," *Newsweek*, August 29, 1977, 47; Jack Kroll, "The Heartbreak Kid," *Newsweek*, August 29, 1977, 49.

58 "John Belushi, 1949–1982," *People Weekly*, March 22, 1982, 28; "What a Long, Strange Trip," *People Weekly*, August 21, 1995, 68.

59 Parke Puterbaugh, "Remembering George," *Us Weekly*, December 17, 2001, 39; Jay Cocks, "The Last Day in the Life," *Time*, December 22, 1980, 21.

60 Mikal Gilmore, "The Road from Nowhere," *Rolling Stone*, June 2, 1994, 44–46.

61 Mark Bechtel, "Crushing," *Sports Illustrated*, February 26, 2001, 38–39.

62 Marjorie Rosen, "The Entertainer," *People Weekly*, May 28, 1990, 94.

63 Lewis Lord, "The Way We Were," *U.S. News & World Report*, March 22, 1999, 19, 20.

64 Margaret Carlson, "Farewell, John," *Time*, August 2, 1999, 31; Nancy Gibbs, "The Lost Horizon," *Time*, July 26, 1999, 28.

65 "In Praise of John Lennon: The Liverpool Lad as Musician, Husband, Father and Man," *People Weekly*, December 22, 1980, 27.

66 Anthony DeCurtis, "After the Beatles," *Rolling Stone*, January 17, 2002, 38.

67 Dana Kennedy and Benjamin Svetkey, "Reality Bites," *Entertainment Weekly*, April 22, 1994, 26.

68 "What a Long, Strange Trip," 64.

69 Mikal Gilmore, "Frank Sinatra, 1915–1998: An Appreciation," *Rolling Stone*, June 25, 1998, 102.

70 Evan Thomas, "Grace & Iron," *Newsweek*, May 30, 1994, 36.

71 "End of the Rainbow," *Time*, July 4, 1969, 64–65.

72 Brad Darrach, "All the World Loved This Clown, Lucille Ball," *People Weekly*, May 8, 1989, 48–49.

73 Harrison, "The Princess We Loved," 19.

74 Table of contents, *Time*, September 8, 1997, 3.

75 Clive James, "Requiem," and Francine du Plessix Gray, "Dept. of Second Thoughts," *New Yorker*, September 15, 1997, 50, 31.

76 Darrach, "All the World Loved This Clown," 49.

77 Ty Burr, "Katharine Hepburn, 1907–2003," *Entertainment Weekly*, July 11, 2003, 24; David Ansen, "A Very Independent Woman," *Newsweek*, July 14, 2003, 59.

78 Table of contents, *Newsweek*, May 25, 1998, 3.

79 David Hajdu, "Frank Sinatra, 1915–1998," *Entertainment Weekly*, May 29, 1998, 23; table of contents, *Time*, May 25, 1998, 3.

80 Burr, "Katharine Hepburn," 24.

81 Richard Ben Cramer, "The DiMaggio Nobody Knew," *Newsweek*, March 22, 1999, 53.

82 Lord, "The Way We Were," 19.

83 Kroll, "John Wayne," 76.

84 Noonan, "America's First Lady," 24.

85 Lynn Rosselini, "From Here to Eternity," *U.S. News & World Report*, May 25, 1998, 12.

86 Richard Lacayo, "Ring-a-Ding Ding," *Time*, May 25, 1998, 72.

87 Orth, "All Shook Up," 46; Kroll, "The Heartbreak Kid," 48.

88 Cocks, "The Last Day in the Life," 22.

89 Spencer, "John Lennon," 13. In *"I Read the News Today,"* Fred Fogo writes: "Lennon's death became an important event in the social drama of contemporary life begun in the 1960s, as an articulate if somewhat self-absorbed generational segment sought to reconcile its earlier ideals with the reality of adulthood and the particular historical and material circumstances of the 1980s and 1990s. . . . [It] opened a mass-mediated space where a generational segment talked to itself about its identity and 'place' in the social order through a ritual grieving process that implicitly strove for unity and consensus" (xi).

90 Mary Weimer, "Letters," *Newsweek*, January 5, 1981, 4; "Special Report: Death of a Beatle," *Newsweek*, December 22, 1980, 36.

91 David Gates, "Requiem for the Dead," *Newsweek*, August 21, 1995, 47.

92 Garrison Keillor, "Goodbye to Our Boy," *Time*, August 2, 1999, 102.

93 Linda Regensburger, "Letters," *Newsweek*, August 23, 1999, 14.

94 Jonathan Alter, "A Death in the American Family," *Newsweek: Memorial Edition: JFK Jr.*, n.d. 1999, 10.

95 Anthony DeCurtis, "Kurt Cobain, 1967–1994," *Rolling Stone*, June 2, 1994, 30; Steve Dougherty, "No Way Out," *People Weekly*, April 25, 1994, 43.

96 Noonan, "America's First Lady," 27.

97 Sarah Crichton, "The Last of the Idols," *Newsweek*, May 30, 1994, 38.

98 Marjorie Williams, "The Princess Puzzle," *U.S. News & World Report*, September 15, 1997, 29–30.

99 Rosen, "The Entertainer," 92.

100 Bechtel, "Crushing," 44.

101 "Hour of Farewell" and "A Final Measure of Peace," *People Weekly*, June 6, 1994, 35, 57.

102 Rosen, "The Entertainer," 92.

103 Lacayo, "Ring-a-Ding Ding," 72.

104 Chet Flippo, "Funeral in Memphis," *Rolling Stone*, September 22, 1977, 38–39.

105 "Taken Too Soon," *People Weekly*, September 15, 1997, 56–63.

106 "The Most Famous Woman in the World: Top Newscasters Explore Diana's Lasting Allure," *TV Guide*, September 20–26, 1997, 22.

107 "John Belushi," 30.

108 Gates, "Requiem for the Dead," 47.

109 "Special Report: Death of a Beatle," 32.

110 Angie Cannon and Peter Cary, "The Final Hours," *U.S. News & World Report*, August 2, 1999, 17; Arthur Schlesinger Jr., "Brought Up to Be a Good Man," *Time*, July 26, 1999, 56.

111 Goody, "Death and the Interpretation of Culture," 5.

112 Gregg Easterbrook, "Who's to Blame for Diana's Death?," *U.S. News & World Report*, September 15, 1997, 23.

113 All three magazines devoted considerable attention to the notion of a "Kennedy Curse," with *U.S. News & World Report* using the phrase as its first-week coverline and suggesting that members of the family have some sort of "risk-taking gene." All three also carried timelines of Kennedy family tragedies, suggesting not only blame but reason: JFK Jr.'s story makes sense (i.e., his death is a tragedy but not a "senseless" one) as part of a larger story that is now mythological (Harold Evans, "The Risk of Being a Kennedy," *U.S. News & World Report*, August 2, 1999, 26; Brian Kelly and Kenneth T. Walsh, "The Curse," *U.S. News & World Report*, July 26, 1999, 16–21).

114 Sarah Saffian, "Untimely Deaths Haunt Extended Beatles Family," *Us Weekly*, December 17, 2001, 37.

115 Cocks, "The Last Day in the Life," 18.

116 Schulberg, "A Farewell to Judy," 27.

117 "'I love you . . . I love you . . . ,'" *Newsweek*, August 20, 1962, 30.

118 Orth, "All Shook Up," 49.

119 Richard Corliss, "The Trip Ends," *Time*, August 21, 1995, 60.

120 Lance Morrow, "A Nasty Faustian Bargain," *Time*, September 15, 1997, 77.

121 Gibbs, "The Lost Horizon," 27; Cannon and Cary, "The Final Hours," 18.

122 Cover, *U.S. News & World Report*, August 2, 1999.

123 Kroll, "John Wayne," 76.

124 Rosen, "The Entertainer," 92; "Backstage Memories," *TV Guide*, May 30–June 5, 1998, 20–22; "The Tribute," *Entertainment Weekly*, May 29, 1998, 28.

125 "Echoes of Love," *Rolling Stone*, September 22, 1977, 52.

126 "Remembering Johnny," *Rolling Stone*, October 16, 2003, 74.

127 "John Belushi: Made in America," *Rolling Stone*, April 29, 1982, 18–26, 57–61.

128 Bonnie Bess Wood, "Letters," *Time*, August 23, 1999, 13.

129 "Outpourings of Grief," *Time*, August 16, 1999, 9.

130 Daniel Collins, "Letters," *Rolling Stone*, January 22, 1981, 8; Gary N. Bourland, "Letters," *U.S. News & World Report*, June 20, 1994, 11; Mark Nigara, "Correspondence Love Letters & Advice," *Rolling Stone*, June 2, 1994, 11; Jean Maxwell, "Letters," *Time*, August 16, 1999, 11.

131 Braudy, *The Frenzy of Renown*, 588.

CHAPTER 4

1 Lerone Bennett Jr., "Why Black History Is Important to You," *Ebony*, February 1982, 66.

2 "Readings: Telling Tales," *American Legacy*, Winter 2003, 89–94.

3 Vogel, *The Black Press*, 1 (this is from his introduction to the book).

4 The term African American is used throughout this chapter except within quotes containing earlier terms such as Negro and black, and in specific references to the "black press," which still is called by that term.

5 Pride and Wilson, *A History of the Black Press*, 13.

6 The most visible recent works on the black press are the 1999 Public Broadcasting Service program *Soldiers without Swords* and Vogel's excellent edited volume of historical essays, *The Black Press*. In addition to older written histories such as Wolseley, *The Black Press, U.S.A.*, recent book-length works include Hutton, *The Early Black Press in America, 1827 to 1860*; Pride and Wilson, *A History of the Black Press*; and Tripp, *Origins of the Black Press*. Much additional historical research on the black press has appeared in scholarly journals.

7 Pride and Wilson, *A History of the Black Press*, 41; Tebbel and Zuckerman, *The Magazine in America, 1741–1990*, 41.

8 Thomas Hamilton, *Anglo-African Magazine*, January 1859, n.p., cited in Pride and Wilson, *A History of the Black Press*, 45.

9 Frank W. Miles, "Negro Magazines Come of Age," *Magazine World*, June 1, 1946, 12–13, 18–21; Pride and Wilson, *A History of the Black Press*, 249–52; Wolseley, *The Black Press, U.S.A.*, 37, 57–64, 90, 142; Digby-Junger, "*The Guardian, Crisis, Messenger*, and *Negro World*."

10 Wolseley, *The Black Press, U.S.A.*, 63–64; C. Johnson, "The Rise of the Negro Magazine," 21.

11 "*Ebony* Interview with John H. Johnson," *Ebony*, November 1985, 50; Miles, "Negro Magazines Come of Age," 13; "Negro Progress Spells Suc-

cess for *Ebony*—Mirror of the 'Bright Side,'" *Advertising Age*, October 24, 1955, 3.

12 J. Johnson, *Succeeding against the Odds*, 156–57.

13 During this time, *Ebony* also faced brief but stiff competition from a Sunday newspaper supplement titled *Tuesday*, a monthly launched in 1965 that quickly reached a readership of 4 million. The nature of its distribution, in "white" Sunday papers (which presumably had many black readers), was ironic given that it was named for the day of the week when black-press papers traditionally were published. (Wilson Sullivan, "It's Tuesday on Sundays," *Saturday Review*, November 13, 1965, 90–91; "Tuesday Every Sunday," *Newsweek*, September 20, 1965, 62.)

14 Wolseley, *The Black Press, U.S.A.*, 142.

15 Myers and Margavio, "The Black Bourgeoisie and Reference Group Change," 303, 296. These researchers found that in the 1950s, 55 percent of articles in the magazine fell into the individualism category, but by the 1970s, 75 percent of articles were in the commonality category.

16 See J. Johnson, *Succeeding against the Odds*, 286–89.

17 *Heart & Soul* initially was owned by Rodale Press and then by Black Entertainment Television before it was bought in 2000 by Vanguarde Media, which had acquired the entrepreneurial *Honey* in 1999 and launched *Savoy* in 2001. Vanguarde filed for bankruptcy in November 2003, but all three magazines were sold to separate, black-owned companies, including the publisher of *Black Enterprise* magazine. As of this writing, all three magazines were being repositioned by those companies and seemed as if they would survive. (Roland S. Martin, "Fade to Black: Vanguard Media Files for Bankruptcy," *New York Amsterdam News*, November 27, 2003, 1; John Fine, "Vanguarde Latest Recession Casualty," *Advertising Age*, December 1, 2003, 4–5; Richard Prince, "Earl Graves Wins Heart & Soul," The Robert C. Maynard Institute for Journalism Education, May 20, 2004, maynardije.org, accessed on June 5, 2004.)

18 The magazine also contained house ads offering readers the chance to "raise money" for their churches or clubs by selling subscriptions (see, for instance, *American Legacy*, Winter 1997, 53).

19 Rodney J. Reynolds, "Letter from the Publisher: Our Legacy Continues," *American Legacy*, February–March 1995, 3.

20 *American Legacy*, which initially was titled just *Legacy*, is a joint venture of the entrepreneurial RJR Communications (publisher Rodney J. Reynolds) and *American Heritage*, which is owned by Forbes. In its second year, it went from semiannual to quarterly frequency, and since its launch it has grown in size from around 50 pages to around 100 pages. It now

has a cable television affiliate, American Legacy Television, and publishes spinoff titles, including *American Legacy Woman, American Legacy, Jr.,* and *Healthcare Advantage,* a health magazine for black people. (Sandra Livingston, "Publisher Has Big-Time Backer," *Cleveland Plain Dealer,* March 14, 1995, 4C; Deirdre Carmody, "Two New Black History Magazines Seek Out a 'Niche within a Niche,'" *New York Times,* February 13, 1995, D6.)

21 This study examines more than twenty years of *Ebony* and all of the issues of *American Legacy* published from its founding through the end of 2004. There has been no scholarship on *American Legacy* and, surprisingly, none on *Ebony* with this focus: although scholars have examined *Ebony*'s content in particular eras of the past, no work has considered the magazine's own significance as a "history book," as a disseminator of information about history (and explainer of history's significance) to African Americans. As discussed later in this chapter, Maren Stange ("'Photographs Taken in Everyday Life'") has written on the cultural and political function of visual images in *Ebony.* The magazine has been studied primarily in terms of specific themes, including its discussion of interracial relations, its conveyance of health information, the varied depictions of ideal skin color over the years, and representations of age, gender, and body imagery in its advertisements. See Atwater and Anoka, "Race Relations in *Ebony*"; Bramlett-Solomon and Subramanian, "Nowhere Near Picture Perfect"; M. Johnson, Gotthoffer, and Lauffer, "The Sexual and Reproductive Health Content of African American and Latino Magazines"; Leslie, "Slow Fade to?"; McLaughlin and Goulet, "Gender Advertisements in Magazines Aimed at African Americans"; and Wormley, Heinzerling, and Gunn, "Uncovering History."

22 Historian Carter G. Woodson created Black History Week in 1926 (he chose a week in February to honor the birthdays of both Abraham Lincoln and Frederick Douglass) but the celebration was not national until half a century later, during the American Bicentennial in 1976.

23 See, for instance, *American Legacy,* Winter 1997, 25, and Summer 2000, inside-back-cover.

24 These examples have been culled from February (Black History Month) issues of *Ebony* published between 1982 and 2002. These particular ads have run more than once, some of them in both magazines.

25 See, for instance, *Ebony,* February 2000, 118–19, and *American Legacy,* Spring 1997, inside-front-cover spread, and Spring 1999, 38–39.

26 See, for instance, *American Legacy,* Spring 1996, 33. In the February–March 1995 issue of the magazine, the title was "Passing It On" (6).

27 See, for instance, *American Legacy,* Summer 2003, 16–17.

28 See, for instance, *American Legacy*, Spring 1997, 43; Summer 1997, between editorial pages 28 and 29; Summer 2000, 53; and Fall 2000, 53.

29 The issue heaviest with historical articles is the one published in February during Black History Month, which contains a special section on history. Over the twenty-year period of material included in this study, those sections grew from an average of about seven pages per issue during the 1980s to about seventeen pages per issue during the 1990s, and peaking in the February 1990 and 1991 issues, each of which contained more than twenty-five pages on history.

30 Personal correspondence (letter) to the author from Audrey Peterson, editor, *American Legacy*, October 5, 2004.

31 Rodney J. Reynolds, "Letter from the Publisher: Passing the Baton," *American Legacy*, Summer 1998, 2.

32 Lerone Bennett Jr., "Voices of the Past Speak to the Present," *Ebony*, February 1985, 27–32 (quotation is from pp. 27–28). This article, which went on to quote the words of famous figures of the past speaking on subjects such as education, work, "struggle," and "self-determination," was reprinted in subsequent February issues, including 1991 (pp. 120–26), 1994 (pp. 78–84), and 2001 (pp. 99–107).

33 Lipsitz, *Time Passages*, 110, 111.

34 Ibid., 115.

35 Describing conventional "truth" as "the sort of error that cannot be refuted because it was hardened into an unalterable form in the long baking process of history," Foucault (himself borrowing from Nietzsche) offered instead a definition of "effective history," in which "an event . . . is not a decision, a treaty, a reign, or a battle, but the reversal of a relationship of forces, the usurpation of power, the appropriation of a vocabulary turned against those who had once used it, a feeble domination that poisons itself as it grows lax, the entry of a masked 'other.'" In requiring "an affirmation of knowledge as perspective," Foucault wrote, counter-memory "reverses the surreptitious practice of historians, their pretension to examine things furthest from themselves. . . . Effective history studies what is closest." (*Language, Counter-Memory, Practice*, 144, 154, 156.)

36 Lipsitz, *Time Passages*, 213. This passage comes from a chapter in which he discusses novels by African American writers including Zora Neale Hurston and Toni Morrison ("History, Myth, and Counter-Memory: Narrative and Desire in Popular Novels," 211–32).

37 Ibid., 227.

38 Lerone Bennett Jr., "Jesse Owens' Triumph over Hitlerism," *Ebony*, December 1983, 140, 142.

39 Jamie H. Cockfield, "All Blood Runs Red," *American Legacy*, February–March, 1995, 7.

40 Personal correspondence (letter) to the author from Audrey Peterson, editor, *American Legacy*, October 5, 2004.

41 Joan W. Gandy, "Portrait of Natchez," *American Legacy*, Fall 2000, 51–58.

42 "King Speaks to the 21st Century," *Ebony*, January 1994, 53–56. This article reprinted excerpts from a column titled "Advice for Living" that King had written for *Ebony*.

43 Kevin Chappell, "Montgomery 40 Years Later," *Ebony*, February 1996, 162–68.

44 Cover, *American Legacy*, Winter 2000.

45 Many of these figures are less well known than the subjects of retrospectives on "greats." They have included, for instance, vaudeville performer Bert Williams, nineteenth-century U.S. senator Hiram Revels, Paris nightclub owner Ada Smith ("Bricktop"), Episcopal priest Pauli Murray, Olympic gold medalist Alice Coachman, education pioneer Inman Page, early-twentieth-century architect Julian Abele, West Point graduate Henry Flipper, abolitionist pamphleteer David Walker, and others.

46 These articles appeared in the February 1999 and February 2001 issues. The people shown included Mary McLeod Bethune, W. E. B. Du Bois, Dr. Martin Luther King Jr., Malcolm X, Madame C. J. Walker, Rosa Parks, and B. B. King.

47 The first article appeared in the February 1991 issue of *Ebony*; the second two appeared in the magazine's February 2002 issue.

48 Bennett, "Why Black History Is Important to You," 66.

49 Lerone Bennett Jr., "Did Lincoln Really Free the Slaves?," *Ebony*, February 2000, 54–60.

50 William Loren Katz, "Black Indians," *American Legacy*, Spring 1997, 31.

51 Lerone Bennett Jr., "The Second Time Around," *Ebony*, September 1995, 86–90, 144. This article was a slightly altered reprint of a piece that appeared under the same title in the October 1989 issue.

52 Mary Pat Kelly, "The Mason Comes Home," *American Legacy*, Spring 1996, 9–18.

53 J. Johnson, *Succeeding against the Odds*, 157.

54 Philip Burnham, "Selling Poor Steven," *American Legacy*, Summer 2003, 44–54.

55 Personal correspondence (letter) to the author from Audrey Peterson, editor, *American Legacy*, October 5, 2004.

56 Jo Cavallo, "Day of the Black Jockey," *American Legacy*, Spring 1996, 22–32; the quotation is from p. 26.

57 Frontispiece, *American Legacy*, February–March 1995, 2.

58 "Completing the Picture," *American Legacy*, Spring 2000, 61.

59 "'I Saw a Foreign Town . . . ,'" *American Legacy*, Winter 2004, 26–38; the passage cited here, which quotes the photographer, Henry Clay Anderson, is from p. 27.

60 For more on the importance of visual images in African American identity, see Willis, *Picturing Us*.

61 Zelizer, *Remembering to Forget*, 11.

62 Sturken, *Tangled Memories*, 19.

63 J. Johnson, *Succeeding against the Odds*, 156–57.

64 Stange, "'Photographs Taken in Everyday Life,'" 208. In her final phrase, she is quoting Rosalind Krauss, "Tracing Nadar," *October* 5 (Summer 1978): 5.

65 Given the importance of visual imagery to racial counter-memory and the long life of this particular editorial department, the author had hoped to be able to illustrate her points (and the material discussed here) with a number of these Memorable Photos pages. Unfortunately, *Ebony* refused the author's request for illustration permissions. The one image reproduced in this chapter, which was used as a Memorable Photo in the magazine, was created and is owned by the U.S. government.

66 All of the content of this department published from 1982 to 2003 (a total of 252 photographs) was studied for this chapter. In its first six years, the department had a multipage, multiphoto format.

67 Memorable Photos from the *Ebony* Files, *Ebony*, September 2002, 210; May 1999, 86; and July 1999, 162.

68 In the issues studied here, this department recognized 138 famous blacks, several of them more than once. Featured most often were entertainers (36 of the subjects, 26 of them musicians). Political figures, including civil rights activists, were the next most common type of person (33), and 20 of the subjects were athletes (8 of them boxers). Also represented frequently were religious leaders, authors-poets, military figures, and scientists-inventors-explorers.

69 Eleven of these were in a photo-essay published under the Memorable Photos title in the January 1986 issue, the month marking the first celebration of the national holiday in his honor ("Memorable Photos of Martin Luther King Jr.," *Ebony*, January 1986, 86–94).

70 Memorable Photos from the *Ebony* Files, *Ebony*, May 1989, 214; June 1989, 178; and December 1988, 78.

71 Memorable Photos from the *Ebony* Files, *Ebony*, September 2001, 210.

72 Only thirty-two identified whites appeared in the 252 photographs studied

for this chapter. The white person shown most frequently was President Lyndon B. Johnson, who appeared five times and was the only white to be the central figure of a photo, signing the 1964 Civil Rights Act into law (Memorable Photos from the *Ebony* Files, *Ebony*, June 1994, 130).

73 Memorable Photos from the *Ebony* Files, *Ebony*, September 1984, 98, and March 1989, 80.

74 Memorable Photos from the *Ebony* Files, *Ebony*, October 1999, 202, and November 1999, 216.

75 Goldberg, *The Power of Photography*, 135.

76 Memorable Photos from the *Ebony* Files, *Ebony*, September 1991, 130, and July 1992, 130.

77 One could explore the use of the word "negative" as meaning not only editorial condemnation, but also photographic reversal, the dark side of "the brighter side" of "pride" imagery, the making of black into white and white into black.

78 S. Hall, "Encoding, Decoding."

79 Memorable Photos from the *Ebony* Files, *Ebony*, May 1989, 214; June 199, 162; and December 1998, 146.

80 Memorable Photos from the *Ebony* Files, *Ebony*, August 1999, 124.

81 Memorable Photos from the *Ebony* Files, *Ebony*, August 2002, 122; October 1992, 142; August 2000, 162; and July 1991, 130. The Till funeral and Baptist church photos are among the few "event" photos (rather than portrait or action shot of an individual) in Memorable Photos, and they appeared in the magazine quite recently, perhaps suggesting an ongoing shift in imagery. Another recent example, published in the March 2002 issue (p. 146), depicted the 1997 Million Woman March in Washington.

82 Memorable Photos from the *Ebony* Files, *Ebony*, January 1990, 146.

83 Memorable Photos from the *Ebony* Files, *Ebony*, August 1993, 138.

84 Memorable Photos from the *Ebony* Files, *Ebony*, August 1990, 146.

85 "Ten Years That Rocked the World," *Ebony*, November 1955, 134.

86 "Flashback," *American Legacy*, Winter 2000, 84.

87 Atiya Butler, "The Art of Black Cinema," *American Legacy*, Spring 1997, 44–49.

88 The latter appeared in Memorable Photos from the *Ebony* Files in the fortieth-anniversary issue of *Ebony*, November 1985, 214, within a ten-page section of photos depicting the range of black life.

89 See, for instance, George Canto, "Touring the Black Past," *American Legacy*, February–March 1995, 26–38.

90 Susan Hensel Dixon, "New Lessons along Freedom's Trail," *American Legacy*, Summer 2003, 57–61. Despite its appearance and presentation with

a title, a byline, and an editorial-like layout, this is a "Special Advertising Section," and thus is another example of the blurring between editorial and advertising messages in the magazine.

91 Currie Ballard, "The Camera Speaks for Them," *American Legacy*, Summer 1996, 42, 44.

92 Rodney J. Reynolds, "Letter from the Publisher: Our Africa," *American Legacy*, Spring 2001, 7.

93 The "Cultural Crossroads" article on stepping, as practiced by black sororities and fraternities, contained an interesting example of counter-memory within counter-memory: "A University of Missouri alumnus adds, 'In the 1970s we modeled ourselves after the Temptations and the Dramatics. . . . To say we were stepping to relate to Mother Africa is disingenuous and inaccurate'" (Elizabeth C. Fine, "Stepping," *American Legacy*, Summer 2003, 20).

94 Curtis Ellis, "The Last of the Cane Fifers," *American Legacy*, Fall 2002, 18.

95 "Flashback: History You Can Own," *American Legacy*, Spring 2004, 104.

96 Lipsitz, *Time Passages*, 99.

97 Bennett, "Why Black History Is Important to You," 66.

CHAPTER 5

1 "The Younger Generation," *Time*, November 5, 1951, 46, 48, 51–52.

2 David Gelman, "A Much Riskier Passage," *Newsweek*, Summer–Fall 1990, 10.

3 The term "generational" memory in this chapter refers to the shared memory of an age- or era-based cohort, as explained in the following paragraphs. It is not the same concept as Tamara Hareven's use of the term, a view in which "generational memory" means a family's inherited oral narrative of its origins ("The Search for Generational Memory"). Some of Hareven's ideas are discussed in the epilogue.

4 Mannheim, "The Problem of Generations," 290.

5 Ibid., 296.

6 Schuman and Scott, "Generations and Collective Memories," 377.

7 Austin and Willard, *Generations of Youth*, 1.

8 Halbwachs, *The Collective Memory*, 67–68.

9 Strauss and Howe, *Generations*, and *The Fourth Turning*, 19.

10 Keller, "Politics and Generations in America."

11 Hollander and Germain, *Was There a Pepsi Generation?*

12 J. Smith and Clurman, *Rocking the Ages*, xiv.

13 Hebdige, "After the Masses," 232.

14 Mission Statement, *My Generation* Media Kit, sent to author (at author's

request) in spring 2001. A media kit is a packet of material sent to advertisers, describing reader demographics and psychographics and listing advertising rates.

15 Jon Fine, "AARP Puts Boomers First with New 'My Generation,'" *Advertising Age*, September 25, 2000, 15.

16 Betsy Carter [editor in chief], "Start Here: It's Our Party," *My Generation*, March–April 2001, 8.

17 Jillian S. Ambroz, "From the Reader's Modem to the Advertiser's Ear," *Folio:*, January 1, 2004, n.p.

18 *MH-18* and *Teen Movieline* had folded by the time this book was written.

19 "The Gennys," *My Generation*, March–April 2002, 19.

20 Tebbel and Zuckerman, *The Magazine in America, 1741–1990*.

21 This change in the late 1960s prompted historian James Baughman to declare that "though still the most popular newsmagazine, *Time* has lost its leading role in opinion leadership" ("The Transformation of *Time* Magazine," 125).

22 "Paid Circulation in Consumer Magazines for Six Months Ending Dec. 31, 2003," adage.com, accessed on July 23, 2004. *Time*'s paid circulation was 4,112,311; *Newsweek*'s paid circulation was 3,115,407.

23 Both *Time* and *Newsweek* give advertisers the opportunity to pinpoint specific groups of readers by buying space only in editions mailed to those particular types of readers (this is accomplished through a demographic breakdown of the mailing list and selective binding in the printing process). Both magazines offer a "Families" edition (distributed to a combination of Generation X and Baby Boomers) and an edition targeted to older people. In *Newsweek*'s case, the latter is a "Fifty-Plus Edition" (combining Boomers and Greatest Generation). Its media kit (sent to prospective advertisers) explains that—while "there are currently over 72 million American adults who are age 50 and over"—the magazine is targeting only some of them: "Reaching over 4.5 million affluent, educated Americans who lead the way in purchase behavior (from investments to travel to technology), *Newsweek* Fifty Plus is an unparalleled vehicle to target this core group of consumers." This page further describes this target group as those older people who "invest wisely . . . travel extensively . . . and live the good life." Similarly, the "*Time* Gold" edition reaches Americans with a median age of fifty-five and a median household income of $85,000. Its media kit urges advertisers to "capture this exploding baby boomer marketplace today—it's soon to be 78 million strong" (*Newsweek* and *Time* Media Kits, 2001).

24 Such a twenty-year framework is common in marketing definitions of generations. One of *Time*'s cover stories (focusing on Generation X but discussing other groups as well) drew on "the New American Dream study," which was a survey of people in their twenties, forties, and sixties (Margot Hornblower, "Great Xpectations," *Time*, June 9, 1997, 58–68). In addition to the four groups discussed here (and named by most marketers), audience researcher Ann Fishman designated a fifth group as "the silent generation"—Americans born between 1925 and 1942, who were young adults in the 1950s and who neither fought in World War II nor were involved in the social-protest movements of the 1960s ("Generational Marketing: Reaching the Hearts and Minds of Consumers," *Circulation Management* 13, no. 7 [1998]: 58–60; the quotation is from p. 58). That group was the subject of the first generational-trend story published in *Time*, cited in note 25.

25 "The Younger Generation," 46–52. The fact that this was the magazine's first "comprehensive assignment on youth" was confirmed in the publisher's letter printed the following week (James A. Linen, "A Letter from the Publisher," *Time*, November 12, 1951, 15).

26 "Man of the Year: Twenty-Five and Under," *Time*, January 6, 1967, 19.

27 Gans, *Deciding What's News*, 167–68.

28 "Hit and Myth," *Adweek*, August 8, 1994, n.p.

29 Evan Thomas, "Growing Pains at 40," *Time*, May 19, 1986, 22–23.

30 Ibid., 41.

31 Bernhard M. Auer, "A Letter from the Publisher," *Time*, January 6, 1967, 3.

32 James S. Kunen, "Strawberry Restatement," *Time*, May 19, 1986, 41.

33 Tom Mathews, "The Sixties Complex," and Mickey Kaus, "Confessions of an Ex-Radical," *Time*, May 19, 1986, 17–21, 24, 28.

34 Lance Morrow, "1968," *Time*, January 11, 1988, 16.

35 "Decade Shock," *Newsweek*, September 5, 1988, 14–16.

36 Cover and table of contents, *Newsweek*, July 3, 1989, 3.

37 "Rock and Roll Forever," *Newsweek*, July 5, 1993, 49.

38 "The New Middle Age: Oh God . . . I'm Really Turning 50!," *Newsweek*, December 7, 1992, 50.

39 Barbara Kantrowitz, "A Boomer's Guide to Happiness," *Newsweek*, April 3, 2000, 57.

40 Ibid., 60.

41 David Brooks, "Why Bobos Rule," *Time*, May 29, 2000, 38.

42 David M. Gross and Sophfronia Scott, "Proceeding with Caution," *Time*, July 16, 1990, 61.

43 Table of contents, *Time*, July 16, 1990, 2.

44 Gross and Scott, "Proceeding with Caution," 57.

45 Ibid., 58.

46 Ibid., 62.

47 Ibid., 58.

48 Jeff Giles, "Generalizations X," *Newsweek*, June 6, 1994, 63.

49 Ibid., 64.

50 "The VIX List: Very Important Xers," *Newsweek*, June 6, 1994, 70.

51 Hornblower, "Great Xpectations," 58.

52 Ibid., 60.

53 Ibid., 68.

54 Ibid.

55 Ibid.

56 Table of contents, *Newsweek*, Summer–Fall 1990, 3.

57 Ibid., 4.

58 David Gelman, "A Much Riskier Passage," *Newsweek*, Summer–Fall 1990, 10.

59 Barbara Kantrowitz and Pat Wingert, "The Truth about Tweens," *Newsweek*, October 18, 1999, 62.

60 Ibid., 64.

61 Ibid., 64–65.

62 Table of contents, *Newsweek*, May 8, 2000, 3.

63 Sharon Begley, "A World of Their Own," *Newsweek*, May 8, 2000, 56.

64 Barbara Kantrowitz and Keith Naughton, "Generation 9-11," *Newsweek*, November 12, 2001, 47–48.

65 Ibid., 48.

66 Nancy R. Gibbs, "Grays on the Go," *Time*, February 22, 1988, 66–75.

67 Jonathan Alter, "So Long, Soldier," *Newsweek*, January 11, 1993, 25.

68 Ibid.

69 Table of contents, *Newsweek*, January 11, 1993, 3.

70 Stephen E. Ambrose, "The Kids Who Changed the World," *Newsweek*, July 13, 1998, 59.

71 Tom Brokaw, "War, Remembrance and Reward," *Time*, May 29, 2000, 38.

72 Gross and Scott, "Proceeding with Caution," 57.

73 Morgan, "The Aging of the Baby Boom," 6.

74 Mannheim, "The Problem of Generations," 283.

75 Liza Featherstone, "Talkin' 'bout Their Generation," *Columbia Journalism Review*, July–August 1994, 40.

76 Lentz, *Symbols, the News Magazines, and Martin Luther King*; Kitch, "Reporting the Birth and Death of Feminism."

CHAPTER 6

1 "Premiere Collector's Edition," *Reminisce*, n.d., 2.

2 [No name given] As told to Margaret L. Tauber, "Pulling Together," *Good Old Days*, August 2001, 10.

3 They are what anthropologists call "memory objects," which are "produced retrospectively, long after the events they depict transpired" (Kirschenblatt-Gimblett, "Objects of Memory," 331).

4 Lash and Urry, *Economies of Signs and Space*, 247.

5 Home page, reminisce.com.

6 Table of contents and Keith Naughton and Bill Vlasic, "The Nostalgia Boom," *Business Week*, March 23, 1998, 2, 58–64.

7 Halbwachs, *On Collective Memory*, 48.

8 Hoskins, *Biographical Objects*, 1.

9 Kaminsky, "The Uses of Reminiscence," 156. In addition to Kaminsky and researchers cited elsewhere in this chapter's notes, other scientists who have confirmed the positive uses and results of reminiscence include Butler, "Successful Aging and the Role of the Life Review"; Haight and Bahr, "The Therapeutic Role of the Life Review in the Elderly"; McMahon and Rhudick, "Reminiscing"; and Reis-Bergan et al., "The Impact of Reminiscence on Socially Active Elderly Women's Reactions to Social Comparisons." Both of the magazines that are the primary focus of this study have been used in memory-recall programs in assisted-living facilities and nursing homes (Bettina Miller, editor, *Reminisce*, personal communication with author, August 27, 2003; Ken Tate, editor, *Good Old Days*, personal communication with author, March 31, 2004).

10 Priefer and Gambert, "Reminiscence and Life Review in the Elderly," 93; Haight and Bahr, "The Therapeutic Role of the Life Review in the Elderly," 297.

11 See, for instance, Kitch, *The Girl on the Magazine Cover*, 150, and Mendelson, "Slice-of-Life Moments as Visual 'Truth.'"

12 *Life: Elvis Remembered* (New York: Warner Books, 1995); *Life: America's Parade* (New York: Time Inc. Home Entertainment, 2001); *America in the '40s* (New York: Reader's Digest Books, 1998).

13 Steve Malanga, "How Sweet It Is on Memory Lane," *Crain's New York Business*, March 19, 1990, 1; Paul Fricht, "*Memories*: Next Major Magazine?," *Folio:*, February 1988, 62–63; Patrick Reilly, "DCI Sees No Lapse in 'Memories,'" *Advertising Age*, October 31, 1988, 31.

14 The *Reminisce* issues studied were published bimonthly from 1995 to 2000; the issues of *Good Old Days* were published monthly from 2001 to 2004.

15 Ken Tate, "Looking Back," *Good Old Days Specials*, July 2003, 6, and personal communication with author, January 19, 2004.

16 See whitebirches.com, accessed on August 27, 2003; "Reader's Digest Completes Reiman Publications Acquisition," *Magazine World*, May 20, 2002, fipp.com/910, accessed on August 26, 2003.

17 Ken Tate, "Looking Back," *Good Old Days*, August 2002, 6. *Women's Household* was one of a number of homemaking magazines published by the New England–based Tower Press, which later became the House of White Birches.

18 *Reminisce* was launched in 1991, and by 1997 it had 1.72 million subscribers, though since the late 1990s circulation has declined to a current figure of 1.1 million (Kevin P. Keef, "Between the Slick Sheets," *Once a Year*, 1997, milwaukeepressclub.org/onceayear/oay97/mags.html, accessed on August 27, 2003; Miller, personal communication with author, August 27, 2003). Even so, Reiman Publications was listed by *Folio*: magazine (the trade magazine of the magazine industry) as being among the top-forty fastest-growing publishing companies, experiencing a 33 percent growth in revenue between 1997 and 2003. In mid-2003, revenues totaled $300 million, with circulation for all of the Reiman magazines totaling approximately $16 million. (Joe Hagan, "The High-Wire Act," *Folio*:, June 11, 2001; Tony Silber, "Reiman Publications," *Folio*:, April 30, 2000, both at foliomag.com, accessed on August 27, 2003.)

19 Ads in this magazine, which are not plentiful and often are partial-page, are for products including recorded music (country, inspirational, big band), health-care products, Bibles, collectibles (model cars, dolls), needlework patterns, inspirational and large-print books, and comfortable shoes and clothing.

20 The audiotapes are advertised regularly in the magazine; for instance, see *Good Old Days*, September 2001, 21. The books are advertised on the company's web site, goodolddaysmagazine.com, accessed on August 26, 2003. Other book titles published by *Good Old Days* include *I'll Be Home for Christmas*, *We Made This Country Great*, *Mother's Favorite Verses*, *Bringing in the Sheaves*, *Good Old Days on the Farm*, *The Little Country Schoolhouse*, and *Working on the Farm*.

21 Like *Good Old Days*, *Reminisce* also publishes books based on the magazine's content. Their titles include *We Had Everything but Money*; *When the Banks Closed, We Opened Our Hearts*; *We Made Our Own Fun!*; *When Families Made Memories Together*; *We Pulled Together . . . and Won!*; *The Victory Era*; *Motorin' Along!*; *Tough Times, Strong Women*; *At Ease* (military memories); and the cookbook *Dining during the Depression*. The com-

pany also runs cooking schools affiliated with *Taste of Home*, which in recent years has become the highest-circulation (4.6 million) food magazine in the United States and has a travel subsidiary, World Wide Country Tours, which is promoted in the magazine and offers trips ranging from a Mississippi riverboat "Big Band Cruise" to an African safari. (Hagan, "The High-Wire Act"; "Travel with Us," in "Premiere Collector's Edition," 51.)

22 The other Reiman magazines are *Birds and Blooms, Backyard Living, Country, Country Woman, Country Discoveries* (a travel magazine), *Crafting Traditions, Farm & Ranch Living,* and three cooking magazines, *Taste of Home, Light & Tasty,* and *Quick Cookin'* (see reimanpub.com). The House of White Birches, which owns *Good Old Days,* publishes other magazines about needlework.

23 Veronis Suhler Stevenson [venture-capital firm], "Reader Digest to Acquire Reiman Publications," March 21, 2002, vss.com/articles/article_239.html, accessed on August 27, 2003.

24 Miller, personal communication with author, August 27, 2003.

25 "Y'all Come See Us . . . ," *Reminisce,* July–August 1999, 11.

26 "Our Visitor Center Has Become a 'Meeting Place,'" *Reminisce,* January–February 2000, 51.

27 Tate, personal communication with author, January 19, 2004.

28 Miller, personal communication with author, August 27, 2003.

29 Ibid.

30 Christina Davis, "Wanted," *Good Old Days,* December 2002, 70.

31 "Look What's Coming!," in "Premiere Collector's Edition," 24. Reader-contributors are paid small fees ($50 for a full-page article) or are sent "a Classic Red '57 Chevy car bank," a "popular keepsake car [that] identifies them as a '*Reminisce* Staffer'" ("Contributors' Guidelines" for *Reminisce,* reminisce.com/guidelines, accessed on August 27, 2003).

32 "Okay, Now It's Your Turn," in "Premiere Collector's Edition," 56.

33 See, for instance, "Look Who's Talking," *Reminisce,* January–February 1997, 59.

34 Ken Tate, "Looking Back," *Good Old Days,* February 2001, 6.

35 Tate, personal communication with author, March 31, 2004.

36 Ellwood F. Reim, "From the Mailbox," *Good Old Days,* March 2003, 8–9.

37 Miller, personal communication with author, August 27, 2003.

38 Ibid.

39 Middleton and Edwards, "Conversational Remembering," 24.

40 Laura Weddle, "The Town Gathering Place," *Good Old Days,* January 2002, 10.

41 McCracken, *Culture and Consumption*, 106.

42 Dale Hultgren, "Doggone Good Business in the '30s," *Reminisce*, March–April 2000, 17.

43 These quotations are from the Short Memories department in these issues of *Reminisce*: "Premiere Collector's Edition," 18; May–June 1997, 24; and March–April 2000, 24.

44 Norman Smith, "My Grandest Birthday Party," *Reminisce*, November–December 1998, 16.

45 Dorothy Saik, "Porch-Cleaning Ritual Wasn't Swept Away," *Reminisce*, July–August 2000, 27.

46 These quotations are from these issues of *Good Old Days* (in order): Georgia Green Fowler, "The Irony of It All," March 2001, 36; V. Frances Hill, "The Long Road Home," April 2001, 28; Don Smart, "The End of an Era," June 2001, 35; Ernest Shubird, "The Rolling Store Era," June 2001, 60; Theresa H. Morr, "'Automatic' Corn Pickers," July 2001, 13; Bernice De Boer, "Strange Funeral," August 2002, 36; Joyce Miller, "From a Silent Movie to Bank Night," August 2002, 50; and Thelma Kesterson Coffey as told to Donna McGuire Tanner, "Childhood Days," January 2003, 82.

47 Halbwachs, *On Collective Memory*, 48–49.

48 Beryl Veldine, "Yes, I'll Rock You," *Good Old Days*, May 2003, 28.

49 "Feed Sack Fashions," *Reminisce*, November–December 1996, 32–33.

50 Iris Hanson, "Threshing Day Was Long, Hard . . . and Memorable," *Reminisce*, September–October 1997, 56.

51 "They Used to Call Them *Service* Stations," *Reminisce*, November–December 2000, 23.

52 Sally Smith Lewis, "Mom Was the Friendly 'Hello Girl,'" *Reminisce*, September–October 1997, 18.

53 Miller, personal communication with author, March 15, 2004; Tate, personal communication with author, January 19, 2004.

54 Helterline and Nouri, "Aging and Gender," 32.

55 Ibid., 34; Webster and McCall, "Reminiscence Functions across Adulthood," 82.

56 Ann Casper as told to Jennie Moore, "Granny's Advice," *Good Old Days*, June 2003, 70; Eleanor P. Heath, "The Mother of Invention," *Good Old Days*, April 2001, 54; Betty Thomason, "Aunt Annie and Her Magical Sewing Machine," *Good Old Days*, June 2001, 72–73; Elyse Kaner, "Grandma's Wisdom Lives On," *Reminisce*, March–April 2000, 22; Doris McCown Capps, one of four memories in "Nicest Thing Anyone Has Done for Me," *Reminisce*, May–June 1996, 64; and Evelyn Smith, "'It's Just a Jar of Peaches,'" *Reminisce*, November–December 1999, 27.

57 Anne Pierre Spangler, "Play It Again, Mom," *Good Old Days*, March 2003, 63.

58 Virginia Lushbaugh, "'Ma' Encouraged My Days on Stage," *Reminisce*, March–April 1997, 22–23.

59 Eileen Higgins Driscoll, "Radio City Music Hall," *Good Old Days*, November 2001, 38–39.

60 Nancy Hasselberger, "When Cinderella Went to Paris," *Reminisce*, November–December 1995, 20.

61 Margaret Gunn, "A Pair of Rosies," *Good Old Days*, July 2003, 62.

62 Dorothy C. Snyder, "The Government Girls," *Good Old Days*, May 2003, 48.

63 Clancy Strock, The Old Party Line, *Reminisce*, September–October 1997, 39–40.

64 The Old Party Line is no longer a regular feature in *Reminisce*, though it was in the five years' worth of issues studied for this analysis.

65 Clancy Strock, The Old Party Line, *Reminisce*, November–December 1995, 36–37.

66 Kirschenblatt-Gimblett, "Objects of Memory," 332.

67 Miller, personal communication with author, August 27, 2003.

68 Ibid.

69 "Cookie Jars We Still Cherish," *Reminisce*, March–April 2000, 8–11.

70 "'We Wish It Was Still Around!'" *Reminisce*, May–June 1996, 41.

71 F. Davis, *Yearning for Yesterday*, 122, 131.

72 Doris M. Kneppel, "Buttons and Bows," *Good Old Days*, November 2002, 29.

73 Hoskins, *Biographical Objects*, 8, 196.

74 Belk, "Possessions and the Extended Self," 145, 160.

75 Lowenthal, *The Past Is a Foreign Country*, 8.

76 Miller, personal communication with author, August 27, 2003.

77 Middleton and Edwards, introduction to *Collective Remembering*, 9; emphasis is in the original.

78 Donna Cryer, "From the Mailbox," *Good Old Days*, October 2001, 8.

79 See, for instance, F. Davis, *Yearning for Yesterday*, and Wallace, *Mickey Mouse History and Other Essays on American Memory*.

80 I am indebted for this insight to journalism historian Janice Hume, who read and commented on an earlier version of this work.

CHAPTER 7

1 Lewis H. Lapham, "Hazards of New Fortune," *Harper's*, June 2000, 57.

2 "Out Front," *Outside*, October 1997, 45.

3 Cover, *Good Housekeeping*, October 1910.

4 Davis, "'Set Your Mood to Patriotic,'" 134.

5 Kammen, *Mystic Chords of Memory*, 667.

6 Zerubavel, "Social Memories," 294.

7 Nevertheless, trade magazines and very specialized consumer magazines have published anniversary issues with the same common characteristics that this chapter identifies. *Photographer's Forum* ("25th Anniversary Edition," Winter 2002) and *Directors & Boards* ("25th Anniversary" issue, Autumn 2001) used the same visual devices, including big numbers and the use of silver color on covers. The latter also personalized its history ("An Oral History of Corporate Governance, 1976–2001," told through stories of individuals) and combined prediction of the future with summary of the past (with section heads including "The Way It Was" and "The Shape of Things to Come"). The cover of the twentieth-anniversary issue of *Transworld Skateboarding Magazine* featured the same skater who had been on its first cover and used personalization in its article on "skaters who have been a big part of history. When you look back, these are the skaters who stood out. . . . They influenced all of us in some way or another, and many continue to kill it in their own special way even today" (Dave Swift, "Speak: Twenty Years," January 2003, 18). *PC Gamer* used a large, gold number "10" on its tenth-anniversary issue, and its special section reviewed each of its years of publication by reprinting covers and excerpting articles from that year ("Ten Years of *PC Gamer* Magazine," May 2004, 34–56). *Wine Spectator* magazine published a twenty-fifth-anniversary issue with the large number "25" in red-wine color in the middle of a clean, glossy, white cover with a wine-colored border; it also included a feature titled "A Gallery of Covers" (pp. 61–80). The *Columbia Journalism Review* published a fortieth-anniversary issue (November–December 2001) that blended its own past into the past of its topic (journalism), which itself was conflated with great events, "history" itself. Also like the others, the magazine reprinted the magazine's original mission statement, organized the story of its past by decades, and profiled one representative journalist to stand for each of the forty years.

8 Several magazines have published issues with an "anniversary" label on their first anniversary; recent examples include *CosmoGirl!* (August 2000), *Savoy* (February 2002), *My Generation* (March–April 2002), and *Rosie* (May 2002). Yet aside from the label, these issues had very little anniversary content (moreover, the latter two have since folded).

9 Conversely, in a few cases, an earlier (rather than the magazine's most recent) anniversary issue has been used.

10 Launched in 1850, *Harper's* is one of only two surviving American consumer magazines more than 150 years old. The other, *Scientific American* (launched in 1845), did not publish a 150th anniversary issue (per author's phone conversation with the magazine's research department, August 31, 2000). The *Atlantic Monthly* will be 150 in 2007.

11 Lewis H. Lapham, Editor's Letter, *Harper's*, June 2000, 5.

12 Lapham, "Hazards of New Fortune," 57.

13 Joan Konner, "Publisher's Note: 100 Years of News," *Columbia Journalism Review* (January–February 1999), 6.

14 *Sports Illustrated: Special Issue: 50th Anniversary, 1954–2004: The Covers, All 2,548*, November 10, 2003.

15 Julia Roberts was first, at thirty-nine times ("The EW Index," *Entertainment Weekly*, Spring 2000, 172).

16 "Best of 5" and "The Big Stories," *ESPN The Magazine*, March 31, 2003, 92–110.

17 These regular departments include Life in These United States, Laughter, the Best Medicine, All in a Day's Work, Campus Comedy, and Quotable Quotes.

18 Paul O'Neil, "Duel of the Four-Minute Men," *Sports Illustrated*, August 16, 1994, 30.

19 These appeared throughout 2003.

20 "Celebrating a Half Century of America's *Life*," *Life*, Fall 1986, 5.

21 "80th Anniversary Celebration: 80 Days That Changed the World," *Time*, March 31, 2003, A1–A78. This special section later was republished as a book with the same title.

22 Jann S. Wenner, "A Letter from the Editor," *Rolling Stone*, October 15, 1992, 37.

23 Wilbur E. Garrett, "Within the Yellow Border," *National Geographic*, September 1988, 270.

24 Williams, *The Long Revolution*, 53.

25 "Year by Year," *Life*, Fall 1986, 33.

26 In 2003, *Time* was eighty years old and *Newsweek* was seventy.

27 F. Davis, "Decade Labeling," 16.

28 *TV Guide*, April 17, 1993; April 4, 1998; and June 15, 2003.

29 Ronald Steel, "Prologue: Life in the Last Fifty Years," *Esquire*, June 1983, 24.

30 "Our First Decade" and "Encore," *Entertainment Weekly*, Spring 2000, 25, 176. The back page showed, for instance, Lucille Ball for the 1950s, the Monkees for the 1960s, the cast of *Welcome Back, Kotter* for the 1970s, and Judd Nelson for the 1980s.

31 "*TV Guide* Presents 40 Years of the Best," *TV Guide*, April 17–23, 1993, 5.

32 Steve Rushin, "How We Got Here," *Sports Illustrated*, August 16, 1994, 36.

33 Quincy Jones, "The Block Is Still Hot," and "VX Time Line," *Vibe*, September 2003, 64, 175.

34 "Our Story," *Utne Reader*, March–April 1994, 51. The magazine defined those "forces"—which it called "the biggest news stories of the past decade"—as including the AIDS crisis, the fall of communism, the environmental movement of the late 1980s and early 1990s, Reaganism, and globalism ("10 Events That Shook the World," 58–74).

35 Anne Mendelson, "The 40s," *Gourmet*, September 2001, 71.

36 Martin Beiser, "Here at *GQ*," *GQ*, September 2002, 131.

37 "A Century of Passions: From Our Pages," *House & Garden*, October 2001, 51.

38 *House & Garden*, October 2001, 308.

39 The quotation within the coverline—"the world and all that is in it"—was attributed (in smaller type on the cover) to Alexander Graham Bell, who was the first president of the National Geographic Society.

40 Garrett, "Within the Yellow Border."

41 *Jane*, September 2002; *Out*, June 2002.

42 "Cover Stories" [supplement], *New Yorker*, February 19 and 26, 2001, 1–32.

43 The history of Eustace Tilley, in the magazine itself and in spoofs of it, was reviewed inside the anniversary issue in an article that also explained the Weimaraner dog face as the work of photographer William Wegman (Francoise Mouly, "Portfolio: Cover Story," *New Yorker*, February 21 and 28, 2000, 79).

44 Back cover, *Esquire*, June 1983.

45 "Big Timers," *Vibe*, September 2003, 194–98.

46 "*Life* Celebrates 50 Years," *Folio:*, November 1986, 59–60.

47 Jane Livingston, "The Art of Photography at *National Geographic*," *National Geographic*, September 1988, 324; advertisement, *House & Garden*, October 2000, 189.

48 Steven Reddicliffe, "From the Editor," *TV Guide*, April 4, 1998, 6. The first quotation was said by the magazine's president and CEO, David Steward, quoted here in the editor's letter.

49 Advertisement, *Outside*, October 1997, 211; advertisement, *Vibe*, September 2003, 297.

50 Ruth Reichl, "Letter from the Editor," *Gourmet*, September 2001, 26; advertisement, *Sports Illustrated*, February 9, 2004, 28.

51 Advertisement, *Esquire*, June 1983, 51.

52 For instance, the program *20/20* on the ABC network aired a special epi-

sode titled "The Great American Magazine" in November 1986 on the occasion of *Life*'s fiftieth anniversary ("*Life* Celebrates 50 Years").

53 Advertisements, *Harper's*, June 2000, 179, 182.

54 Bill Clinton, letter, *Harper's*, June 2000, 1.

55 Sally Koslow, "From the Editor," *McCall's*, November 1996, 12.

56 Jane Pratt, "Diary: Where Are They Now?," *Jane*, September 2002, 53.

57 "Celebrating a Half Century of America's *Life*," *Life*, Fall 1986, 5.

58 "How a Little Magazine Went around the World," *Reader's Digest*, n.d. 1997, 14; Eric Utne, "Under the Volcano," *Utne Reader*, March–April 1994, 2.

59 "*TV Guide* Presents 40 Years of the Best," 5.

60 Peter Bauer, "President's Letter," *People* [by this time the magazine had dropped "*Weekly*" from its title], April 12, 2004, 12.

61 Andrew Chaikivsky, "Our Longest Subscriber (or Close to It)," *Esquire*, October 2003, 113–14.

62 "Just One More," *Life*, Fall 1986, 415. See chapter 1, note 11, on the publication history of *Life*. George Story also appeared on the back page of the magazine's sixtieth-anniversary issue published in 1996. In the spring of 2000, just after the magazine announced its most recent closing, George Story died.

63 *Outside*, October 1997 and October 2002, 38–42.

64 Mark Mulvoy, "To Our Readers," *Sports Illustrated*, August 16, 1994, 1.

65 Table of contents, *TV Guide*, April 4, 1998, 3.

66 "The 10 Most Important Black Business Luminaries," *Black Enterprise*, August 2000, 71–78.

67 "Icons," *GQ*, September 2002, 438–45.

68 "American Icons," *Rolling Stone*, May 15, 2003, 69–124; the quotation is from p. 69. These "icons" ranged from people (Elvis Presley, Bob Dylan, Bruce Springsteen) to objects ("The Backstage Pass," "The Harley-Davidson") to roles ("The Blonde Bombshell," "The Leading Man," "The Superhero," "The Dead Rock Star").

69 Jann S. Wenner, "A Letter from the Editor," *Rolling Stone*, June 11, 1992, 31.

70 Koslow, "From the Editor," 12.

71 "Generations," *Ms.*, September–October 1997, 81.

72 "60-On-Up Women Give You Their Self-Esteem Secrets," *Glamour*, March 1999, 290.

73 "Revisiting Some Special Friends," *Life*, Fall 1986, 140–62.

74 "American Anthem: A Recollection of the Way We Were," *Life*, Fall 1986, 278–95.

75 This vision has been the subject of a good deal of scholarship on *Life* maga-

zine, including two books: Kozol, *Life's America*, and Doss, *Looking at* Life *Magazine*.

76 Cover, *Newsweek*, Spring 1983.

77 William Broyles Jr., "A Celebration of America," *Newsweek*, Spring 1983, 3.

78 Wally McNamee, "Our Town," *Newsweek*, Spring 1983, 10.

79 Christopher Willcox, "Dear Friends," *Reader's Digest*, n.d. 1997, 8.

80 Garrett, "Within the Yellow Border," 270.

81 "21 for the 21st," *Ms.*, September–October 1997, 102.

82 "100 Young Women of Promise," *Good Housekeeping*, May 1985, 124; "Watchworthy Women: 60 Years Strong," *Glamour*, March 1999, 222; Wetzler, "To Do," *Outside*, October 1997, 66.

83 "Teens in Charge" and "The *Teen People* Poll: What Will Your Future Look Like?," *Teen People*, February 2003, 110–11, 122–28.

84 "20 Young Scientists to Watch in the Next Twenty Years," *Discover*, October 2000, 58–61, 68–73.

85 Sonja Brown Stokely, "30 for the Next 30," *Black Enterprise*, August 2000, 179; Robyn D. Clarke, "Generation XCeptional," *Black Enterprise*, August 2000, 193.

86 Earl G. Graves, "Publisher's Page," *Black Enterprise*, August 2000, 14.

87 "Letter from *Discover*," *Discover*, October 2000, 49; "Letter from the Editors: A Restatement of Purpose," *Fast Company*, October 2001, 20.

88 Walter Isaacson, "Luce's Values—Then and Now," *Time*, March 9, 1998, 195–96.

89 Lapham, "Hazards of New Fortune," 57.

90 Wright, *Six Guns and Society*, 11–12.

91 Schwartz, "Collective Memory and History," 491.

EPILOGUE

1 *Time: Special Issue: Man and Woman of the Year*, 1, 10, 12, 13.

2 Jacob M. Schlesinger, "Operation Serenade: Laying Groundwork for Reagan's Funeral," *Wall Street Journal*, June 10, 2004, A1. This plan was later referred to in other news media also as "Operation Sunset."

3 Marilyn Berger, "Ronald Reagan Dies at 93," *New York Times*, June 6, 2004, sec. 1, p. 1.

4 Tom Sinclair, "Ray Charles, 1930–2004," *Entertainment Weekly*, June 25–July 2, 2004, 43.

5 "Remembering Ray," *Rolling Stone*, July 8–22, 2004, 104.

6 Christopher John Farley, "The Genius of Brother Ray," *Time*, June 21, 2004, 90.

7 Sinclair, "Ray Charles," 44.

8 Ibid.

9 Another interesting bit of counter-memory was present in the same issue of *Newsweek* that contained a one-page tribute to Ray Charles amid thirty pages of Reagan funeral coverage: an article about a book-based exhibit of photographs of African American war veterans at the National Constitution Center in Philadelphia (Lisa Helem, "Periscope: 'I Had to Be the Best I Could Be,'" *Newsweek*, June 21, 2004, 11). This brief report was illustrated with photographs of proud, African American World War II veterans, another example of visual counter-memory at work in the same month when news media were full of the faces of (largely) white World War II veterans.

10 Kerry himself tied his Vietnam experience to World War II by describing his fellow veterans today as a "band of brothers" (John Kerry acceptance speech, Democratic National Convention, aired on NBC and other television networks July 29, 2004, also reprinted as "Kerry's Acceptance: 'We Have It in Our Power to Change the World Again,'" *New York Times*, July 30, 2004, P6–P7).

11 Advertisement, *New York Times*, September 26, 2004, sec. 1, pp. 12–13. The quotation is attributed to Tony Toscano, *Talking Pictures*.

12 Lisa Schwarzbuam, "Review: *Ladder 49*," *Entertainment Weekly*, reposted on www.ew.com on September 29, 2004, accessed on November 12, 2004.

13 James Poniewozik, "All Fired Up," *Time*, July 26, 2004, 61–62.

14 *Rescue Me* (FX network), written and starring Denis Leary. This phrase was used in a short "behind-the-scenes" program including interviews with the cast that aired on the same night as the first episode, July 21, 2004.

15 *Miracle* (Disney, 2004).

16 Halbwachs, *The Collective Memory*, 69.

17 *Saving Private Ryan: D-Day 60th Anniversary Commemorative Edition* (Dreamworks, 2004). This edition was packaged in a box made to look like an "authentic" (khaki-colored, scratched, with pretend latches) bullet-cartridge box.

18 Interestingly, it was during this very decade, the 1980s, that psychologists began to declare the "loss" of virile masculinity in American culture. The recuperated Trump, whom (according to television critics) America now regards with fondness, and the hockey heroes of yesteryear suggest otherwise—or, at any rate, their current portrayal may help to erase that "memory" of American culture in the 1980s.

19 David Thomson, "The Madness in His Method," *New York Times*, July 3, 2004, A31.

20 Richard Schickel, "Hostage of His Own Genius," *Time*, July 12, 2004, 74.

21 Hareven, "The Search for Generational Memory," 138.

22 Shriver, "Journalists and Democratic Memory," 133. He adds: "Their goal
    should be to remember the past with the fullness, accuracy and empathy
    that prevent people from stereotyping one another," as well as the negative
    aspects of history even if they problematize a national narrative of unity,
    the "'necessary griefs' which journalists and other public leaders may have
    to invite, if not force, their constituents to remember" (133, 138).

23 Sturken, *Tangled Memories*, 8.

Bibliography

PRIMARY SOURCES: MAGAZINES

American Legacy

Atlantic Monthly

Black Enterprise

Business 2.0

Columbia Journalism Review

CosmoGirl!

Directors & Boards

Discover

Ebony

Entertainment Weekly

ESPN The Magazine

Esquire

Fast Company

Gear

Glamour

Good Housekeeping

Good Old Days

Gourmet

GQ (Gentlemen's Quarterly)

Harper's

House & Garden

Jane

Ladies' Home Journal

Latina

Life

Maxim

McCall's

Men's Health

Men's Journal

Ms.

My Generation

National Geographic

New Republic

Newsweek

New York

New Yorker

New York Times Magazine

Out

Outside

Parade

PC Gamer

People (formerly People Weekly)

Photographer's Forum

Reader's Digest

Reminisce

Rolling Stone

Rosie

Savoy

Sports Illustrated

Talk

Teen People

This Old House

Time

Transworld Skateboarding Magazine

TV Guide

U.S. News & World Report

Us Weekly

Utne Reader

Vibe

Wine Spectator

SECONDARY SOURCES

Anderson, Benedict. *Imagined Communities: Reflections on the Origins and Spread of Nationalism.* Rev. ed. London: Verso, 1991.

Arendt, Hannah. *The Human Condition*. Chicago: University of Chicago
    Press, 1958.

Ariès, Philippe. "The Reversal of Death." In *Death in America*, edited by
    David E. Stannard, 134–58. Philadelphia: University of Pennsylvania
    Press, 1975.

Atwater, Tony, and Kwadwo Anoka. "Race Relations in *Ebony*." *Journal of
    Black Studies* 21, no. 3 (March 1991): 268–78.

Austin, Joe, and Michael Nevin Willard, eds. *Generations of Youth: Youth
    Cultures and History in Twentieth-Century America*. New York: New York
    University Press, 1998.

Bakhtin, Mikhail M. *The Dialogic Imagination: Four Essays by M. M. Bakhtin*.
    Edited and translated by Michael Holquist. Austin: University of Texas
    Press, 1981.

Barkin, Steve M. "The Journalist as Storyteller: An Interdisciplinary
    Perspective." *American Journalism* 1, no. 2 (Winter 1984): 27–33.

Barta, Tony, ed. *Screening the Past: Film and the Representation of History*.
    Westport, Conn.: Praeger, 1998.

Barthes, Roland. *Image — Music — Text*. Translated by Stephen Heath. New
    York: Hill and Wang, 1977.

Baughman, James L. "The Transformation of *Time* Magazine." *Media Studies
    Journal* 12, no. 3 (Fall 1998): 120–27.

Beisecker, Barbara A. "Remembering World War II: The Rhetoric and Politics
    of National Commemoration at the Turn of the 21st Century." *Quarterly
    Journal of Speech* 88, no. 4 (November 2002): 393–409.

Belk, Russell W. "Possessions and the Extended Self." *Journal of Consumer
    Research* 15 (September 1988): 139–68.

Bellah, Robert N., Richard Madsen, William M. Sullivan, Ann Swidler, and
    Steven M. Tipton. *Habits of the Heart: Individualism and Commitment in
    American Life*. Berkeley: University of California Press, 1985.

Bennett, W. Lance, and Murray Edelman. "Toward a New Political Narrative."
    Journal of Communication 35, no. 4 (Autumn 1985): 156–71.

Berger, Arthur Asa. *Narratives in Popular Culture, Media, and Everyday Life*.
    Thousand Oaks, Calif.: Sage, 1997.

Betcher, R. William, and William S. Pollack. *In a Time of Fallen Heroes: The
    Re-Creation of Masculinity*. New York: Atheneum, 1993.

Bird, S. Elizabeth. *The Audience in Everyday Life: Living in a Media World*. New
    York: Routledge, 2003.

Bird, S. Elizabeth, and Robert W. Dardenne. "Myth, Chronicle, and Story:
    Exploring the Narrative Qualities of News." In *Social Meanings of News*,
    edited by Dan Berkowitz, 333–50. Thousand Oaks, Calif.: Sage, 1997.

Bly, Robert. *Iron John: A Book about Men*. Reading, Mass.: Addison-Wesley, 1990.

Bodnar, John. *Remaking America: Public Memory, Commemoration, and Patriotism in the Twentieth Century*. Princeton, N.J.: Princeton University Press, 1992.

Boer, Roland. "Iconic Death and the Question of Civil Religion." In *Planet Diana: Cultural Studies and Global Mourning*, edited by Re: Public, 81–88. Kingswood, Australia: Research Center in Intercommunal Studies, 1997.

Borman, Ernest G. "Symbolic Convergence Theory: A Communication Formulation." *Journal of Communication* 35, no. 4 (Autumn 1985): 128–38.

Bramlett-Solomon, Sharon, and Ganga Subramanian. "Nowhere Near Picture Perfect: Images of the Elderly in *Life* and *Ebony* Magazine Ads." *Journalism & Mass Communication Quarterly* 76, no. 3 (Autumn 1999): 565–72.

Braudy, Leo. *The Frenzy of Renown: Fame and Its History*. New York: Oxford University Press, 1986.

Britton, Diane F. "Public History and Public Memory." *Public Historian* 19, no. 3 (Summer 1997): 11–23.

Butler, Robert N. "Successful Aging and the Role of the Life Review." *Journal of the American Geriatrics Society* 22, no. 12 (December 1974): 529–35.

Carey, James. "Communication and Economics." In *James Carey: A Critical Reader*, edited by Eve Stryker Munson and Catherine A. Warren, 60–75. Minneapolis: University of Minnesota Press, 1997.

———. *Communication as Culture*. Boston: Unwin Hyman, 1989.

———. "Why and How?: The Dark Continent of American Journalism." In *Reading the News*, edited by Robert Karl Manoff and Michael Schudson, 146–96. New York: Pantheon, 1987.

———, ed. *Media, Myths, and Narratives: Television and the Press*. Newbury Park, Calif.: Sage, 1988.

Carnes, Mark C. *Past Imperfect: History According to the Movies*. New York: Henry Holt, 1995.

Caughey, John L. *Imaginary Social Worlds: A Cultural Approach*. Lincoln: University of Nebraska Press, 1984.

Cohn, Jan. *Creating America: George Horace Lorimer and "The Saturday Evening Post."* Pittsburgh: University of Pittsburgh Press, 1989.

Dahlgren, Peter. "Television News Narrative." In *Framing Friction: Media and Social Conflict*, edited by Mary S. Mander, 189–214. Champaign: University of Illinois Press, 1999.

Darnton, Robert. "Writing News and Telling Stories." *Daedalus* 104, no. 2 (Spring 1975): 175–94.

Davis, Fred. "Decade Labeling: The Play of Collective Memory and Narrative Plot." *Symbolic Interaction* 7, no. 1 (1984): 15–24.

———. *Yearning for Yesterday: A Sociology of Nostalgia.* New York: Free Press, 1979.

Davis, Susan. "'Set Your Mood to Patriotic': History as Televised Special Event." *Radical History Review* 42 (1988): 122–43.

Dayan, Daniel, and Elihu Katz. *Media Events: The Live Broadcasting of History.* Cambridge, Mass.: Harvard University Press, 1992.

DeConcini, Barbara. *Narrative Remembering.* Lanham, Md.: University Press of America, 1990.

Digby-Junger, Richard. "*The Guardian, Crisis, Messenger,* and *Negro World*: The Early-20th-Century Black Radical Press." *Howard Journal of Communications* 9, no. 3 (July 1998): 263–82.

Doss, Erika. *Looking at "Life" Magazine.* Washington, D.C.: Smithsonian Institution Press, 2001.

Drucker, Susan J., and Robert S. Cathcart. "The Hero as a Communication Phenomenon." In *American Heroes in a Media Age,* edited by Susan J. Drucker and Robert S. Cathcart, 1–11. Cresskill, N.J.: Hampton Press, 1994.

Dubbert, Joe L. *A Man's Place: Masculinity in Transition.* Englewood Cliffs, N.J.: Prentice-Hall, 1979.

Dyer, Richard. *Heavenly Bodies: Film Stars and Society.* London: BFI/Macmillan, 1986.

Eason, David. "Telling Stories and Making Sense." *Journal of Popular Culture* 15, no. 2 (Fall 1981): 125–29.

Edy, Jill. "Journalistic Uses of Collective Memory." *Journal of Communication* 49, no. 2 (Spring 1999): 71–85.

Elson, Robert T. *Time Inc.: The Intimate History of a Publishing Enterprise.* 3 vols. New York: Atheneum, 1973.

Faludi, Susan. *Stiffed: The Betrayal of the American Man.* New York: Perennial, 1999.

Fisher, Walter R. "The Narrative Paradigm: In the Beginning." *Journal of Communication* 35, no. 4 (Autumn 1985): 74–89.

Fogo, Fred. *"I Read the News Today": The Social Drama of John Lennon's Death.* Lanham, Md.: Rowman & Littlefield, 1994.

Foss, Sonja K. *Rhetorical Criticism: Exploration and Practice.* 2nd ed. Prospect Heights, Ill.: Waveland Press, 1996.

Foucault, Michel. *Language, Counter-Memory, Practice: Selected Essays and Interviews.* Edited with an introduction by Donald F. Bouchard. Translated by Donald F. Bouchard and Sherry Simon. Ithaca, N.Y.: Cornell University Press, 1977.

Frisch, Michael. "What Public History Offers, and Why It Matters." *Public Historian* 19, no. 2 (Spring 1997): 41–42.

Fussell, Paul. "Images of Anonymity." *Harper's*, September 1979, 76–81.

———. "Time Life Goes to War!" *New Republic*, August 18, 1979, 21–22.

Gamson, Joshua. "The Assembly Line of Greatness: Celebrity in Twentieth-Century America." *Critical Studies in Mass Communication* 9, no. 1 (March 1992): 1–24.

Gans, Herbert J. *Deciding What's News: A Study of "CBS Evening News," "NBC Nightly News," "Newsweek," and "Time."* New York: Pantheon, 1979.

Goldberg, Vicki. *The Power of Photography: How Photographs Changed Our Lives.* New York: Abbeville Press, 1991.

Goody, Jack. "Death and the Interpretation of Culture." In *Death in America*, edited by David E. Stannard, 1–8. Philadelphia: University of Pennsylvania Press, 1975.

Grele, Ronald J. "Whose Public? Whose History? What Is the Goal of a Public Historian?" *Public Historian* 3, no. 1 (Winter 1981): 40–48.

Gripsrud, Jostein. "The Aesthetics and Politics of Melodrama." In *Journalism and Popular Culture*, edited by Peter Dahlgren and Colin Sparks, 84–95. London: Sage, 1992.

Gronbeck, Bruce E. "Character, Celebrity, and Sexual Innuendo in the Mass-Mediated Presidency." In *Media Scandals*, edited by James Lull and Stephen Hinerman, 122–42. New York: Columbia University Press, 1997.

Haight, Barbara Kavanagh, and Sister Rose Therese Bahr. "The Therapeutic Role of the Life Review in the Elderly." *Academic Psychology Bulletin* 6 (November 1984): 287–99.

Halbwachs, Maurice. *The Collective Memory.* Translated by Francis J. Ditter Jr. and Vida Yazdi Ditter. New York: Harper & Row, 1950.

———. *On Collective Memory.* Edited and translated with an introduction by Lewis A. Coser. Chicago: University of Chicago Press, 1992.

Hall, Edward T. *The Silent Language.* New York: Doubleday, 1959.

Hall, Stuart. "Encoding, Decoding." In *The Cultural Studies Reader*, edited by Simon During, 90–103. London: Routledge, 1993.

Hareven, Tamara K. "The Search for Generational Memory: Tribal Rites in Industrial Society." *Daedalus* 107, no. 4 (Fall 1978): 137–49.

Hebdige, Dick. "After the Masses." In *Culture/Power/History: A Reader in Contemporary Social Theory*, edited by Nicholas B. Dirks, Geoff Eley, and Sherry B. Ortner, 222–35. Princeton, N.J.: Princeton University Press, 1994.

Helterline, Marilyn, and Marilyn Nouri. "Aging and Gender: Values and Continuity." *Journal of Women and Aging* 6, no. 3 (1994): 19–37.

Herman, Gerald. "Creating the Twenty-First-Century 'Historian for All Seasons.'" *Public Historian* 25, no. 3 (Summer 2003): 93–102.

Herzstein, Robert E. *Henry R. Luce: A Political Portrait of the Man Who Created the American Century.* New York: Scribner's, 1994.

Hollander, Stanley C., and Richard Germain. *Was There a Pepsi Generation before Pepsi Discovered It?* Lincolnwood, Ill.: NTC Business Books, 1992.

Horrocks, Roger. *Masculinity in Crisis: Myths, Fantasies and Realities.* London: Macmillan, 1994.

Hoskins, Janet. *Biographical Objects: How Things Tell the Stories of People's Lives.* New York: Routledge, 1998.

Hume, Janice. "Changing Characteristics of Heroic Women in Midcentury Mainstream Media." *Journal of Popular Culture* 34, no. 1 (Summer 2000): 9–29.

———. "'Portraits of Grief,' Reflectors of Values: *The New York Times* Remembers Victims of September 11." *Journalism & Mass Communication Quarterly* 80, no. 1 (Spring 2003): 166–82.

Hutton, Frankie. *The Early Black Press in America, 1827 to 1860.* Westport, Conn.: Greenwood Press, 1993.

Jeffords, Susan. *The Remasculinization of America: Gender and the Vietnam War.* Bloomington: Indiana University Press, 1989.

Jennings, Peter, and Todd Brewster. *The Century.* New York: Doubleday, 1998.

Johnson, Charles S. "The Rise of the Negro Magazine." *Journal of Negro History* 13, no. 1 (January 1928): 7–21.

Johnson, John H., with Lerone Bennett Jr. *Succeeding against the Odds.* New York: Warner Books, 1989.

Johnson, Melissa A., Alyse R. Gotthoffer, and Kimberly A. Lauffer. "The Sexual and Reproductive Health Content of African American and Latino Magazines." *Howard Journal of Communications* 10, no. 3 (July 1999): 169–87.

Jorgensen-Earp, Cheryl R., and Lori A. Lanzilotti. "Public Memory and Private Grief: The Construction of Shrines at the Sites of Public Tragedy." *Quarterly Journal of Speech* 84, no. 2 (1998): 150–70.

Kaes, Anton. "History and Film: Public Memory in the Age of Electronic Dissemination." *History and Memory* 1, no. 2 (1990): 111–29.

Kaminsky, Marc. "The Uses of Reminiscence: A Discussion of the Formative Literature." *Journal of Gerontological Social Work* 7 (1984): 137–56.

Kammen, Michael. *Mystic Chords of Memory: The Transformation of Tradition in American Culture*. New York: Vintage Books, 1993.

Kear, Adrian, and Deborah Lynn Steinberg, eds. *Mourning Diana: Nation, Culture and the Performance of Grief*. London: Routledge, 1999.

Keller, Morton. "Politics and Generations in America." In *Generations*, edited by Stephen R. Graubard, 123–35. New York: W. W. Norton, 1978.

Kimmel, Michael S. *Manhood in America: A Cultural History*. New York: Free Press, 1996.

Kimmel, Michael S., and Michael Kaufman. "Weekend Warriors: The New Men's Movement." In *Theorizing Masculinities*, edited by Harry Brod and Michael Kaufman, 259–88. Thousand Oaks, Calif.: Sage, 1994.

Kipnis, Aaron R. *Knights without Armor: A Practical Guide for Men in Quest of Masculine Soul*. Los Angeles: Jeremy P. Tarcher, 1991.

Kirschenblatt-Gimblett, Barbara. "Objects of Memory: Material Culture as Life Review." In *Folk Groups and Folklore Genres*, edited by Elliot Oring, 329–39. Logan, Utah: Utah State University Press, 1989.

Kitch, Carolyn. *The Girl on the Magazine Cover: The Origins of Visual Stereotypes in American Mass Media*. Chapel Hill: University of North Carolina Press, 2001.

———. "Reporting the Birth and Death of Feminism: Three Decades of Mixed Messages in *Time* Magazine." Paper presented at the Association for Education in Journalism and Mass Communication Annual Conference, New Orleans, August 1999.

Kozol, Wendy. *"Life"'s America: Family and Nation in Postwar Photojournalism*. Philadelphia: Temple University Press, 1994.

Krishnaiah, Jothik. "Television News Magazines: Analysis of Mythic Structure." Paper presented at the Association for Education in Journalism and Mass Communication Annual Conference, Anaheim, Calif., 1996.

Kuhn, Annette. "Special Debate: Flowers and Tears: The Death of Diana, Princess of Wales." *Screen* 39, no. 1 (Spring 1998): 67–68.

Kumar, Deepa. "War Propaganda and the (Ab)uses of Women: Media Constructions of the Jessica Lynch Story." *Feminist Media Studies* 4, no. 3 (November 2004): 297–313.

Kunhardt, Philip B., ed. *"Life": The First Fifty Years*. Boston: Little, Brown, 1986.

Landy, Marcia, ed. *The Historical Film: History and Memory in Media*. New Brunswick, N.J.: Rutgers University Press, 2001.

Lang, Kurt E., and Gladys Engel Lang. "Collective Memory and the News." *Communication* 11, no. 2 (1989): 123–39.

Larson, Stephanie Greco, and Martha Bailey. "ABC's 'Person of the Week': American Values in Television News." *Journalism & Mass Communication Quarterly* 75, no. 3 (Autumn 1998): 487–99.

Lash, Scott, and John Urry. *Economies of Signs and Space*. London: Sage, 1994.

Lentz, Richard. *Symbols, the News Magazines, and Martin Luther King*. Baton Rouge: Louisiana State University Press, 1990.

Leslie, Michael. "Slow Fade to?: Advertising in *Ebony* Magazine, 1957–1989." *Journalism & Mass Communication Quarterly* 72, no. 2 (Summer 1995): 426–35.

Levi-Strauss, Claude. *Structural Anthropology*. New York: Basic Books, 1968.

Linenthal, Edward Tabor. *Changing Images of the Warrior Hero in America: A History of Popular Symbolism*. New York: Edwin Mellen Press, 1982.

Lipsitz, George. *Time Passages: Collective Memory and American Popular Culture*. Minneapolis: University of Minnesota Press, 1990.

Lowenthal, David. *The Past Is a Foreign Country*. Cambridge: Cambridge University Press, 1985.

Lule, Jack. *Daily News, Eternal Stories: The Mythological Role of Journalism*. New York: Guilford Press, 2001.

Lumby, Catharine. "Vanishing Point." In *Planet Diana: Cultural Studies and Global Mourning*, edited by Re: Public, 105–9. Kingswood, Australia: Research Center in Intercommunal Studies, 1997.

Mannheim, Karl. "The Problem of Generations." In *Essays on the Sociology of Knowledge*, edited by Paul Kecskemeti, 276–332. London: Routledge, Kegan & Paul, 1952.

Manoff, Robert Karl. "Writing the News (By Telling the 'Story')." In *Reading the News*, edited by Robert Karl Manoff and Michael Schudson, 197–229. New York: Pantheon Books, 1986.

Marshall, P. David. *Celebrity and Power: Fame in Contemporary Culture*. Minneapolis: University of Minnesota Press, 1997.

Mazzarella, Sharon R., and Timothy M. Matyjewicz. "'The Day the Music Died'—Again: Newspaper Coverage of the Deaths of Popular Musicians." In *Pop Music and the Press*, edited by Steve Jones, 219–32. Philadelphia: Temple University Press, 2002.

McConnell, Frank. *Storytelling and Mythmaking: Images from Film and Literature*. New York: Oxford University Press, 1979.

McCracken, Grant. *Culture and Consumption: New Approaches to the Symbolic Character of Consumer Goods and Activities*. Bloomington: Indiana University Press, 1988.

McLaughlin, Tara L., and Nicole Goulet. "Gender Advertisements in

Magazines Aimed at African Americans." *Sex Roles* 40, nos. 1–2 (January 1999): 61–71.

McMahon, Arthur W., and Paul J. Rhudick. "Reminiscing." *Archives of General Psychiatry* 10 (January–June 1964): 292–98.

Mendelson, Andrew. "Slice-of-Life Moments as Visual 'Truth': Norman Rockwell, Feature Photography, and American Values in Pictorial Journalism." *Journalism History* 29, no. 4 (Winter 2004): 166–78.

Merck, Mandy, ed. *After Diana: Irreverent Elegies*. London: Verso, 1998.

Meyrowitz, Joshua. "The Life and Death of Media Friends: New Genres of Intimacy and Mourning." In *American Heroes in a Media Age*, edited by Susan J. Drucker and Robert S. Cathcart, 62–81. Cresskill, N.J.: Hampton Press, 1994.

Middleton, David, and Derek Edwards. "Conversational Remembering: A Social Psychological Approach." In *Collective Remembering*, edited by David Middleton and Derek Edwards, 22–45. London: Sage, 1990.

———. Introduction. In *Collective Remembering*, edited by David Middleton and Derek Edwards, 1–22. London: Sage, 1990.

Molotch, Harvey, and Marilyn Lester. "News as Purposive Behavior: On the Strategic Use of Routine Events, Accidents, and Scandals." *American Sociological Review* 39 (February 1974): 101–12.

Morgan, David L. "The Aging of the Baby Boom." *Generations* 22, no. 1 (1998): 5–9.

Myers, Gloria, and A. V. Margavio. "The Black Bourgeoisie and Reference Group Change: A Content Analysis of *Ebony*." *Qualitative Sociology* 6, no. 4 (Winter 1983): 291–307.

Ohmann, Richard. *Selling Culture: Magazines, Markets, and Class at the Turn of the Century*. London: Verso, 1996.

Pride, Armistead S., and Clint C. Wilson II. *A History of the Black Press*. Washington, D.C.: Howard University Press, 1997.

Priefer, Beverly A., and Steven R. Gambert. "Reminiscence and Life Review in the Elderly." *Psychiatric Medicine* 2, no. 1 (1984): 91–100.

Propp, Vladimir. *Morphology of the Folktale*. Translated by Laurence Scott. 2nd ed. Austin: University of Texas Press, 1968; originally published in 1928.

Radley, Alan. "Artefacts, Memory and a Sense of the Past." In *Collective Remembering*, edited by David E. Middleton and Derek Edwards, 46–59. London: Sage, 1990.

Raphael, Ray. *The Men from the Boys: Rites of Passage in Male America*. Lincoln: University of Nebraska Press, 1988.

Re: Public, ed. *Planet Diana: Cultural Studies and Global Mourning*. Kingswood, Australia: Research Center in Intercommunal Studies, 1997.

Reis-Bergan, Monica, Frederick X. Gibbson, Meg Garrard, and Jan F. Ybema. "The Impact of Reminiscence on Socially Active Elderly Women's Reactions to Social Comparisons." *Basic and Applied Social Psychology* 22, no. 3 (September 2000): 225–36.

Ricoeur, Paul. "Narrative Time." In *On Narrative*, edited by W. J. T. Mitchell, 165–86. Chicago: University of Chicago Press, 1980.

Rivers, Caryl. *Slick Spins and Fractured Facts: How Cultural Myths Distort the News*. New York: Columbia University Press, 1996.

Rock, Paul. "News as Eternal Recurrence." In *The Manufacture of News*, edited by Stanley Cohen and Jock Young, 226–43. London: Sage, 1973.

Rodden, John. *The Politics of Literary Reputation: The Making and Claiming of "St. George" Orwell*. New York: Oxford University Press, 1989.

Rollins, Peter C., ed. *Hollywood as Historian: American Film in a Cultural Context*. Rev. ed. Lexington: University Press of Kentucky, 1983.

Rose, Vivien Ellen, and Julie Corley. "A Trademark Approach to the Past: Ken Burns, the Historical Profession, and Assessing Popular Presentations of the Past." *Public Historian* 25, no. 3 (Summer 2003): 49–59.

Rosenstone, Robert A. *Visions of the Past: The Challenge of Film to Our Idea of History*. Cambridge, Mass.: Harvard University Press, 1995.

Rosenzweig, Roy. "Marketing the Past: *American Heritage* and Popular History in the United States." In *Presenting the Past: Essays on History and the Public*, edited by Susan Porter Benson, Stephen Brier, and Roy Rosenzweig, 21–49. Philadelphia: Temple University Press, 1986.

Rothenbuhler, Eric W. *Ritual Communication: From Everyday Conversation to Mediated Ceremony*. Thousand Oaks, Calif.: Sage, 1998.

Rushing, Janice Hocker. "Putting Away Childish Things: Looking at Diana's Funeral and Media Criticism." *Women's Studies in Communication* 21, no. 2 (Fall 1998): 150–67.

Schneirov, Matthew. *The Dream of a New Social Order*. New York: Columbia University Press, 1994.

Schudson, Michael. *The Power of News*. Cambridge, Mass.: Harvard University Press, 1995.

———. *Watergate in American Memory: How We Remember, Forget and Reconstruct the Past*. New York: Basic Books, 1992.

Schuman, Howard, and Jacqueline Scott. "Generations and Collective Memories." *American Sociological Review* 54 (1989): 359–81.

Schwartz, Barry. "Collective Memory and History: How Abraham Lincoln Became a Symbol of Racial Equality." *Sociological Quarterly* 38, no. 3 (1977): 469–96.

———. "Frame Images: Towards a Semiotics of Collective Memory."
Semiotica 121, nos. 1–2 (1998): 1–40.

Shriver, Donald W., Jr. "Journalists and Democratic Memory." *Media Studies
Journal* 9, no. 3 (Summer 1995): 133–40.

Silberstein, Sandra. *War of Words: Language, Politics and 9/11.* London:
Routledge, 2002.

Smith, J. Walker, and Ann Clurman. *Rocking the Ages: The Yankelovich Report
on Generational Marketing.* New York: HarperCollins, 1997.

Smith, Robert Rutherford. "Mythic Elements in Television News." In *Social
Meanings of News*, edited by Dan Berkowitz, 325–32. Thousand Oaks,
Calif.: Sage, 1997.

Sorokin, Pitirim A. *Sociocultural Causality, Space, Time.* New York: Russell &
Russell, 1964.

Stange, Maren. "'Photographs Taken in Everyday Life': *Ebony*'s
Photojournalistic Discourse." In *The Black Press: New Literary and
Historical Essays*, edited by Todd Vogel, 207–27. New Brunswick, N.J.:
Rutgers University Press, 2001.

Strauss, William, and Neil Howe. *The Fourth Turning: An American Prophecy.*
New York: Broadway Books, 1997.

———. *Generations: The History of America's Future, 1584 to 2069.* New York:
William Morrow, 1991.

Sturken, Marita. *Tangled Memories: The Vietnam War, the AIDS Epidemic, and
the Politics of Remembering.* Berkeley: University of California Press, 1997.

Tebbel, John, and Mary Ellen Zuckerman. *The Magazine in America,
1741–1990.* New York: Oxford University Press, 1991.

Toplin, Robert Brent. *History by Hollywood: The Use and Abuse of the American
Past.* Urbana: University of Illinois Press, 1996.

———. *Reel History: In Defense of Hollywood.* Lawrence: University Press of
Kansas, 2002.

Tripp, Bernell. *Origins of the Black Press: New York, 1827–1847.* Northport,
Ala.: Vision Press, 1992.

Tuchman, Gaye. *Making News: A Study in the Construction of Reality.* New
York: Free Press, 1978.

Turner Victor. *From Ritual to Theater: The Human Seriousness of Play.* New
York: Performing Arts Journal Publications, 1982.

———. *The Ritual Process: Structure and Anti-Structure.* Ithaca, N.Y.: Cornell
University Press, 1977; originally published in 1969.

van Gennep, Arnold. *The Rites of Passage.* Chicago: University of Chicago
Press, 1960; originally published in 1908.

Vogel, Todd, ed. *The Black Press: New Literary and Historical Essays*. New Brunswick, N.J.: Rutgers University Press, 2001.

Wainwright, Loudon. *The Great American Magazine: An Inside History of "Life."* New York: Knopf, 1986.

Wallace, Mike. *Mickey Mouse History and Other Essays on American Memory*. Philadelphia: Temple University Press, 1996.

Walter, Tony, ed. *The Mourning for Diana*. Oxford: Berg, 1999.

Webster, Jeffrey Dean, and Mary E. McCall. "Reminiscence Functions across Adulthood: A Replication and Extension." *Journal of Adult Development* 6, no. 1 (1999): 73–85.

White, Hayden. "The Value of Narrativity in the Representation of Reality." In *On Narrative*, edited by W. J. T. Mitchell, 1–23. Chicago: University of Chicago Press, 1980.

Williams, Raymond. *The Long Revolution*. London: Chatto & Windus, 1961.

Willis, Deborah, ed. *Picturing Us: African American Identity in Photography*. New York: New Press, 1994.

Wills, Garry. *John Wayne's America*. New York: Simon & Schuster, 1997.

Winfield, Betty Houchin. "The Press Response to the Corps of Discovery: The Making of Heroes in an Egalitarian Age." *Journalism & Mass Communication Quarterly* 80, no. 4 (Winter 2003): 866–83.

Winfield, Betty Houchin, and Janice Hume. "Remembrances Past: Nineteenth-Century Press and the Uses of American History." Paper presented to the Association for Education in Journalism and Mass Communication, Baltimore, 1998.

Wolfe, A. J. "'I Read the News Today, Oh Boy': Irony, Ambiguity, and Meaning in CBS Television Network News Coverage of the Death of John Lennon." Ph.D. diss., Northwestern University, 1988.

Wolseley, Roland E. *The Black Press, U.S.A.* Ames: Iowa State University Press, 1971.

Wormley, J. Carlyne, Barbara Heinzerling, and Virginia Gunn. "Uncovering History: An Examination of the Impact of the *Ebony* Fashion Fair and *Ebony* Magazine." *Consumer Interests Annual* 44 (1998): 148–50.

Wright, Will. *Six Guns and Society: A Structural Study of the Western*. Berkeley: University of California Press, 1975.

Zelizer, Barbie. "Achieving Journalistic Authority through Narrative." *Critical Studies in Mass Communication* 7, no. 4 (December 1990): 366–76.

———. *Covering the Body: The Kennedy Assassination, the Media, and the Shaping of Collective Memory*. Chicago: University of Chicago Press, 1992.

———. "Reading the Past against the Grain: The Shape of Memory Studies." *Critical Studies in Mass Communication* 12, no. 2 (June 1995): 215–39.

————. *Remembering to Forget: Holocaust Memory through the Camera's Eye.* Chicago: University of Chicago Press, 1998.

Zerubavel, Eviatar. *Hidden Rhythms: Schedules and Calendars in Social Life.* Chicago: University of Chicago Press, 1981.

————. "Social Memories: Steps to a Sociology of the Past." *Qualitative Sociology* 19, no. 3 (1996): 283–99.

Index

Italic page numbers refer to illustrations.

Anonymity, 41, 104, 105
Arendt, Hannah, 5
Ariès, Philippe, 64
Athletes, 21, 48, 62, 100, 103
Atlantic Monthly, 10, 40, 57
Audiences. *See* Magazine audiences
Austin, Joe, 110

Baby Boom generation: identity of,
    10, 64, 79, 110, 112–13, 116, 118,
    119, 120, 121, 127, 128, 179; and
    newsmagazines, 114, 116, 117–18,
    121, 123, 127; and nostalgia, 152
Bakhtin, M. M., 5
Ball, Lucille, 76, 77
Barthes, Roland, 4
Baughman, James, 214 (n. 21)
Beatles, 113, 155. *See also* Harrison,
    George; Lennon, John
Beisecker, Barbara, 43
Belk, Russell, 150
Bell, Alexander Graham, 224 (n. 39)
Bellah, Robert, 4
Belushi, John, 74–75, 81, 82, 83
Bennett, Lance, 26
Bennett, Lerone, 95
Bennett, Lerone, Jr., 92–93, 108
Bethune, Mary McLeod, 100, 101
Bird, S. Elizabeth, 4, 20
Black Enterprise, 89, 162, 168, 172–73
Black Entertainment Television, 89
Black History Month, 90, 91, 208
    (n. 22), 209 (n. 29)
Black press, 88–89, 206 (n. 6)
Black pride movement, 89, 90
Bodnar, John, 5, 6, 182
Boer, Roland, 71
Boesky, Ivan, 22
Boorstin, Daniel, 14

Borman, Ernest, 19
Brando, Marlon, 179–80
Braudy, Leo, 86
Britton, Diane F., 6
Brokaw, Tom, 43, 124, 127
Brown, James, 176
Brown, Linda, 103
Brown, Tina, 71
Bunche, Ralph, 98, 101
Bush, George H. W., 125
Bush, George W., 54, 175, 199 (n. 87)
Business 2.0, 47
Business Week, 132

Calloway, Cab, 101, 103
Capa, Robert, 59
Capitalism, 34, 182, 183
Carey, James, 4, 9, 19, 63–64
Carter, Jimmy, 26, 83
Cash, Johnny, 62, 65, 67, 74, 83
Cathcart, Robert S., 40–41
Caughey, John, 68
Celebrities and celebrity memorials:
    and public mournings, 1, 62; and
    special magazine issues, 8, 10, 187
    (n. 45); and newsmagazines, 21–
    22, 32, 69, 71, 72, 73; criticism of,
    62, 63, 200 (n. 8); and ordinary
    people, 62, 74–77, 85–86, 176,
    181; and emotions, 63, 71–72, 86;
    and sacrificial symbolic status, 63;
    and values, 63, 64, 65, 68, 69, 78,
    86; and commemorative issues,
    64–65, *66*, 68; and generational
    identity, 64, 78–80, 85, 180, 204
    (n. 89); identification with, 68,
    69; narrative of, 68, 72–76, 81–
    82, 175, 179–80; and *communitas*,
    69; and public/private line, 71; and

uniformity of stories, 72–73; and class, 74–75, 77; and conflation of celebrities and social groups, 80; and untimely death, 80–81; and responsible villains, 81–82, 176; and martyrdom, 82; and funeral coverage, 83, 175; and readers' response, 83, 85–86; and anniversary issues, 157. *See also specific celebrities*

Charles, Ray, 176–77, 227 (n. 9)

Civil rights movement, 89, 94, 95, 101, 103–4, 180, 181, 182, 207 (n. 13)

Civil War: and African American soldiers, 95

Class: and ordinary people, 22; and nostalgia, 39; and masculine heroism, 43, 53, 54, 59, 60, 177–78; and firemen images, 45; and celebrity memorials, 74–75, 77; and African American market, 90; and counter-memory, 96, 98, 99, 104, 105; and American Dream, 182

Clinton, Bill, 125, 162, 166–67

Clinton, Hillary, 118

Coal-mine accident and rescue of miners (2002), 39, 53–54, 57, 195 (n. 1), 198–99 (n. 79)

Cobain, Kurt, 63, 64, 75, 76, 79, 82, 85, 155

Cold War, 20, 21, 26

Collectibles, 7, 8–9, 15, 64–65, 148, 189 (n. 12)

Collective amnesia: and cultural narratives, 2; and nostalgia, 11; and newsmagazines, 29; and generational identity, 110, 128, 179; and anniversaries, 155; and celeb-

rity memorials, 175; and media memory, 182, 183

Collective memory: and cultural narratives, 2; race's role in, 10; and nostalgia, 11; and newsmagazines, 29; and World War II, 53, 55; and African American magazines, 92; and African retentions, 93; and generational identity, 128; and reminiscent journalism, 142; and anniversaries, 155

Columbia Journalism Review, 157

Commemoration, 60, 182, 183

Common man. *See* Ordinary people

Communitas, 64, 69

Core plots, 26–29, 34, 35, 37, 73, 192 (n. 77)

Counterculture, 78, 179

Counter-memory: as reconstitution of history, 10, 93–94, 107; Foucault on, 93, 209 (n. 35); and magazine audiences, 95; and class, 96, 98, 99, 104, 105; and white histories and settings, 96; and role of visual images, 98, 100–101, 103, 211 (n. 65); and family, 105; and travel, 106; and Charles' death, 177, 227 (n. 9)

Coupland, Douglas, 111

Crisis, 88

Dardenne, Robert, 4, 20

Davis, Benjamin O., Jr., 101

Davis, Fred, 3, 26, 27–28, 150

Davis, Sammy, Jr., 74, 75, 80, 81, 83

Davis, Susan, 155

D-Day anniversary, 1, 58, 59, 155, 179

Dean, James, 69

DeConcini, Barbara, 5

Gamson, Joshua, 65

Gans, Herbert, 27, 115, 195 (n. 4)

Garcia, Jerry, 64, 69, 73–74, 75, 76, 79, 81, 82, 83

Garland, Judy, 63, 69, 71, 73, 76, 82

Garvey, Marcus, 88, 168

Gates, Bill, 22, 34

Gear, 48

Gender, 4, 39, 53, 56–57, 60, 76–77, 144–47, 152–53

Genealogical research, 181

Generation 9–11, 124

Generational archetypes, 111

Generational identity: and role of journalistic memory, 4; magazines' definition of, 10–11; and nostalgia, 11, 110, 113, 117, 118, 123, 128, 129, 130, 152, 179; and celebrity memorials, 64, 78–80, 85, 180, 204 (n. 89); and collective amnesia, 110, 128, 179; elastic distinctiveness of, 110–11; and watershed events, 110, 113, 117, 124, 127–28; and young adulthood experiences, 110, 114, 117, 120, 123, 127, 130; and advertising, 111–12, 214 (n. 23); and lifestyle markers, 111, 120, 123, 128; and marginal groups, 114, 215 (n. 24); and newsmagazines, 114–18, 120–21, 123–25, 127–30; and erasures, 123, 124, 128; and progressive narrative, 128–29; and discursive connections, 151; and ordinary people, 182

Generational memory, 110, 213 (n. 3)

Generation gap, 78, 111

Generation X: identity of, 10, 110, 115, 120, 121, 122, 124; and celebrity memorials, 64, 79; and news-

magazines, 114, 115, 118, 120–21, 123, 127

Generation Y: identity of, 10, 110, 113, 128, 179; and newsmagazines, 114, 118, 121, 123–24

Gibbs, Nancy, 57–58

Gibson, Althea, 101

Giuliani, Rudolph, 166

Glamour, 156, 169, 172

Goldberg, Vicki, 101, 103

Good Housekeeping, 54, 155–59, 162, 165, 167, 168, 169, 172

Good Old Days: and nostalgia, 11, 132, 134, 136, 138, 153; circulation of, 134; supplemental titles of, 134–35, 218 (n. 20); editorial content of, 135–36; covers of, 136, 137; reader characteristics, 136, 145; and readers' personal reminiscences, 136, 139, 142–44, 146–47, 151–52; and Wanted department, 139, 148; and physical objects of past, 148–49; and values, 151

Goody, Jacky, 81–82

Gorbachev, Mikhail, 21

Gould, Mary, 144–45

Gourmet, 156, 157, 158, 160, 162, 166, 168

GQ, 162, 165, 168

Grace, Princess, 65, 72, 73, 82

Great Depression, 136, 145–47, 176, 182

Greatest Generation, 10, 110, 112, 114, 116, 124–25, 125, 127, 128

Grele, Ronald J., 5

Gripsrud, Jostein, 190–91 (n. 41)

Gronbeck, Bruce, 71

Hadden, Britton, 15

Halberstam, David, 125

Halbwachs, Maurice, 2, 5, 110–11, 132, 144, 178

Haley, Alex, 90

Hall, Stuart, 103

Hamilton, Thomas, 88

Hareven, Tamara, 181

Harlem Writers' Guild, 88–89

Harper's, 2, 156, 162, 164, 166–67, 173, 223 (n. 10)

Harrison, George, 69, 71, 75, 76, 82, 83

Heart & Soul, 90, 207 (n. 17)

Hebdige, Dick, 112

Helmsley, Leona, 22, 26

Henson, Matthew, 100

Hepburn, Katharine, 77

Herman, Gerald, 6–7

Heroes: masculine heroism, 9–10, 41–42, 43, 51, 53–55, 56, 58–59, 60, 177–79, 181; heroic template, 10, 39, 45, 55–58, 59, 60, 181, 195 (n. 1), 198 (n. 65), 198–99 (n. 79); and summary issues, 19–22, 24–25, 34, 41; and myth, 40–41, 43, 54, 60; and celebrity memorials, 73–74, 78, 83, 85, 177; and generational identity, 124, 125; and reminiscent journalism, 151

Hine, Darlene Clark, 96

Historians, 6–7, 182, 186 (n. 36), 209 (n. 35), 228 (n. 22)

History Channel, 14, 188 (n. 7)

Hitler, Adolf, 36, 93

Holocaust, 18, 20

Honey, 90, 207 (n. 17)

Horne, Lena, 100, 101

Hoskins, Janet, 133, 150

House & Garden, 156, 162, 164, 166

Howe, Neil, 111

Hsu, John, 129

Hume, Janice, 2, 40, 47

Identity: and collectibles, 8; social identity, 10, 114, 129, 151; identity-affirmation, 11; and celebrities, 68, 69; African American identity, 88, 89, 95, 98, 105, 107; and reminiscence, 133, 152; and anniversaries issues, 156; and media, 183. *See also* Generational identity; National identity

Individualism: and core plots, 26, 27, 29, 34, 35, 37; commonality vs., 89, 105; individual and collective, 181

Inside Edge, 129

Iraq War, 10, 55–58, 60, 175, 177, 179, 198 (nn. 65, 79), 199 (nn. 81, 82)

Iwo Jima flag-raising photograph, 41, 45, 197 (n. 42)

Jackson, Mahalia, 101, 103

Jane's, 164, 167

Jeffords, Susan, 42

Jennings, Peter, 14, 188 (n. 7)

Johnson, Charles S., 89

Johnson, John H., 89, 96, 98

Journalism: role in articulation of history, 1, 2, 3; role of nostalgia in, 2, 90; and social identity formation, 4; narrative structure of, 5; and public history, 5, 7, 12; photojournalism, 15, 41, 89, 96, 98, 100–101, 103–6, 211 (n. 65), 212 (n. 77); personalization in, 19–20, 35, 93, 168–70, 172, 173, 182; as public forum, 41; and firemen images, 53; and Iraq War, 55;

and heroic template of September 11th, 60; and public mourning, 62, 64; function of, 63–64; and public/private line, 71; and heroes' characteristics, 74; and African American identity, 88; and novelty, 115; and national identity, 182, 228 (n. 22); and dramatization of stories, 190–91 (n. 41). *See also* Reminiscent journalism; Summary journalism

Joyner, Florence Griffith, 103

Julian, Percy, 101

Kaes, Anton, 6

Kammen, Michael, 11, 155

Kaufman, Michael, 42

Kay, Richard, 81

Keller, Morton, 111

Kennedy, Bobby, 20, 117

Kennedy, Edward, 83

Kennedy, Jacqueline. *See* Onassis, Jacqueline Kennedy

Kennedy, John F., 2, 7, 20, 23, 113, 125, 160, 162

Kennedy, John F., Jr.: and celebrity memorials, 1, 62, 69; and values, 63; and commemorative issues, 65; and narrative, 68; and emotions, 72; and core plots, 73; and ordinary people, 75–76; and generational identity, 79, 85; and untimely death, 81; and cult of celebrity as villain, 82–83; and "Kennedy Curse," 82, 205 (n. 113); and funeral coverage, 83, 84; and readers' response, 83, 85

Kennedy, William, 83

Kerry, John, 36, 177, 227 (n. 10)

Kesey, Ken, 82

Kimmel, Michael, 42, 43

King, Coretta Scott, 20, 100, 117

King, Martin Luther, Jr., 20, 91, 100, 103, 211 (n. 69)

Kirschenblatt-Gimblett, Barbara, 148

Kirshnaiah, Jothik, 192 (n. 77)

Konner, Joan, 157

Kozol, Wendy, 22

Kumar, Deepa, 57

Ladies' Home Journal, 45, 54

Lance, Bert, 69

Landy, Marcia, 6

Langewiesche, Will, 57

Lapham, Lewis, 156

Lash, Scott, 132

Lennon, John: and celebrity-death coverage, 1, 69; and September 11th dedication, 39; and values, 63; and generational identity, 64, 78–79, 204 (n. 89); identification with, 68; and narrative, 73–74, 75, 76; and untimely death, 81, 82; and responsible villain, 82; and funeral coverage, 83; and readers' response, 85; scholarship on, 200 (n. 8)

Levi-Strauss, Claude, 60

Life: and historic issue reprints, 7, 187 (n. 40); summary issues of, 8, 9, 14, 15; circulation of, 15, 189 (n. 11); half-century-review issue of, 15, *16*, 25, 29, 35; goals of, 17, 18; audience of, 18, 19; and decade-end reviews, 19, 21, 23, 24, 28, 35, 191 (n. 51); and dramatization of stories, 20, 23; and ordinary people, 22, 23–24, 25, 26–27;

and predictions of future, 30, 193 (n. 86); millennium-review issue, 34–35; and century-review issue, 37; and Vietnam War, 42; and celebrity-death coverage, 69, 71, 73, 82; and *Ebony*, 89; and generational identity, 113; and reminiscent journalism, 133; anniversary issues of, 155, 158, 159, 164, 165, 166, 167, 168, 169–70

Life-review process: and reminiscence, 133, 145

Lincoln, Abraham, 2, 162

Linenthal, Edward, 41

Lipsitz, George, 93, 107

Long, Huey, 20

Look, 42

Lorimer, George Horace, 2

Lowenthal, David, 35, 151

Luce, Henry, 15, 18, 19, 20, 34, 173

Lule, Jack, 40

Lumby, Catharine, 71

Lynch, Jessica, 56–57

Magabooks, 7, 69, 133, 199 (n. 85)

Magazine audiences: and media, 4, 6, 183; producer/receiver relationship, 4, 133, 155; influence of film makers on, 6; as ordinary people, 6, 22–23; and social meaning of magazines, 8–9; loyalty of, 9; older audiences, 11, 132, 134, 151, 153; as national audience, 17; as participants and spectators, 18–19, 134, 135, 136, 139, 153; range of, 40; and celebrity memorials, 63, 65, 68, 83–84, 86; and discourse theory, 92–93; and counter-memory, 95; and advertising, 112; and generational identity,

113; and anniversary issues, 155, 167, 168, 174

Magazines: and industry specialization, 2–3; and social memory, 3, 175; as vernacular culture, 6; archival functions of, 7–8; and public history, 7, 11–12; as dialogic, 9; specialized magazines, 11, 189 (n. 22); national audience of, 17; and celebrity-death coverage, 64–65, 69; and black press, 88–89; and generational memory, 110; historians on, 186 (n. 36). *See also* African American magazines; Newsmagazines

Malcolm X, 20, 101

Mannheim, Karl, 110, 128

Manoff, Robert Karl, 5

Margavio, A. V., 89

Marshall, David, 71

Masculine heroism, 9–10, 41–42, 43, 51, 53–55, 56, 58–59, 60, 177–79, 181

Masculinity, crisis of, 42, 53, 59, 227 (n. 18)

Matyjewicz, Timothy, 64, 202 (n. 55)

Mauldin, Bill, 41, 55

Mazzarella, Sharon, 64, 202 (n. 55)

McCall's, 167, 169

McCracken, Grant, 140

Media: and history as heritage, 1; and memory, 3, 6, 180–83; dialogic media, 4, 9, 92–93, 103, 133, 134, 151, 152, 183; role of, 6, 17; as public forum, 41, 182; and public mourning, 62; and celebrity memorials, 63, 71, 86; and African American history, 90, 91; and generational identity, 113; and anniversaries, 155; contradictions in, 175; and narrative, 183–84. *See also* News media

Memorials: and September 11th, 1; role in journalism, 2

Memories, 133–34

Memory: and media, 3, 6, 180–83; social memory, 3, 116, 175; and narrative, 5, 39; and African Americans, 88; and African American magazines, 91, 107–8, 173; public memory, 93, 96; and photographic images, 98; generational memory, 110, 213 (n. 3); and generational identity, 114; and cleaned-up heritage, 132, 151; and elderly, 132–33, 143–44; and physical objects, 150; national memory, 156, 167; and ordinary people, 181. *See also* Collective amnesia; Collective memory; Counter-memory

Memory objects, 132, 217 (n. 3)

Men's Health, 40, 51

Men's Journal, 48, 49

Meyrowitz, Joshua, 65, 68

Middleton, David, 60, 140, 151

Miller, Bettina, 136, 148, 151

Mirror of Liberty, 88

Modern Maturity, 112

Monroe, Marilyn, 69, 71, 73, 82

Morgan, David, 127

Morrow, Lance, 82

Ms., 158, 164, 168, 169, 172

Myers, Gloria, 89

My Generation, 45, 46, 47, 112–13, 134

Myth: national mythology, 9, 177; and heroes, 40–41, 43, 54, 60; and anniversary issues, 174

Narrative: public narrative, 2; news narratives, 3, 4–5, 115; paradigm of, 4–5, 183; and memory, 5, 39; and summary journalism, 7, 28–29, 35; recovery narrative, 53, 56, 179; of celebrity memorials, 68, 72–76, 81–82, 175, 179–80; white historical narratives, 96, 98, 104; and media, 183–84

National Association for the Advancement of Colored People, 88

National Geographic, 8, 157, 159, 162, *163*, 164, 166, 172

National identity: and public narratives, 2; and media, 6; and magabooks, 7; and newsmagazines, 17, 18; and masculine heroism, 43, 53, 60; and pluralism, 88, 182; and African Americans, 98, 104; and advertising, 111; and individual identity, 181

Nationalism, 39, 183

National mythology, 9, 177

National Urban League, 88

Negro Digest, 89

New Republic, 155

Newsmagazines: and public history, 9, 14; influence of, 15; voice of, 15, 17, 18, 19, 22; and national identity, 17, 18; and audience's importance, 18, 22–23; and dramatization of stories, 19–22, 23, 31, 190–91 (n. 41); and personalization in journalism, 19–20; and celebrities, 21–22, 32, 69, 71, 72, 73; and world leaders, 21, 26–27, 34; and ordinary people, 22, 23–27, 30, 31, 32, 34; and core plots, 26–29, 34, 35, 192 (n. 77); and collective amnesia, 29; and predictions of future, 29–31, 32, 36, 193 (n. 86), 194 (n. 114); and trend reporting, 113–14, 115, 116, 118, 129–30; and generational identity, 114–18, 120–21, 123–25, 127–30

News media: and civic rituals, 1–2; and maintenance of society, 4; and erasures, 29; and September 11th, 39; and American heroes, 40; and American soldiers in Iraq, 57, 58–59; celebrity coverage of, 62, 64, 71, 179; generational characterizations in, 111, 129; and campaign rhetoric, 157

Newspapers, 17, 88

News values, 27, 195 (n. 4)

Newsweek: summary issues of, 9, 14; circulation of, 15; goals of, 17, 18, 20; and dramatization of stories, 20–21; and ordinary people, 24, 32, 34; and decade-end issues, 28, 29; and half-century review issues, 29–30; and predictions of future, 30–31, 32, 36, 193 (n. 86), 194 (n. 114); and century-review issues, 31, 32, 34, 36, 37, 194 (n. 114); and firemen images, 40, 44, 45, 51, 52; and patriotism, 47; and American soldiers in Iraq, 56, 57; and celebrity-death coverage, 62, 69, 71, 72, 73, 74, 76, 77, 78, 79, 81, 82, 83, 227 (n. 9); and generational identity, 114, 115, 117–18, 119, 121, 123, 125, 126, 127, 214 (n. 23); and anniversary issues, 159, 162, 170, 171, 172; and advertising, 214 (n. 23)

New Yorker, 39, 40, 54, 71, 76–77, 158, 164, 195 (n. 1)

New York magazine, 47–48

New York Times, 8, 47, 56, 176, 180, 198–99 (n. 79)

New York Times Magazine, 14, 57

Nixon, Richard, 21, 26

Noonan, Peggy, 71–72

Nostalgia: role in journalism, 2, 90, 152–53, 175; appeal among audiences, 3; and generational identity, 11, 110, 113, 117, 118, 123, 128, 129, 130, 152, 179; magazines specializing in, 11, 132–34; and nationalism, 39; and masculine heroism, 42, 60; and firemen images, 45, 48; and World War II, 51, 59, 125, 179; as social experience, 133; and television, 133–34, 180; definition of, 151; and anniversaries, 155; and anniversary issues, 170; and celebrity memorials, 176; and narrative, 180; and ordinary people, 181. *See also* Reminiscent journalism

Novelty/familiarity: in news narratives, 5, 115

Oklahoma City bombing, 62

Onassis, Jacqueline Kennedy, 20, 65, 71–72, 73, 76, 78, 79–81, 83, 85

Opportunity, 88–89

Ordinary people: and vernacular culture, 5, 182; magazine audiences as, 6, 22–23; and African American magazines, 10, 103–4, 105; newsmagazines' featuring of, 22, 23–27, 30, 31, 32, 34; and values, 25, 175; and firemen images, 45; and September 11th, 47, 182, 183; and American soldiers in Iraq, 55, 56, 57, 177, 198 (n. 65); and masculine heroism, 59, 177–79, 181; and celebrities, 62, 74–77, 85–86, 176, 181; and anniversary issues, 169, 170, 172

Out, 157, 164
Outside, 156, 166, 168, 172
Owens, Jesse, 93

Parade, 10, 40, 57
Parks, Rosa, 103
Patriotism, 45, 47, 55, 125, 147, 152,
　175, 177, 178
Penn, Irving, 162
People: and masculine heroism, 10;
　and firemen images, 40, 51; and
　patriotism, 47; and coal-mine acci-
　dent, 54; and space shuttle Colum-
　bia, 55; and American soldiers in
　Iraq, 56; and celebrity memorials,
　66, 68, 69, 74–75, 76, 77, 79, 80–
　81; and generational identity, 113;
　and anniversary issues, 157, 164,
　167, 169
Peterson, Audrey, 92, 94, 96
Photojournalism, 15, 41, 89, 96, 98,
　100–101, 103–6, 211 (n. 65), 212
　(n. 77)
Pickett, Bill, 96
Pluralism, 23–24, 88, 182
Powell, Colin, 34, 95
Pratt, Jane, 167
Presley, Elvis: and celebrity-death
　coverage, 1, 63, 69, 70, 201 (n. 13);
　and heroes, 34; and narrative, 72,
　73, 74; and generational identity,
　78; and untimely death, 81; and
　martyrdom, 82; and responsible
　villain, 82; and funeral coverage,
　83; and reminiscent journalism,
　133
Propp, Vladimir, 4
Public history: and journalism, 5,
　7, 12; and film, 6, 186 (n. 29);
　media's role in, 6; and magazines,

7, 11–12; and summary journalism,
7, 9, 14, 37; and African Americans, 88; and ordinary people, 181
Pyle, Ernie, 41–42, 43, 45, 55, 59, 179

Race. *See* African Americans
Radio, 17, 149
Randolph, A. Philip, 88
Raphael, Ray, 42
Reader's Digest, 40, 89, 133, 158, 167,
　168, 172
Reagan, Nancy, 83, 191 (n. 51)
Reagan, Ronald: memorial for, 1, 2,
　59, 175–76, 177, 179, 227 (n. 9);
　and summary journalism, 21,
　167, 191 (n. 51); and masculine
　heroism, 42; and nostalgia, 180
Recovery narrative, 53, 56, 179
Reeves, Richard, 83
Reiman, Roy, 135
Reiman Publications, 134, 135, 219
　(n. 22)
Reminisce: and nostalgia, 11, 132, 134,
　153; circulation of, 134, 218 (n. 18);
　editorial content of, 135–36, 142,
　149–50; supplemental titles of,
　135, 218–19 (n. 21); reader char-
　acteristics, 136, 145; and readers'
　personal reminiscences, 136, 140,
　142, 144, 147–48, 151; and reader
　interaction, 139–40, 148; settings
　of, 140, *141*; and physical objects of
　past, 148, 149
Reminiscent journalism: nature of,
　2–3; and nostalgia, 11, 132; and
　newsmagazines, 14; and values,
　39, 140, 142, 145, 150, 151, 176;
　and generational identity, 117–
　18; and cleaned-up heritage, 132,
　151; and readers' personal remi-

niscences, 136, 139, 140, 142–44, 146–48, 151–52, 153; settings of, 140, *141*, 142, 152; and ideals, 142; and hardship stories, 143–47; and physical objects of past, 148–51, 153; criticism of, 152–53

Reynolds, Rodney J., 90

Rhetoric, 3–4, 55, 71, 105, 151, 157

Ricoeur, Paul, 192 (n. 66)

Rivers, Caryl, 74

Robinson, Jackie, 21, 94, 98, 101, 103

Rockwell, Norman, 2, 133

Rodden, John, 68

Rolling Stone: and September 11th, 48; and celebrity-death coverage, 62, 65, 67, 68, 69, 70, 71, 74, 75, 76, 78, 79, 176; and anniversary issues, 156, 159, 164, 168–69, 225 (n. 68); mission of, 159

Roosevelt, Eleanor, 101, *102*

Roots (Haley), 90

Rosenblatt, Roger, 63, 68, 72

Rothenbuhler, Eric, 4

Rushing, Janice Hocker, 63

Saturday Evening Post, 2, 7, 133

Saturday Review, 69

Savoy, 48, 90, 207 (n. 17)

Schlesinger, Arthur, Jr., 81, 83, 125, 158, 166

Schudson, Michael, 40

Schuman, Howard, 110

Schwartz, Barry, 43, 45, 174

Scott, Jacqueline, 110

September 11th: and memorials, 1; and masculine heroism, 9–10, 43, 53, 54, 59; and national mythology, 9; and heroic template, 10, 39, 53–58, 59, 60, 195 (n. 1), 198–99 (nn. 79, 87); and firemen images,

39–40, 44, 45, 47–48, 51, 52, 53, 57, 59, 62, 177–78, 195 (nn. 6, 8), 197 (n. 42); heroic ideal of, 39; and news media, 39; and patriotism, 45, 47; and military story shift, 47; and ordinary people, 47, 182, 183; and Gibb, 57–58, 199 (n. 80); and public mourning, 62; and generational identity, 124, 128; and intelligence failures, 175; and individual and collective, 181

Shriver, Donald, 182

Silberstein, Sandra, 195 (n. 8)

Silent generation, 114, 124, 215 (n. 24)

Sinatra, Frank: and commemorative issues, 65; and narrative, 68, 71, 72, 74, 76; and ordinary people, 77; and generational identity, 78; and Davis, 80, 81; and funeral coverage, 83

Small-town values: and core plots, 27, 37; and September 11th, 45, 47; and coal-mine accident, 54, 57; and American soldiers in Iraq, 56; and nostalgia, 133, 140; and anniversary issues, 170, 172

Social history, 5, 162, 181, 182

Space shuttle Challenger, 62

Space shuttle Columbia, 39, 54–55, 62

Sports Illustrated: and anniversary issues, 8, 156, 157, 158, 160, 166, 168; and masculine heroism, 10; and September 11th, 48; and celebrity memorials, 75, 80

Stange, Maren, 98

Status quo, 6, 183

Steinem, Gloria, 34, 172

Stolley, Richard, 68

37; and decade-end reviews, 21,
22; and ordinary people, 22,
27; and predictions of future,
30, 193 (n. 86); and century-
review issues, 31–32, 34, 37, 193
(n. 96); and dramatization of
stories, 31; and space shuttle
Columbia, 55; and celebrity-death
coverage, 72, 75, 77–78, 80, 81,
82, 83, 84
Underdogs, 26, 34, 41, 75–76
Urry, John, 132
Us Weekly, 75, 82
Utne, Eric, 167
Utne Reader, 160–61, 167, 224 (n. 34)

Values: and ordinary people, 25, 175;
news values, 27, 195 (n. 4); and
reminiscent journalism, 39, 140,
142, 145, 150, 151, 176; and firemen
images, 43, 53; regained social
values, 45; and September 11th,
60; and celebrity memorials, 63,
64, 65, 68, 69, 78, 86; and generational identity, 111, 128; and
anniversary issues, 156, 170, 172,
173; and Reagan, 176; and national
identity, 181. *See also* Small-town
values
Van Gennep, Arnold, 64
Vernacular culture, 5, 6, 182
Vibe, 8, 157, 160, 164, 165, 166, 168
Vietnam War, 42, 117, 127, 128, 177,
179, 180, 227 (n. 10)
Vogel, Todd, 88
Voice of the Negro, 88

Wall Street Journal, 175
Walton, Sam, 22, 34
War on terrorism, 179

Wayne, John, 63, 68, 69, 73–74, 78,
83, 117
White, Hayden, 5
Wilder, L. Douglas, 95
Will, George, 29–30
Willard, Michael Nevin, 110
William, Raymond, 159
Williams, Brian, 63
Wills, Garry, 68
Winfield, Betty Houchin, 2, 40
Wolfe, Tom, 28, 162
Wolseley, Roland, 89
Women's Household, 134
Woodson, Carter G., 101, 208 (n. 22)
Woodstock music festival, 7, 113, 118,
128, 178
World War II: and anniversaries, 1,
58, 59, 155, 179; and masculine
heroism, 10, 41–42, 43, 51, 53, 59,
179; and summary issues, 17–18,
20, 21, 26, 28, 41; as good war, 39,
41, 43, 128, 177; and nostalgia, 51,
59, 125, 179; and collective memory, 53, 55; and celebrity memorials, 77; and African American
soldiers, 95, 227 (n. 9); anniversaries of, 124–25; and reminiscent
journalism, 147–48; and individual and collective, 181; and
personalization in journalism,
182. *See also* Greatest Generation
World War II Memorial, 41, 58, 179
Wright, Will, 174
Wright Brothers, 34

Yankelovich firm, 111, 112
Young, Whitney, 101

Zelizer, Barbie, 7, 98
Zerubavel, Eviatar, 14, 155–56